The Other Mother

The Other Mother

a rememoir

teresa bruce

JogglingBoardpress

Stories that Matter

THE OTHER MOTHER: A REMEMOIR.

Joggling Board Press books may be purchased for
educational, business or sales promotion use. For information,
please contact sales@jogglingboardpress.com.

FIRST EDITION

Edited by Susan Kammeraad-Campbell
with Thomas Gasque Smith, Ph.D., Elizabeth Palmieri and Isabelle Altman
Cover design by Torborg Davern
Interior design by Shanna McGarry

Library of Congress Cataloging-in-Publication Data applied for.
ISBN 978-0-9841073-9-1

Contents

For Gary, the man Byrne always knew was out there for me.

Prologue

In the beginning there was dance,
because people just needed to move.

~*Byrne*

Hello, Friend

SHE'S WEARING HEADPHONES, listening to something that has transported her far from here. Her magenta sweat suit and costume earrings, normally so bright and cheery, look garish. It's the fluorescent lighting, I tell myself, pulling the headphones away from her springy silver hair.

"Hello, gorgeous. Is your dance card empty?" I ask.

She doesn't recognize my voice. She does not tell me it's wonderful to see me. She does not ask me about the drive. She does not give me a kiss. Instead, I touch the top of the hand whose fingers hang onto the bedrail like a ballet *barre*.

"Byrne, it's me," I say. Her shoulders, coat-hanger thin, carry the unmistakable frame of a lifetime of training.

"I'm not hungry," she says. A smile of benign politeness drifts over her face – run along now, don't bother me. Instead of introducing her to Gary, the man I am about to marry, I will have to introduce myself. "It's me, Teresa."

Wipeout pulls away from her leash, jamming her wet nose between the railing and Byrne's broken hip. Byrne drops her hand onto the silky fur between Wipeout's ears.

9

"Oh! Hello, friend," she says in a deep, breathy tone of recognition. It's the voice she always reserved for Wipeout, the voice that reminds me of a cello. Hearing it is like eavesdropping on a secret password spoken through the peephole of a speakeasy. Wipeout nuzzles even more insistently, like there might be a stick hidden under the magenta sweat suit. Byrne reaches for my hand.

"Come, darling," she says. "Let's have a glass of wine on the porch."

A black patch covers where one eye used to be. The other catches only peripheral, ephemeral shapes, certainly not the bottle of champagne I kept chilled in a cooler on the nine-hour drive from Washington, D.C., to Beaufort, South Carolina.

"How about I open the window, so we can catch the breeze off the river?" I propose. There is no porch or river, only an empty assisted living parking lot outside her window. She lifts her chin, elongating her neck as if her ears and nose need to be a little higher to find the breeze. I open the window, then quickly flick on the ceiling fan – a river breeze without the low note of decaying pluff mud.

"Byrne, I have wonderful news." I wait for a sign that she is with me. "I found my Duncan, remember?"

"Pleasure to meet you," she says, in the come-hither voice she uses with men. She thinks my Duncan is here in the room at Helena House.

"Please, pull up a chair." Her wrist leads an open palm on a graceful swoop through the air, a dancer's grand gesture of hospitality and flirtation.

"He stepped outside," I tell her, "to let us girls catch up."

"Is he a handsome man?" Byrne asks. I squeeze her hand so she can feel the affirmation in my answer. "Good," she says. "Because you are a handsome woman and when the two of you step out together, heads should turn."

I know, with settled certainty now, that she is describing herself and Duncan. Handsome, hell, they were magnificent. I know the Byrne-and-Duncan love story by heart. For a long time, it was my only fairy tale. Now it is my turn to tell the storyteller of how my Duncan proposed on the steps of the Alhambra in Spain, and how, in a few months, we will elope. She responds purely to the rhythm of my voice. I could be reading a beautiful poem in a language she doesn't speak. Her verbal responses to my presence are out of sync, her one eye not quite tracking. She isn't following, so instead, I listen.

The words she assembles on this imaginary porch lift in the breeze before they start to circle, a little confused, like a kite that's lost its string. The updraft of memories is all that keeps them dancing.

"It's going to be a disaster," she tells me, sitting straight up from the waist in her mechanical bed. White sheets fan out from her hips like a Martha Graham skirt. The black-and-white framed photo of Duncan on the wall is now level with her head. He's smoking his pipe and listening.

"What is going to be a disaster?" I ask. The dreamy smile is gone. Every tendon in her arms is tense. The eye patch twitches.

"The entire first act," she answers, in a stage whisper.

"Is there anything I can do?" I whisper back. I think maybe I should get Gary to come open the champagne. The sound of a cork popping might snap her out of this. But she turns her head in the direction of my voice, considering it.

"Can you charm the conductor?" she asks. "Perhaps the orchestra can just keep tuning up until I can make that damn girl remember."

I must tread gently now. I'm not sure if she's the damn girl or I am. "Remember what?" I ask.

"The choreography," she says, irritated. "We've rehearsed and rehearsed but she can't seem to hear the music. She goes blank after the first 32 counts. And stage presence? The silly thing's a pretty fish, apologizing for flopping around on stage."

"Don't any other dancers know the steps?" I ask. "Maybe you can move pretty Miss Flop-About into the chorus and let someone else perform the lead."

"But I need someone sexy, with legs worth watching."

A piece of her biography drifts back to me, like the hint of a familiar fragrance. "I wasn't one of the great ones," Byrne once told me. I had thought her modest, knowing as I did that she had danced in New York, Connecticut, St. Thomas, New Mexico, Mexico and Ireland before she landed in Beaufort in 1969.

"No darling," she had said. "It was these perky bosoms that got me noticed. That and legs that wouldn't quit. It was the Great Depression, remember, men needed a lift."

It is dawning on me what to do.

"Byrne, you're going to have to step in," I tell her.

An eyebrow, half hidden behind the patch, lifts up in an *arabesque* of interest.

I continue. "You did the choreography, am I right?"

She nods, still tense.

"So who could possibly know the dance better? And you said yourself the legs have to be worth the ticket price."

She reaches for her long legs under the over-starched sheets, rubbing the tops of her thighs. I am shocked at how thin they've gotten. She is the elegant skeleton of a lifelong knockout.

"But I'm not warmed up," she says. "I haven't even stretched."

I reach for her feet, loose them from the too-tight tuck of hurried housekeepers. I begin to rub the high arches and calloused balls. Her bones are so brittle my fists could crush them, but I tell myself it's just that a dancer's foot never fills out or settles with ordinary gravity. All I need to do is get the blood flowing. One hand cradles her heel while I stretch her toes back, gently, with the other. Her calf muscles lengthen, releasing the tension of inactivity. She'll need the elasticity for her imaginary *pliés* to bend and spring into grand *jetés* across the stage.

"Oh, that feels so good," she says. "Now the other foot. Hurry, can't you hear the strings? They're the last to tune."

"Hang on. I'll sweet talk the conductor into giving us more time. What are they playing?"

"*Carmina Burana*, of course," she says.

Of course. It was the soundtrack of a lifetime of Byrne seducing strangers to dance. From isolated Navajo reservations in the Southwest to Gullah communities in the Southeast where descendants of slaves still held community sings. Wherever Byrne lived, this pounding drama accompanied her.

"Start your head rolls," I tell her as I slip from my chair. "Slowly, keep those shoulders down. I'll be right back."

I go only as far as her dresser, where a stack of CDs leans up against a boom box. It still smells of musty dance studios, the southern kind with walls that sweat the musky cologne of trapped humidity. There, on the top, is Carl Orff's cantata. I put it in, but don't press play. She's not ready. I know this warm-up. Every finger will extend and every vertebra will align before it's done. I look over at the bed. Byrne is marking the movements her body can no longer manage. Her neck and torso gently sway, touching off the invisible follow-through. She is wind through a grove of trees, when all that blows is ghostly moss.

"Can you check on the men?" she asks. "There are lifts we must adjust."

Ah, the lifts. Duncan called them "worth wearing tights for." In rehearsals, he volunteered to hold Byrne's dancers overhead, but never Byrne herself. She was too tall. This is what still worries her. I can see it in her sinking posture. The dancer she's replacing must have been a tiny thing – all legs and no brains.

"Why not shake things up a bit?" I tell her. "You are strong enough to lift the men."

She sits up straight again, vertebra by vertebra. "Scandalous," she says with a thin, mischievous smile. Her hands flutter down to her hips and she pivots one shoulder to a jaunty angle. Her chin lifts. "Just what this town needs. Call the newspapers. Get the TV cameras. You and I are going to turn things on their heads."

O Fortuna fills the room, timpani and snare drums drowning out the pitiful, piped-in muzak. Helena House is a concert hall today. Byrne is back where she was born to be and I am in the front row, mesmerized. And when Wipeout hears the cello, low as hello friend, she throws her head back and howls.

1

Balancing Act

It is hard to feel graceful in a rat costume, especially when you are a 12-year-old girl. Perhaps in my twenties, I could have suspended humiliation long enough to appreciate the innate grace in scurrying rodents, seen their artistic possibilities. By that age, I had observed plenty of rats. We lived in an Oregon farmhouse whose owner rented out the slowly collapsing building to tenants willing to wake to geese honking and step in the occasional pile of cow dung. I'd even kept a bald white rat with pitiful skin lesions as a pet, until the box he slept in proved insufficient protection from a particularly athletic farm cat. Chasing the rat-snatching cat over the fence to save Scabby's life was how I wound up taking ballet class with my arm in a cast for six weeks. Still, I didn't love rats enough to want to play one in *The Nutcracker.*

I was a dancer and a nationally ranked rhythmic gymnast, capable of contortions of flexibility far outshining a dingy rat. Clara, dream-dancing in her long, lacy nightgown with the Nutcracker Prince in his royal blue leggings, now that was the role for me. After all, I had earned the right to wear toe shoes *before* my 12th birthday, which is the age when the Beaverton Dance Academy deemed most girls developed enough to stuff their tender feet into what are essentially tiny cement cages camouflaged with shiny pink satin. My friend Caitlin got her toe shoe privileges the same day I did, but she was already 12.

Together we mastered the art of standing in third position, *en pointe*, and propelling ourselves across the dance floor without the use of heels or the undulation of the foot's natural arch. The French ballet term for this insanely redundant step is *bourrée* – an effortless-appearing staple of any *corps-de-ballet*. It is how dancers appear to float over a stage, wearing tutus that quiver as their tiny hip sockets hold spindly legs in loose rigidity. Not unlike a wind up doll, or a rat, for that matter.

There was no mention of rats when our ballet teacher, Patti, told us that the Pacific Northwest Ballet would be staging auditions for children in the Christmas classic. "If you want to try out, I'll submit both of you as advanced," she said at the end of class.

Caitlin grabbed my hand and tried to squeeze it, just as I was reaching up to cover my gaping mouth. I did not intentionally wrench her arm almost out of its socket; this was decades before Tonya Harding made Oregon famous for disabling prettier, taller competitors. I was simply transported by the thrill, the honor, the sudden glory of my beloved ballet teacher officially declaring me "advanced."

Ours was not a sophisticated family and the closest thing I'd seen to live ballerinas were the highland dancers at the Scottish Games, where girls in plaid skirts jumped over crossed swords on the spongy, rain-squelching grass of an Oregon summer. "Now that's talent," my father said as he pointed out the tartan of our Scottish clan: Bruce. "One day you'll put them all to shame. I know you will."

I always knew my father was proud of me, but Patti thought I was destined for tights and tutus, not muddy knee-highs and scratchy wool skirts. The day she announced *Nutcracker* auditions in ballet class, she earned a nickname she never knew she had: Patti Who? When you are 12, and the teacher who has danced on stages in New York and Europe invites you into her rarified world, she becomes the queen of yours. I spoke of no one else in my waking hours.

Patti had short strawberry blond hair that tucked perfectly under a tortoise-shelled headband. Mine was dishwater brown, perpetually frizzed out from my mother's home perms. Patti's legs were longer than my whole body and when she pointed her feet, her arches looked like rainbows from the side.

Patti knew George Balanchine, or George Balancing, I wasn't exactly sure which one, but he was terribly important. The only terribly important person I'd ever even met was Tammy Wynette when I was a toddler. My father took me backstage so he'd have a better shot at getting her autograph. "Stand By Your Man" was his shower song.

Patti got a dance scholarship and left home to live in New York City when she was still a teenager. Unless my father quit his job as a truck driver and robbed a bank, I was pretty sure my teenage years would unfold in the same room I shared with my little sister Jenny, with a blue tarp permanently stapled over the leaky window.

Patti said lots of ballerinas could extend their legs as high as their ears, but hardly any could hold that position as long as I could. She didn't know I was expert in holding positions for a long time. Like hiding outside my parents' bedroom door when they fought, not making a peep until my mother stopped crying and I could hear the sounds they made in bed after my father apologized.

I had remarkable strength and potential. Patti said so.

"Patti says this. Patti says that," my mother teased me. "Do you tell her everything that I say?"

I was in the middle of an exaggerated eye roll when my father chimed in. "Patti Who?" he asked, and proceeded to repeat whenever I brought up another fascinating fact about her.

"Dad," I said, drawing the word into at least three syllables. "She's my ballet teacher, duh."

As the auditions neared, and my mentions of her became even more frequent, Patti Who became an owl's hoot under my father's roof: "Patti Hoo Hoo." It was funny how far he could rotate his head around as he ridiculed my adoration. Later, her nickname got a sing-song Indian accent. "Paddi-who, Paddi-who" trilled my father, accompanied by a charming head bobble.

If Patti ever found out, or worse if he ever did it in front of her, it would be even more embarrassing than the time my father took my mother shopping at K-mart on Valentine's Day. She held her hands over her eyes, like she thought it was going to be a good surprise. "Can I look now?" she asked. He pulled her hands down. "Pick out whichever color you like," he said. "If you learn to keep house you might get a necklace next year." We were standing in front of a stack of plastic laundry baskets.

So each day after ballet class, I crossed my fingers that it was my mother who would pick me up in our blue van with the $100 Earl Scheib paint job and back seats replaced with floor-to-wall-to-roof shag carpeting.

"When you get older, you'll understand what the padded carpeting is for," my father said when he brought the van home. I understood then that I desperately wanted to be a ballerina, living in New York City, where I would ride to the theater in a shag-carpet-free, horse-drawn carriage through Central Park.

Caitlin's mom drove a brand new Volvo station wagon. I knew because she waited for Caitlin through every 90-minute ballet class, watching through the glass observation window and videotaping her daughter's technique at the long wooden ballet *barre* with a VHS handi-cam. I wondered if she taped me, too.

"Those little legs of yours sure have muscles," she'd tell me. "Must be the gymnastics. I've never seen calves like that on a girl."

"Patti says that's why she leaps so much higher than everyone else," Caitlin would defend me. In those moments, I hated her even more than when she gave me garbage bags full of clothes she outgrew. "They're still nice, I promise," she'd say. If she wasn't so nice all the time, I could just concentrate on beating her, which is how I saw the upcoming *Nutcracker* auditions. Just like gymnastics, there would be a winner and a loser; the girl picked to be Clara and the girl who wasn't. I still didn't see a rat coming.

"The Balanchine version is the most evocative of all the *Nutcrackers*," Patti told us. "Just listen to this music and watch what he does with the choreography."

She pulled a worn Tchaikovsky album from its cardboard cover and put the needle in the groove just before the part where the record slinks into the Arabian Dance. The haunting clarinet was a cobra unwinding from a coiled basket and wrapping its way up my spine. I looked up at Patti in a trance, with my legs stretched out in side splits and elbows on the floor in front of me so my hands could hold up my head.

She didn't dance full out, and it was all the more delicious for the hint of what she was holding back. Her rainbow feet flexed instead of arched. The normally continuous line of her hands broke at the wrists. Her *développés* were sinuous and fluid, her long legs never reaching a pose and stopping. When she slid into a forward split, arching her back over her back leg, I jumped up to copy her movements. *Let me show you,* I wanted to say, *let me be just like you.*

"Now you realize, girls," she told us when the record stopped, "parts like these are saved for the company dancers. But there are as many as 60 other parts they'll need to fill with students, and whichever role you get, your job is to dance it as beautifully as you are capable."

I heard the part where she said "whichever role you get," and understood that the teacher I worshipped was sure we would get roles. And I was sure that mine would be Clara.

My mother made my seven-year-old sister come along with me in the shag-carpet van on the long drive to the auditions in downtown Portland. "The paper said they need little kids, too," she said, "and daddy says she's too young to stay home by herself anyway."

"It's an audition for the ballet, not the circus," I protested, melting only when Jenny made a face at me upside down, from a headstand position as we drove along Sunset Highway. She had balance; I gave her that much. "Point your toes at least," I told her, then tickled her grubby bare feet until she fell over.

It was Jenny who first pointed out the problem at the studios where the auditions were held. "Where are you supposed to wait in line for the part you want?" she asked. "All these signs only go by ages." She was right. There were no lines specifically for would-be Clara's. I already had my number pinned to the front of my black scoop-neck leotard. My toe shoes were in a backpack over my shoulder, just in case the judges wanted to see my effortless *bourrées.* I squeezed Jenny's hand goodbye and stood behind a hundred other girls in scoop-neck leotards waiting under the sign that said "Ages 12 and up."

On stage, I was in the fourth row that stretched from wing to wing, but I knew the lines would rotate so I figured it was better to start near the back. I'd have plenty of time to master the steps the audition mistress called for by the time I was in front of the judges. I couldn't even see Caitlin, but I was so focused on keeping my shoulders down and toes pointed she could have been one pair of pale pink tights in front of me and I wouldn't have said hello.

The lines rotated. My certainty of becoming Clara grew each time. The steps were easy. My legs were higher than anyone else's. My muscles memorized the movements and all I had to do was feel the music and remember to smile. I could practically feel a splendid Christmas tree growing behind me so I wasn't surprised when they called my number. The first cut and the second weeded out two-thirds of the girls, and I could finally see Caitlin dance. She was remembering to smile, too.

She smiled even through the next phase of the audition, which involved each dancer standing against a tape measure on a wall and having a wardrobe assistant press down on the top of each head with a silver ruler and call out her height to another assistant with a clipboard. My whole body felt like a foot crammed into a metal heel cup and adjustable width bar at the JC Penny's shoe department. I kept picturing Clara's costume: a waif-like, waistless nightgown that surely couldn't be too hard to hem shorter for a dancer of my caliber.

After the measuring, the selected dancers from each age group filed onto the stage. Jenny ran over to me and sat in my lap when everyone was told to take a seat. I let her, my confidence translating into unusual magnanimity. Caitlin sat right next to us and whispered, "Good luck. I hope you get it."

The audition mistress started with Act 1 party dancers, children who get to open presents and "ooh" and "ahh" when Clara gets the super cool nutcracker. Kid's stuff. Then it was time for Clara to be called, and I heard my number over and over in my head. But it was Caitlin whose number got called. She even had to ask me to read the front of her leotard to make sure. She just kept sitting there, smiling at me, as if some other role would cheer me up. Even Jenny forgot to feel sorry for me after she got picked to be one of the little kids who tumble out from under Mother Ginger's giant hoop skirt. "Cool," she said, "maybe I'll get to do cartwheels."

She did get to do cartwheels. Watching from the wings on opening night, I could see layers of bloomers under the pretty yellow skirt that was her costume. I could see Caitlin's long legs silhouetted under the nearly transparent gossamer gown that was Clara's costume. Her face glowed in the soft spotlight that followed her every move. I could see her perfect white teeth when she smiled. Luckily, no one in the audience could tell it was me inside my rat costume.

I had plenty of stage time, being tossed from toy soldier to toy soldier in the battle scene that closes the first act. I did flips and back spins and huge *assemblé* jumps through the air. But my entire body was disguised in what the costume designers of TV's *Barney* clearly ripped off a generation later. The rats in that year's *Nutcracker* looked like giant, grey Hershey Kisses with grotesque paper mache head masks that stunk of newspaper ink and paste. They didn't even have whiskers – we had to scurry around waving our fingers under our chin.

I'm not sure who was more embarrassed, me or my mother. She had dreamed of being a ballerina when she was growing up and she understood the power of the stage as portal to a world beyond plastic laundry baskets and vans with shag carpeting.

"You would have made a much better Clara," she consoled me. "We'll try stretching exercises next year, if you don't get a growth spurt in time."

"Just don't tell Daddy I'm a rat," I made my mother promise. It was humiliating enough that Patti and Caitlin knew it was me under that hideous, shapeless costume. For my father, nothing other than me being Clara would warrant all the time and money we were spending driving back and forth to Portland for the performances.

"What," he said, raising both palms. "Am I supposed to work three jobs so you three can put on airs?" He finally agreed to it once Jenny and I promised to do our homework in the van and keep our rooms clean. Watching me play a rat would be all the proof he needed that ballet was ridiculous.

Keeping secrets from my father felt natural to me, nothing more than habit grown from watching my mother. She could never match my father's charisma, so secrets kept her dreams alive. She called me her princess and lived through my potential glory. We collected newspapers and scoured construction sites for recyclable soda cans to pay for my ballet classes and competition fees. She got me out of bed at 5:30 a.m. to practice, helped me stretch, drove me to ballet classes and studied judging manuals to make sure my routines had all the required elements. She sewed leotards for other gymnasts and hid the money she earned under bolts of fabric in her sewing room. It was just between us, like how she saved her most dazzling costume designs for me, alone, to wear. She signed notes to get me out of school for extra practice, all without my father knowing.

I thought her fear of him finding out was paranoid, until I was 13 and Patti told me about another audition. "This one has nothing to do with height or fitting into costumes," she said. "They'll judge you just on your talent.

You bring so much athleticism to your dancing they'll be dazzled."

This time it wasn't either Caitlin or me, winner take all. We both auditioned and both got accepted into a summer ballet intensive that fed promising dancers into the New York City Ballet. They even offered me a scholarship. All my parents would have to pay was airfare and living expenses. Patti said she was as excited for me as she had been when she was awarded the same scholarship at the beginning of her career.

"You'll learn so much," she said, smoothing a strand of my perm-frizzed hair. "It's the start of a whole new life." She even hugged my mother. "Don't be nervous," she told her. "They'll take good care of her and you can always ask me if you have any questions."

The only question my mother had was whether I was ready to choose ballet over gymnastics. There wouldn't be time for both; ballerinas don't get to compete in the Olympics. I didn't blink. The Olympics came around only every four years. The ballet scholarship started that very summer, which turned out to be the one detail that derailed it.

The intense schedule of the residency would mean I couldn't come on the yearly family camping trip. This summer we were going to drive our truck and camper down to Mexico. So we had to tell my father about the scholarship while there was still time to make other plans. I wasn't worried, like my mother was. I had the confidence of a beloved 13-year-old, convinced my father would not only understand but be proud of me for getting the scholarship.

"No daughter of mine is going to go off to that faggot-infested city," he said. The words sailed over my understanding but not the way he said them. "You're too young. No telling what kind of crap they'd fill your head with."

That was the first time I saw what happened when secrets spill. My mother begged my father on my behalf, sobbed for me, gave him the hidden leotard money to cover any living expenses in New York. This fight didn't end with funny noises coming from their bedroom. It dragged on for days of food served cold with resentment, un-laundered work pants, and gravel spitting out from under car tires on our driveway. And late one night, when they didn't know I was watching from the stairs, they wrestled over a rifle in the living room. The long black barrel pitched and lunged over their heads, wildly pointing at the leak-stained ceiling.

Girls raised in the backwoods of Oregon know what guns can do. I'd watched a doe go down in the pine straw, smelled the blood that clung to our rusted truck bed long after the carcass was removed. So I cowered in speechless horror until my father wrenched the rifle from my mother's shaking arms. I never knew if my mother meant to shoot him, or herself, but the next day I told my father the scholarship didn't matter.

"I'm quitting ballet anyway," I said, not looking at my mother. "You just dress up in stupid rat costumes and pretend to have whiskers."

I think he saw through me, but not enough to change his mind. "I knew you were the smart one," he said. "Just tell that dance teacher of yours to butt out of our business."

"Patti Who?" I said, and I have hated *The Nutcracker* ever since.

2

Mediocrity is distasteful.
          —Byrne

Byrne and Fanny

WASHINGTON HEIGHTS, NEW York – 1920s

BERNICE ROSALIE MILLER spent the last 68 years of her life parading in front of mirrors, but the first 24 avoiding them altogether. She had too many disorganized teeth, for one thing, a fact magnified by proximity whenever brushing them required opening a mirrored medicine cabinet to retrieve the paste. It wasn't difficult to escape her early reflection; there weren't many mirrors in the long railroad flat she shared with her little brother Sherman and their parents in Washington Heights, Manhattan. There was, however, the highly polished baby grand piano in the front room, whose luster was such that it had mirror-like qualities. For at least an hour every day, after Hebrew and elocution lessons, Byrne squinted directly at the sheet music in front of her face, not an inch to either side of the instrument's reflective rack or fall board. When she mastered Liszt's *Sonata in B Major*, it was her Hungarian father whose big smile reflected in the gleaming beechwood lid.

"My *tzigane*," Michael Miller said, wrapping her in the warmth of his pride. "One day you will be a concert pianist, my little gypsy."

Concert pianist or gypsy, maybe, but only a doting father could possibly see anything little in Byrne. By 13, she stood a head taller than all the boys in school, could fold in half at the waist and pretend to swallow Sherman like the clams they picked from the muddy flats of the Hudson River. By middle school, she was five feet nine inches tall and the mirrors in the girls' restroom cut her off at the neck. So it was with all the fervor a self-conscious introvert could muster that she railed against the social dancing classes her mother Fanny insisted every well-rounded young Jewish woman needed.

"Mother, my glasses will fall off. They're expensive," began the pleading.

"You don't need to read anything in order to follow instructions," Fanny replied, ready to engage in the clash of wills.

"My piano lessons will suffer," Byrne continued.

"Not if your father has anything to say about it," came Fanny's answer.

"I'm awkward. You said so yourself. Look, my feet are twice the size of yours. I'll trod on toes, flail off the stage. Become an embarrassment."

"All the more reason to learn to control your body."

"I'll check out a book from the library and learn the steps myself," Byrne pleaded.

"Your eyesight is bad enough with your nose always in a book. You will attend the classes and you will thank me on your wedding day."

Here, perhaps, was the one loose brick in her mother's wall.

"That's just it. I'll never have one. My reputation will be ruined."

Fanny leaned back against the sink, a half-smile parting her lips in anticipation of Byrne's rationale.

"How so?"

Byrne peered past her mother, checking to see if her father was at the keys of the baby grand, within earshot. He was, softly playing *Un Sospiro* by memory.

"I'm so tall the boys will be pressing their faces into my bosoms!"

This did not evoke the shocked silence or discordant minor key pounded by mistake that Byrne hoped for. There was no kindly or even slightly embarrassed fatherly intervention. From the next room over came simply a pause, a breath in his unceasingly gentle playing. It was Fanny who redirected the path of Byrne's life in that single uncomfortable instant.

"Lower your voice, young lady. We'll enroll you in ballet instead."

For a moment, Byrne thought of telling Fanny how ballet was ancient history, how even the famous Fanny Brice made fun of it in her Zeigfeld parody of a dying swan. But she knew her mother disapproved of the comedienne who shared her name because she found Brice's Yiddish accent affected and her humor undignified. She would be equally unimpressed if Byrne argued the case of the new German modern dancer, Harald Kreutzberg, who made the teenager quiver in anticipation of the Saturday matinees where he performed. He was muscular, thrilling and deeply menacing. His movements were wild and trapped at the same time, emotions pouring out in free-form mime as much as choreography. His costumes were prop and backdrop both.

At one matinee, Byrne had gasped at the narrow arcs of metal that encircled his head like Medusa's snakes transformed into a warrior's helmet. In another, his bald head had looked to Byrne like a bare white exclamation point against priestly black robes that fanned out around him when he spiraled down to the floor. Byrne was in the balcony, almost frightened to look down on the stage. His glowing head hovered over the darkness of the silk, a buoy bobbing in what might as well have been a spreading pool of black blood.

Harald Kreutzberg didn't perform what Byrne knew as steps and turns and poses; his body exhorted, lamented, cried out to her. Byrne knew that if she told her mother anything about this exotic modern dancer, she would end up confessing the massive crush that held her in its grip, the silly schoolgirl letters she had written him.

So, dutifully, Byrne reported to ballet class along with her cousin Irma and her best friend Ruth. She stood in the very back, at the teacher's suggestion, behind the plump and curvy bodies of her friends and sank deep into her pelvis for the privacy of a sagging inch. Her long arms flailed a beat behind everyone else's.

"Bernice, we begin on the one," the teacher barked, "not the two and loose change."

Byrne squinted and slumped a little lower, seething inside her outsized limbs. She, Michael Miller's darling gypsy, was meant to be a concert pianist. There was no girl in the room better tuned to the timing of musical notes. She was a beat behind to create her own dance space, to spare the humiliation of her gangly arms and legs colliding with Ruth's or Irma's.

"TURN AROUND, GIRLIE," a Vaudeville casting director said on a cold January afternoon 10 years later. "Lemme get a look at those gams."

3

A Surfer and a Dog

Sonny spotted the dog seller on the side of the road first. I was too busy trying not to rear-end the produce trucks and *collectivo* mini-vans that seemed to ooze out of Guadalajara in a fume-belching, volcanic flow toward the Pacific Ocean. My diesel VW Rabbit had a stick shift, so driving the toll-free highways of Mexico felt more like intermittent lurching, one honk on the horn at a time. I barely heard Sonny the first time he said to stop. I only paid attention when he switched from English to Spanish.

"Pull over, *ahora ahora!*" Sonny shouted, slapping the dashboard in front of the passenger seat. He was pointing to a corner just ahead and two lanes over, where a man in a soot-stained straw cowboy hat held up three white puppies in one brown hand. "That's the one! My dog," he said. His voice was coming from deeper in his scrawny chest than normal, genuine excitement somehow excreting through the practiced veneer of a half-Mexican, half-Canadian, 22-year-old surfer with a macho reputation to preserve. "That's it! That's it, Teresa, that's my dog!"

He meant it in epiphany, as though his whole life flashed

in front of him and a squirmy puppy on the side of the road was central to it. In the six months I'd known him, I had never seen his eyes blaze like that, not even when he described perfect beach breaks. He was in a trance and I wouldn't have pierced it even if I'd understood.

So I inched the VW diagonally forward, angling through the raised fists of drivers and insults I only half understood. Sonny's fingers drummed the armrest, his muscles involuntarily twitching under his brown, salt-softened skin. He didn't even wait to open the door when I pulled onto the gravel shoulder. In one fluid move, he torqued himself up and through the open passenger window and began haggling for the puppy.

I watched through the rear-view mirror as my moody, enigmatic Latino boyfriend transformed into a little boy bargaining with Santa Claus. His desperation couldn't have been more obvious. I heard what sounded like *"ciento,"* 100, and then the dog seller's unmistakable insistence on dollars – turning the word into something sounding closer to Dolores – the woman's name.

Unbelievable – he must have seen me, a gringa *behind the wheel,* I thought to myself. There's no way a puppy on the side of any street in Mexico would sell for 100 U.S. dollars. Sonny's surfboards didn't even cost that much. We could rent an apartment for less.

Watching him in the rearview window, I saw a street-grace in Sonny's body language, a pre hip-hop way of pulling his chin into his neck and snaking his head into an attitude of almost arrogant astonishment. The dog seller looked down at his sandaled feet, the outrageousness of his opening price acknowledged. I watched as Sonny's arm went from palm raised in respectful consideration to outstretched, behind his back. I thought I saw in this the familiar stance of a surfer, extending an arm like a rudder to stabilize the body in the face of a five-foot wave. Then I realized he was simply pointing back to me, in the car. Somehow, in the dog seller's eyes at least, I must have become a bargaining chip in the power struggle, a girlfriend to convince, perhaps, a soft heart to manipulate. And then they were three silhouettes coming toward me like a Western showdown: the dog seller, a surfer and a squirming ball of fur.

The dog seller stuck the puppy through the passenger side window and plopped it on the seat like a small sack of dried beans.

"What's going on?" I asked Sonny. I didn't even want to look at the puppy, afraid of how pathologically cute it would be. It wasn't practical. We were living at the mercy of Sonny's harpy mother, a woman pointedly not happy with an unemployed *gringa* sharing her son's upstairs bedroom. I had exactly $60 in cash in my wallet, and that was supposed to be our contribution to Gloria's grocery bill when we returned.

"*Ay mierde*," said the dog seller. The bags under the man's eyes compressed a little when his eyes bulged at the sight of the puppy, squatting indelicately on the front passenger seat of my car. Now his was the face of desperate compromise, sensing a deal slipping away.

"*Lo siento, lo siento*," he apologized. I looked down. The puppy was standing in a pool of piss slowly sinking into the plush seat cushion.

"Whatever he wants, it's too much," I told Sonny. "And besides, it's too young to be separated from its mother. Look, not even potty trained."

"Teresa, this is the dog I've always wanted," Sonny insisted. "I'll pay you back. Eighty bucks and I am the happiest *cabron* in fucking Mexico."

I leveled with him. Even if he gave this puppy dealer every last dollar in my wallet, we'd be $20 short with not quite enough gas to get back to Puerto Angel.

"My father always said I could have a white husky. He promised. Since I was a little kid. Teresa, I did everything he said. I was promised. I deserve to have this dog."

There is a point beyond pleading, when a man's voice threatens to dissolve into a silent howl of pain. I didn't understand what particular pain it was, but I heard it coming. I handed Sonny my three last twenties and watched as he took the gold stud earring from his left lobe and pressed it into the dog seller's palm along with the cash.

Now it was the dog seller's palms raised. What would he do with one gold earring? I took the silver loops from my ears and handed them to Sonny to add to the collection. The dog seller's eyes were sinking back into their sockets, calculating our collective worth.

Sonny reached behind his neck and untied the knot that held a shark's tooth to a strap of leather. His brother had given it to him when he'd caught his first wave. The dog seller scraped the serrated edges of the tooth against the dry calluses of his hands, impressed. But then he reached into the car, picked up the puppy and started bouncing it, belly first, like he was weighing it.

"*Su camisa*," he said, pointing to Sonny's brand new Quick Silver t-shirt. "*Quanto vale?*" It would never fit him; but he must have recognized the logo, known that he could sell it to some kid who dreamed of being as cool as a surfer with an American girlfriend who owned her own car.

Sonny grabbed the back of his collar with one hand and yanked the shirt off his back. He stood on the side of a Guadalajara highway, naked from the waist up, the most vulnerable and passionate person I had ever known.

The three of us – Sonny, me and a terrified, trembling puppy no more than three weeks old – drove away from the city. The sun stretched through the agave-studded fields and transformed the hills into swaths of silvery purple, but

Sonny had eyes only for the puppy he cradled in the palm of his hand.

"We have to give her a good name," Sonny said. "Otherwise I'm not kidding you, my mother will start calling her Snowflake or Snowball or some shit like that."

I laughed, imagining the reaction of Sonny's band of surf buddies to a wimpy, girlie name. I looked down at the puppy, so exhausted that her feet dangled on either side of Sonny's wrist, and the perfect name came to me: Wipeout. Sonny turned to me and smiled – the smile of the happiest *cabron* in all of fucking Mexico.

I HAD FALLEN IN LOVE with Sonny the year before, watching him surf. Swells rose to lift him, crests of breakers curled over his head like a crown. He was a dancer on a watery stage – effortlessly, unknowingly graceful. I had never met anyone so free from gravity, so full of pure possibility.

I was an overachieving 22-year-old who was supposed to have been an Olympic rhythmic gymnast. I skipped grades and started college at 16, the only member of my family ever to finish. My competitive ranking was on an equally fast track, rising from twelfth among the nation's rhythmic gymnasts to fourth in less than two years. Three girls would make the 1988 Olympic team, but when I broke my back in a training accident, I realized I wouldn't be one of them and raced straight into grad school to study broadcast journalism instead, chasing a different kind of fame. I interned in the summer, applied for every scholarship, and made it through in a year and a half. A trip to Puerto Angel, near the Guatemala border, watching surfers was a graduation reward from my father. It was the last vacation as a family before I was meant to take the TV world by storm.

Sonny didn't care about any of that. He chased me like a perfect wave. Where every aspect of my life was regimented, part of a bigger plan, he jumped from chance to chance, thrilled by risk. His devil-may-care confidence was intoxicating. On the day he first followed me back to my hotel room, I laughed at his Latin lover lines. He declared that his life would be meaningless without me, and that I would never be satisfied with pale *gringos* after trying a hot-blooded Mexican.

"Do you like those flowers?" he asked one day when we passed a high brick wall enclosing a private courtyard. Above it was a wooden trellis cloaked in bougainvillea.

I looked behind us, embarrassed. We were being followed by a merry band of adolescent surfers, whistling and cheering Sonny on. He was their prince, the one whose English gave him the chance to make it out of Mexico. Any one of them could have been my brother's age, if I still had a brother.

"They're beautiful," I said.

Sonny whistled for his entourage and the boys formed a human ladder for him to scale the wall. He couldn't have weighed more than 120 pounds, even with long black curls still wet from the waves. He balanced atop the wall, bare feet dancing around shards of glass, and plucked fists full of flowers.

"Beautiful flowers for the beautiful Teresa," he sang out as he tossed them down.

My name sounded magical on his lips, breathy and sibilant, the rolled "r" fluttering like my heart. No college boy had ever stolen flowers for me or serenaded me in front of all his friends. Yet here was a stranger willing to be rejected, sure that I was worth the risk of humiliation. When Sonny hopped down from the wall, I was the one who reached for his hand, letting his fingers thread between my own. I saw the triumphant, macho look he threw the boys behind us and I didn't care. Our family vacation was drawing to a close, but I would come back to this man. Be with him. Be like him, if only for a while.

After my parents fell asleep that night, he pitched tiny shells at my hotel window until I joined him on the moonlit beach. He wanted to stay up all night, to commit it to memory. I promised I'd return and I did. Six months later we were a little family of our own – the two of us and Wipeout.

The night we returned from Guadalajara, I drove my VW straight to the beach. Wipeout was still asleep on the front seat and Sonny insisted I lock the door and bury the keys in the sand to keep his new puppy safe from thieves.

We floated, naked, under Orion's Belt and the Seven Sisters. I told him how, long before I wanted to be a gymnast or a ballerina, I had resolved to become a mermaid. I imagined it just like this, the mermaid splashing her handsome prince on a beautiful beach. Sonny didn't smile or splash me back. He waited until I was wrapped around his tiny waist, tracing my fingers down his spine, to tell me that his father had shot himself. In the living room. When Sonny was 10 years old. I let his wounds swallow mine.

"It all disappears in the ocean," he said. "When you catch a wave it's as if you're flying and being flown at the same time."

It seemed possible, and wildly romantic, when he told me of his dream to become a pilot.

"Wherever you are, I will find you," he whispered. "Wherever you want to go I will fly you there."

It was inevitable that Sonny would follow me. Our fates were tangled since the day I fell in love with Mexico itself.

That was when I was seven, and Puerto Angel was the first place I dared to hope might make everything all right again, that my parents might forget about my little brother John John. I had been much younger than Sonny had been when death came to our house. On the steep driveway in front of our trailer in the Oregon woods, my brother climbed into my father's truck and knocked the gear shift into neutral, releasing the truck to roll backward downhill. John John panicked and pushed open the heavy drivers' side door that flung him under the wheels of the runaway truck, crushing him instantly.

Mexico was far enough away from the grave of a three-year-old boy for my parents to stop mourning for a few nights at least. It was Christmas Eve, 1973. Just down the beach in this quiet Pacific fishing village, a boy named Sonny was getting his first surfboard for Christmas. His father was still alive at that point, more alive than mine.

4

Innate intelligence is surpassed by impeccable instincts.

~*Byrne*

The Casting Call

Byrne's flat secretarial shoes gripped the floor in first position, as if she were still in the back row of ballet class instead of a third-story warehouse in front of a man who wanted a look at her "gams." She was certain that the frigid air was making her nipples point through her brassiere and cardigan. She arched her left foot to its ball, tucked it behind the heel of her right foot and pivoted precisely 180 degrees. At least the wall she now faced couldn't see her blush. She had no idea what to do with her gangly arms. They dangled off her sides like fireplace pokers.

"Sweet Jesus, those legs could kick my arse from a block away," came a voice behind her.

Byrne put her hands on her tiny waist and cocked her head to reveal her profile. "Or kick higher than any chorus girl you've ever seen," she said, hoping for a tone somewhere between don't-come-any-closer and you'd-be-lucky-to-hire-me.

It was a different kind of luck that had led to Byrne's first and only Vaudeville dance audition. The ballet lessons, Saturday matinees, summers picking strawberries with her

Aunt Cornelia in Cream Hill, Connecticut, pocket change to ride the new Manhattan subway system – all evaporated when Michael Miller went bankrupt in 1933. His was a business that catered to Manhattan's middle class: a chain of drycleaners. When jobs disappeared, so did the need for professionally cleaned suits and dress shirts. Of all of Byrne's nine uncles, not one could find a job. So Byrne and her mother found work, each for the first time in their lives, and each for lower pay than any man would accept.

Fanny's job was at the Home Relief Bureau. Byrne worked at *Nature's Path Magazine*. Combined, their salaries still weren't enough to support the family. So when the Mildred Strauss Dancers put a classified ad in the *New York Post* for "tall, beautiful dancers to go on tour," Byrne looked in a full-length mirror in the *Nature's Path* ladies room and decided that, at the very least, she was tall.

"This horrible little man had a wet cigar dangling from the corner of his mouth," she told her best friend after the audition.

"Probably longer than anything in his pants," Ruth warned. "Be careful. Desperate men do desperate things."

He hadn't, actually. After the initial spin-around look-see, he called in a wardrobe mistress who handed Byrne a glittering, gold-colored silk tank suit – the kind that looked like a spaghetti strap, all-in-one bathing suit ending high on the thigh, except with pointier pleats and lower neckline. Behind a burlap curtain, Byrne unzipped herself down to her stockings and slipped her first foot through the leotard opening.

Point the toes, she told herself, clinging to the dancers' way of referring to parts of the whole. *Now extend the leg, keep the hip turned out.* If she thought of her body as an instrument she could create a distance between the girl who was still her father's little gypsy and the grown woman who would do almost anything to help him.

It was working, up until the leotard left the leg far below and wrapped around parts more personal. The silky fabric clung to the curve of her hips, tapered in to accent her high waist and molded itself around her firm breasts like a second skin. She was gold-plated, jutting out and shielded all at once. For the first time in her life, Byrne wished for a mirror. She felt like a goddess.

"Now that's how to fill a costume," the wardrobe mistress said when Byrne emerged from behind the burlap curtain, smiling as if she'd created the body, not just the leotard. "She'll be stunning mounted up on the velvet dais."

"That's if she can dance," the casting director mumbled over the fat wet stogie still dangling from his lip. "Let's see you improvise."

Byrne froze, certain that any classical ballet combinations would mean never getting to wear the costume again.

"I haven't anything prepared," she mumbled.

"That's why they call it improvisation, girlie. Just move."

She couldn't.

"Listen, girlie, this ain't the job for prudes. We got 18 other girls and most of them worked the corners before I discovered 'em, if you follow me."

Byrne nodded. She, the well-bred daughter of a kosher-keeping drycleaner, would be working alongside former prostitutes.

"I don't have all day. Just say something, without talking."

Her body was already speaking on her behalf, fists clenched and shoulders ratcheting up her long neck. *I need this job,* she told herself, *just close the door on me and be someone else for a few minutes.*

The someone else who flashed behind her squeezed-shut eyes was Fanny. Not Fanny her loving and practical mother but the famous Jewish performer who grated on Fanny

Miller's last nerve. Fanny Brice wasn't a born dancer or an all-American beauty, but she'd found a way to incorporate her awkwardness and otherness into every act and make it charming. *Use what you have,* Byrne told herself, *even if you have to fake it.* She grabbed the sheet of ratty burlap that served as dressing room divider and yanked it off the nails.

"Stop that!" the wardrobe mistress shrieked, but Byrne was already ripping it into long ribbons. Five in each fist, she swooped them through the air like propellers on either side of her body.

"Picture these as palm fronds masquerading as ostrich plumes," she said, winking at the casting director. Then she launched into the parody of fan dancing chorus girls that had made Fanny Brice the sweetheart of the Ziegfeld Follies. Byrne curtsied and shimmied, all the while flapping the limp strips of burlap. She strutted and kicked behind her vented veil. She blinked and blushed, then, for a finale, climbed atop a metal chair and flung her faux feathers as wide as her smile full of disorganized teeth.

The casting director pulled the wet cigar from his mouth, balanced it on the chair Byrne towered over and applauded. Then he held up his plump, sweaty hand.

"How long does it take you to pack a suitcase?" he said, helping her down. "The Sara Mildred Strauss Dancers leave for Washington on Tuesday."

Her mind raced. *Tuesday? As in next week Tuesday?*

"Tuesday would be fine," she said, still carrying on another conversation in her head. *Rushed, it's so rushed. I won't be able to give notice at the magazine. Maybe mother can take over and we can keep the salary.* Even a year ago, Fanny would never have been a party to this. A would-be concert pianist "improvising" atop a velvet-covered dais would have been a secret to keep from her mother forever. But witnessing the man they both loved wallow in unfamiliar despair had erased the normal lines of propriety and expectation. Fanny and Byrne were partners in survival now, not simply mother and daughter. Byrne knew she would understand. Pulling in a showgirl's salary would keep the whole family afloat, maybe even pay for the baby grand piano to be tuned and a breath of hopeful melody to float from Michael Miller's nail-bitten fingers.

"I'll be at Grand Central bright and early," she said.

Suddenly the chair seemed wobblier than it had when she pounced upon it as Fanny Brice. The color drained from Byrne's face; her knees hyper-extended and she all but fell into the casting director's arms.

"Something the matter?" he asked.

There was. Never mind her mother's reaction. Byrne had been married not even a month. What would she tell Duncan?

5

An Island of Our Own

Beaufort – 1989

For a brief, thrilling moment, the Whale Branch River Bridge releases all who travel over it from gravity. You look down from an Osprey's eye view into a fish-full ribbon of life. The water is a shimmering membrane, wide and porous. Salt and sweet, past and present glide through in opposite directions.

The first time we crossed the Whale Branch River I rolled down the windows of a rented U-haul truck and let Wipeout stick her wet nose into the sulfurous wonder of it. She was nearly grown now, 60 pounds of pure white, furry enthusiasm. We were towing my car, going slow enough that the warm slobber on my shoulder blended with the humidity rushing into the cab. Her panting doggy breath was at one with the gases of the salt marsh.

"We're finally here!" Sonny exclaimed, crumpling up the ragged map we'd used to navigate the last 3,000 miles. "It smells like home."

Beaufort perches on an island that French explorers named Port Royal, surrounded by brackish rivers like the Whale Branch. Jump in at the wrong place and you'll sink to your knees in tar-thick, black mud that hides razor-sharp oyster shells. If Wipeout had made a leap for it, the outgoing tide would have carried her past Half Moon and Ballast islands, down the Intracoastal Waterway, and dumped her out onto the beach where it empties into the Atlantic Ocean.

On the promise of this unseen beach, I had dragged Sonny with me when I got my first reporting job at the town's only television station: WJWJ. Moving to a coastal town south of Charleston and north of Savannah wasn't a hard sell, compared to the alternative of living off his mother in Mexico or with my parents in Oregon.

We figured that as soon as we got settled in Beaufort and had paychecks rolling in, Sonny would get his private pilot's license and fly planes for a living. But the only job he could get right away was washing dishes, using his cousin Ricardo's fake social security card.

It was in Beaufort that Sonny became the illegal alien known as "Rick." We thought the name sounded Southern, not that Sonny looked it with his dark, brooding eyes, defiant nose and caramel skin. The romance of our tidal island life was pricked the first time he got fired.

"Fucker said I'm living the Mexican dream," Sonny told me as I swabbed his split lip after the ensuing fist fight. "A white girlfriend and a part-time job."

I didn't dare say it aloud but it seemed to me that the fight was more than just a reaction to a perceived insult. I tended to his bleeding face with the steady calm possessed by the truly treasured. *He loves me. He will never let anything happen to me.* Sonny had put himself in danger to defend the bond between us. I was much more than just a white girlfriend to Sonny and he wasn't afraid to prove it.

"It's only temporary," I tried to soothe him, "until we save up enough for flight school. Then you'll be a pilot, above all this."

Beaufort County is made up of more than 200 islands, yet it is 20 miles to Hunting Island, the nearest public beach, where Sonny could paddle a board out into the cleansing waters. My VW Rabbit was in the shop with pistons that hadn't made it through the drive from Mexico, and once we'd returned the U-haul, we were stranded. I didn't want to live with a trapped man. I'd spent the first 16 years of my life trying to please a father who would rather have been anywhere but where his marriage landed him.

So I called my grandmother to ask for a loan to set my boyfriend free.

"How's the next Barbara Walters doing?" she said, the pride in her voice scraping against my conscience. "Your father showed me how to work my VCR machine so I've been watching all your stories."

I groaned. "Gran, me prattling on about mosquito control ordinances can't possibly be interesting."

"No, sweetheart, but that lipstick you're wearing is. It looks orange next to your skin tone. I'll send you some better shades."

I leaned back against the faux wood paneling of the tiny house we'd rented and took a deep breath. "That'd be great Gran, but I'm wondering if you could loan me some money too – just until things get settled."

I crossed my fingers for not telling her the money was for a truck for Sonny and squashed a cockroach with my shoe. Beaufortonians call them palmetto bugs, as if proud that South Carolina roaches have the distinction of being good fliers. Calling it something prettier than the truth still made my skin crawl.

When my grandmother sent the money, I bought Sonny a white Toyota pickup from a used-car dealer on Boundary Street and three lives transformed. The truck bed was long enough to carry Sonny's surfboards with room leftover for a long-haired husky to sprawl. Instead of hitchhiking to the beach and leaving Wipeout tied to her doghouse in our dirt backyard scratching fleas, he could take her with him. The subtropical, palm-fanned, lushly primeval landscape of Hunting Island State Park was alive with smells that must have reminded her of Mexico. Where the forested park gives way to the Atlantic Ocean, she had sand and sun and a boy who threw sticks into the waves.

On weekends I spread out a beach towel and watched them both, just as I had in Mexico. Wipeout galloped in and out of the ocean and then rubbed her itchy, salty back on a coastal carpet of pine needles and sweet grass. Sonny wedged the tail of his board into soft piles of sand and squatted on his haunches, scanning the horizon. He could stay like that for hours, serene and patient as the Indian women in Mexico who hover over piles of vegetables and fruits at outdoor markets. But when he spotted the makings of a swell in the distance he sprung up from his tensile crouch like a projectile. He jerked the board from its sentry stance and ran with it under his arm, stopping only to Velcro the leash around his tattooed ankle.

In Mexico, there would have been an entourage of lost boy surfers behind him, whooping with the thrill of the hunt. In Beaufort the waves weren't worthy of such howls. Sonny had to sneak up on them, holding back his own expectations. He didn't have to duck and bob under row after row of breakers to get into position. His board sliced across the still Atlantic surface. Instead of paddling in place while he waited for waves, he dangled – conserving energy. When a set finally rolled his way, he swam ahead of it, never glancing backward. He knew when to stand as intuitively as I knew when to breathe.

In Puerto Angel the power of the surf had dictated Sonny's technique. At Hunting Island he had to carve his own waves out of limp curls of sea foam. His thighs and knees pumped each swell like a jockey whipping a racehorse. He leaned out over his board, cutting back and forth across the face of the wave to squeeze every possible moment from the ride. This was not a man who accepted disappointment. He thrashed and wrestled with it, determined to make the most out of any hand he was dealt.

With one of his first paychecks he bought a shallow aluminum jon boat that he could hitch to the truck and launch from the Pigeon Point public landing.

"What are we going to do with that?" I asked. The boat looked as sea worthy as a peeled-open sardine tin, shallow and wide. There wasn't even a steering wheel. Sonny had to sit in the back next to the noisy two-stroke motor and maneuver through the winding creeks with his hand on a taped-together wooden tiller.

"We're going to discover all the places where people threw booze bottles into the water a hundred years ago," he answered. "I checked out a bunch of books on it from the library. They're worth a ton of money now, and you don't need a green card to collect them."

And so began an expedition to recover all remaining South Carolina Dispensary bottles from the oyster banks of the Beaufort River. Sonny was right; the hand-blown bottles were worth money on the antique market. From 1893 to 1907, they were the South Carolina governor's solution to calls for early prohibition. Liquor consumed in the state had to be bottled at a South Carolina dispensary so that at least some of the spoils of vice went into the public kitty.

I sat in the middle of the jon boat, atop a Styrofoam cooler filled with tuna sandwiches, Pringles and beer, and watched another world glide by. At low tide the Whale Branch River slid down its glistening banks and exposed vast mud flats and thick stands of spartina marsh grass. Wipeout stood wobbly guard at the bow, ears twitching at the sound of oysters squirting water from their long, jagged shells. Sonny cut off the motor and beached the boat on a river-ringed mound of sun-bleached, discarded oyster shells.

He hopped over the side of the boat into murky, knee-high water and held out both arms in front of him, a cradle to carry me to shore. *My bare-chested knight,* I thought. After a few mud-sucking steps Sonny grinned down at me, splashed out into deeper water and tossed me in, diving over my head before I came up for air.

"Are you crazy?" I sputtered. "This whole estuary is a breeding ground for bull sharks."

"Actually it's more like a nursery," he said, squirting water at me through clasped-tight hands. "They're too little to bite off more than a finger or two."

We splashed enough to scare away any baby sharks or their protective mothers, letting the buoyancy of the brackish water substitute for actual exertion. When we got hungry, we pulled the boat higher up the bank and shared the contents of the cooler with our panting, mud-covered dog.

"Be nice," Sonny said, stretching the length of the word past its breaking point. It was his way of warning Wipeout, the tone of voice that told her he could still grab her snout, pry open her jaws, reach down her throat and take away whatever food she wanted. I felt my own jaw-bone clench, remembering the violent way he had trained Wipeout not to snatch at offered treats. "It's for her own good," he had said in front of me and his band of pre-teen surfers on the beach in Mexico. "Otherwise she'll end up biting someone."

For her own good I had doubted, even then. Now I watched with the itching, guilty skin of a bystander as Wipeout went down on her belly in front of Sonny and tentatively licked a lump of tuna fish from his salty palm.

"That's my good girl," he said, and tossed Wipeout his entire sandwich as reward. She wolfed it down before he changed his mind and Sonny laughed and wrestled in the black pluff mud with the dog he'd always wanted. The heavy white sky of summer was kite high above our heads, drifting without purpose or border, and we were alone on our own private island.

It was Sonny who first spotted a reflection in the shell-speckled mud. Sun glinted off the weathered neck of a bottle the color of sea glass.

"Help me dig it out," he said, dropping to his knees and scooping pluff mud with his bare hands. The bottle made a sucking sound as he pried it from its viscous tomb. I splashed water over the flat front panel of what once had been a half-pint of rum or bourbon, and Sonny massaged the crusty surface until the raised ridges of a design began to show.

Slowly the river released an image straight out of a pirate story: the splaying fronds of a palmetto tree with two crossed logs at its base. I held in my hands something more than 100 years old and suddenly I felt like a trespasser, marooned in a place with a history not her own. I thought of telling Sonny to bury it again, that it might be a bad omen to take something so beautiful from the river.

But one look at Sonny's face and I knew taking something so beautiful from him would bring only worse luck. On the shores of our private island, Sonny was no longer a dishwasher with a fake Social Security card or a surfer betrayed by his ocean. He was adventurer, explorer and treasure hunter all in one, and I was the woman for whom he would name all his discoveries, at whose feet he would pile his hard-won loot. *He's already traveled to another country for me. The least I can do is let him keep an old bottle,* I said to myself.

For hours Sonny scoured the oyster mound for more South Carolina Dispensary bottles until the tide began to reclaim our private island. Wipeout drank all the melted ice water from the cooler and fell asleep with her head across my thighs. The bottom of the boat made sloppy, slapping noises as the tide tugged it out into deeper waters where the dorsal fin of a bottlenose dolphin broke the surface.

"Look! Dolphins!" I called out to Sonny.

He looked up from the pile of mud and shells at his feet.

"You know what that means, don't you?" he asked. "Every time you see a dolphin, it means you're going to have a perfect day."

"But what if the day's already over?"

He paused, bringing a mud-covered hand to his chin. "I never thought about it, but I guess it works retroactively. Didn't we have a perfect day?"

It was the logic of the hopeful, the rationale of a dreamer, and I have judged the perfection of a day by dolphin hindsight ever since.

It was dolphins I thanked when Sonny stopped calling me at the TV station every couple of hours, bored and wasted. He had a truck, a boat and a quest to keep himself busy and he didn't have to ask me for money anymore. "Rick" drove his truck to a string of jobs at bars, bakeries and delis. Each one lasted until his payroll tax deduction got red flagged and his bosses were notified that the number on his social security card didn't match up to an actual person. Like every illegal immigrant with a fake social security card, "Rick" paid taxes on behalf of someone who doesn't exist and could never claim benefits. The Social Security Administration has a great name for this giant slush fund, the "earnings suspense file," but it wasn't the kind of suspense Sonny needed.

"I don't owe these fuckers anything," he told me every

time he quit a job. "I do the work, Rick pays taxes. It's not like perfect little *gringa* gymnasts with master's degrees in journalism are lining up to do this shit."

Between jobs, there was more time for him to surf, smoke pot and search for bottles. The months flowed past in liquid, opposite directions. Sonny moved in the world of the none-of-your-business, don't-ask-questions service industry. He categorized his coworkers as just let outs, kicked outs or dropouts. I covered city council, circuit court and cultural features on the Gullah people, descendants of freed slaves who still spoke a form of the languages that connected them to Africa. Old black ladies from the islands, who couldn't afford cable TV, patted my shoulder when they recognized me at the checkout line of the Piggy Wiggly. "Might talk a little slower," they suggested. "But you doin' a good job, sugar, real good."

On weekends we packed up the truck for the beach. Sonny always drove and I would roll the windows down and turn up the volume on his favorite Doors' song.

Now that we know each other a little bit better, why don't you come over here?

Wipeout would howl at the sound of Jim Morrison's voice and I'd scoot over on the bench seat closer to Sonny.

Make me feel all right.

Some days, it seemed as if he was fine with being "Rick" forever – like the days when he and his kitchen-staff pals got high in the service alley off Bay Street, or the days leading up to a hurricane when the waves at Hunting Island could top four feet. Other days I knew it ate away at him. He would wait outside the TV station for my lunch break, and then eat his tuna fish sandwich next to me. If there were no waves, he would return to the station to watch the newscast at 6 o'clock. He would sit, with his feet up on my desk, teasing me about each teleprompter mistake.

The male reporters would hang around, listening to Sonny describe tubular waves that take a mile to break, or peyote you can ball into beads for a necklace and walk right by the cops without them knowing. He charmed them, with his Mexican street handshakes and promises of teaching them how to surf.

One sunny Saturday, on the way to Hunting Island, Sonny smiled at me and reached for my hand. Then he squeezed, three times.

"What's that for?" I asked.

"It'll be our private code," he said. "One squeeze for each word in 'I love you'."

I inhaled Sonny's rebel scent of saltwater and coconut wax, breathed deeply his devotion. I closed my eyes as I twisted proof of his love around my wrist, the hemp bracelet entwined with cowry shells he had braided for me when we first met. A charm bracelet, he had called it. *Para mi sirena* – for my mermaid.

"Bitch," Sonny said, suddenly shoving me away. "Think you're too good for me?"

I turned to look at him but he wouldn't meet my eyes.

"What did I do?" I asked.

"It's what you didn't do," he said, still not looking at me. "How fucking hard is it? You should have squeezed me back four times."

What was he talking about? *Oh, the private code, one squeeze for each word in I love you.*

"But I thought you said three."

"I did."

A farm truck, overflowing with tomatoes, was bearing down on us but Sonny chose that moment to take his eyes off the two-lane road and glare at me.

"If you loved me too, that's four words. Four squeezes back." He held up four fingers, poised, like a backhand.

"Maybe I can't count good enough for you either."

If there were dolphins in the Whale Branch River that day, I didn't see them.

6

It does a man good to flirt.
~Byrne

Secret Marriage

BYRNE NEVER SET OUT to hide her job from her lover or her lover from her job. She told herself she was only thinking of Duncan. What young newlywed wants to imagine other men leering at his bride on a velvet-covered Vaudeville dais? Or, for that matter, what burlesque casting director wants to discover that his leggy new star is actually a respectable married lady? There is a fine line between discretion and dishonor, and Byrne wasn't at all sure she was graceful enough to balance along it.

She berated herself for not auditioning for a touring Vaudeville dance act long before settling down with a husband. In the libretto of her life, she would have gotten this flashy, exhibitionist dance business out of her system before her husband even met her. The income from her scandalous dance troupe days would have mysteriously bolstered her family finances enough for a nice Jewish wedding reception in Washington Heights. She would have saved tales of being on stage alongside scantily clad former prostitutes for private giggle material, just in case any children resulting from her marriage grew up to consider their mother boring or repressed.

But that would have been the story line of a traditional ballet, a three-act structure described in glossy programs handed out in hushed performance halls. Byrne was all modern dance – plot-less, earthy, leading from the torso instead of pointed toes and fluttering fingers. And so her married life started *in medias res*, secretive and tumultuous. She met her future husband at a writers' group that gathered to share work every week in Central Park's Shakespeare Garden. It was the same day Duncan had decided to quit the group.

In the moment their lives intersected, Byrne hadn't even heard of the Sara Mildred Strauss Dancers, let alone imagined herself among them. The serendipity of her meeting Duncan at all was only because belonging to a writers' group scratched the itch of creative yearning. Each week, for an hour at least, she could pretend she was something more than a daughter struggling to pay her father's rent. The group didn't know she spent her days at *Nature's Path* churning out articles touting the miracles of drugless therapies, massage and nude sunbathing. Under the leafless trees of Central Park, she was iambic pentameter and internal rhyme, never too tall or gangly to lean and sway with the rhythm of her own words. Instead of a girl stooping in the back row of ballet class, she was a woman reading her poetry out loud and out front.

Until the day she met Duncan, there had been only nods of encouragement and eyes closed in dreamy solidarity. Until him, no one had ever leaned against the trunk of a tree and listened wide-eyed, screwing up his lips as though tasting her words and deciding whether to spit them out. Duncan seemed to her a beautiful man-child with bushy eyebrows that anchored what otherwise would have been an impish face. His clean-shaven chin, his long nose, even his earlobes ended in points instead of curves. Despite the cluster of people around them, she felt naked and alone with him. It seemed like hours between her last couplet and his first words to her.

"Promising," he pronounced. "But in my estimation real writers simply write. They have no need for groups."

Duncan was 18; Byrne was a 24-year-old who actually made a living, however meager, writing. His cocky certainty slid under her thin skin like a bamboo point, prying up the sense that she was treading water, waiting for the Depression to end and her life to begin. She dallied after the rest of the would-be writers adjourned for coffee, not quite ready to allow the arrogant upstart to assume he'd won but not wanting to let him slip away either. In the moment before she'd decided exactly how to put him in his place, Duncan pounced first.

"Away before me to sweet beds of flowers," he quoted the garden's namesake, snapping a stalk of flax from a newly planted bed. "Love thoughts lie rich when canopied with bowers."

"Is that your idea of asking me to quit with you?" she asked.

"Count Orsino, Act one, Scene one, *Twelfth Night*," he replied, as if to a student unfamiliar with the Bard.

But Byrne's instinct was right. Duncan did want her to run away with him. He was quitting precisely so that she would join him and together they would be the beginning of something new. He leaned over and picked up Byrne's books.

"You may find it interesting to note that we share the same surname," he said. "I'm Duncan Miller and I'm walking you home."

"You have no idea how far away that is," Byrne said before giving in to the outstretched hand before her.

"It doesn't matter now," he replied, his thin red lips parting into what she hoped was a smile and not a smirk.

It was winter, not a day for a leisurely stroll through Central Park. Byrne was bundled under cardigans and a thick wool pea coat which, even conspiring together, could not disguise the lanky power of her figure. Duncan wore only a Greek fisherman's cap and a cream cabled sweater. He was compact and loose at the same time. He seemed to her lit from someplace deep within.

"I'm a Southerner who misses the water," he said. It was a genuine smile; she was certain of it once she saw the sparkle in his eyes. His accent didn't seem as natural – he spoke with more British prep school than down-home Dixie. "We'll take in the lake on the way."

Byrne laughed. "Wrong direction. I'm 70 blocks north, give or take," she said, wrapping her scarf a little tighter. He was already striding south, leading the way with the swagger of a young man who'd just convinced an older woman to run away with him.

Her irritation surfaced again, just enough to needle him. "Do you always quit things before you've even given them a try?" she asked, when her long legs overtook him. She meant the writers' group, and how insultingly he'd dismissed everyone who took it seriously.

He paused, wiping his hand under the nose that had begun to run in the cold.

"Not always. I tried Duke University for almost a whole year."

So he was a college dropout. It wasn't uncommon in the few bleak years since the stock market had crashed. But to Byrne it made him a little more human, less intellectually intimidating.

"I tried Columbia," she said. "I was studying philosophy. And journalism."

It was then that she saw him smirk, not at her but at the concept of journalism. In the hours that he managed to stretch the task of accompanying Byrne to her parents' home in Washington Heights, Duncan railed against all things propaganda, never acknowledging that in his earnestness he was using those very tactics to persuade her.

"The best intellects are in the East," he said. "And opportunities. I might apply for papers to emigrate to Russia." A millisecond later his declaration collided with the spark of another thought traveling in the opposite direction. "Loads of us already have though. The moment's probably passed."

He told her he had written a paper for *The New Republic* and decided to send it not to the magazine itself but to a writer whose work for it had once inspired but now disgusted him: Edmund Wilson. He'd just read *The American Jitters* and thought it naively glorified Soviet Russia as a utopia.

"You'd like to move in with Stalin and you want Wilson's magazine to publish your work, yet you called his writing naive?" Byrne asked.

"Of course," Duncan answered. "If he doesn't respect my integrity then how will he recognize the truth of my words?"

He gripped Byrne's hands as he spoke, turning to face her so that she understood he wasn't just a boy trying to hold a girl's hand. He meant to arrest her, to hold her scattered thoughts and palpitating heart hostage. She knew the sensation of her father's adoration, bathed in the spotlight of her mother's critical attention. She was accustomed to the stares and whistles of men twice her age. But Duncan made her feel like audience and star at the same time. It was more than her talent or opinion that mattered to him. It seemed he craved her belief in him.

Duncan's voice pierced through the sounds of the busy streets surrounding them, rendering normal distractions mute. The rumble of subway cars dulled, even the multisyllabic braying of Ford Model A horns receded into distant annoyance. The monochromatic greys and blacks of men shuffling along the sidewalks made Duncan leap from the background in stark relief. He was sharp edges and burning energy, all of it bearing down on her. If it weren't for the way his eyes softened and enveloped her, his withering focus would have made her shoulders tense and her jaw click. But those eyes made her feel as though each word she uttered in reply was the most interesting he had ever contemplated.

Byrne would later say she fell in love with Duncan Miller on that long walk through New York's Upper West Side to Washington Heights, that she knew then that she would marry this much younger, more certain man. She did not know she would be the one to comfort him when Edmund Wilson sent a dismissive reply.

"Dear Mr. Miller," the letter began, respectfully enough. "The socialist dictatorship of the proletariat – as Lenin and Trotsky always insisted – is in fundamental ways a very undesirable state of things. It is merely the necessary first step in the direction of communism."

Duncan saved the letter, almost proud of his first rejection by such a noted intellectual. "I don't like to see people trying to make political opinions do duty for artistic ability," it concluded. "I'm afraid that *The New Republic* couldn't very well use your paper … and by the way 'American Jitters' was not my first book but my sixth. Yours sincerely, Edmund Wilson."

Duncan found a more receptive audience in Fanny Miller. Byrne's mother noticed his red pointed ears and even redder, runny nose and insisted that this underdressed young man who'd walked her daughter all the way home in the dead of winter stay for supper. Byrne thanked Fanny with complicit eyes. She knew her mother was extending the magic of an evening like she had when Byrne was a little girl and wanted to stay up past her bedtime listening to her father play piano. Fanny would stretch the ritual of brushing out her daughter's hair for shiny, soft hours on end, and somehow she knew it was a different man's performance Byrne wanted to extend that night.

Byrne settled down in the front row to watch Duncan's story unfold but quickly realized his was a performance not commanded. He artfully steered the dinner conversation to his hostess's interests and opinions and away from his own background. It was the first time Byrne ever heard the story of her Polish grandfather John, a sometimes cruel itinerant peddler, or of her grandmother Bessie who became an invalid after bearing seven children. She was vaguely aware, perhaps a tad embarrassed, that her mother had quit school in the eighth grade. What Duncan's presence revealed was how proud Fanny was of managing to bathe, feed and protect her siblings so her beloved, beleaguered mother could finally rest.

So distanced and disconnected were Duncan's references to his own family that Byrne felt as if he sprung from a place and not a people. He spoke of the weight of Charleston summers, how just-short-of-drowning it was to simply breathe the air there. She yearned to pull him from the dark currents that he swam against. She leaped in and swept the conversation to safer, lighter topics; it was their first *pas de deux*.

It would be decades before Byrne, or any American audiences, saw the Russian ballet *The Nutcracker Suite* performed on stage. But when she did, she recognized the opening party scene as a mimed version of the night Duncan made his debut on the Miller stage. Duncan was Herr Dosselmeyer – the charismatic councilman who makes a grand entrance bearing gifts and enchanting all the children. His gifts were the ways he extricated laughs from her father and blushes from her mother, how he drew out responses from Sherman with attentive patience and the grace with which he made each member of Byrne's family feel like a guest in their own home.

To Edmund Wilson he may have seemed impudent and accusatory, but to Fanny Miller, Duncan was a polite, hungry boy who devoured every morsel of his first Kosher meal with unaffected appreciation and hopped up to help clear the table between courses. He was just as direct and unassuming with Byrne's father and younger brother. He didn't condescend to ask Sherman about girls or popular Yankees players of the day like Lou Gehrig. He treated the teenager like the working man he had just become and promised to drop by the soda shop where Sherman manned the counter when he called on Byrne again.

Duncan stayed until Michael Miller tired of playing the piano. He even coaxed a song out of Fanny's repertoire before she insisted on giving Duncan a token for the subway home. Byrne was equal parts astounded and intrigued. This Shakespeare-quoting communist sympathizer had seduced her family in a single sitting.

Years later, she would tell friends that she and Duncan consummated their affair soon after they met, skipping the next writers' group meeting to plunge into each other's bodies in Central Park's neglected Ramble.

"We hadn't two dimes to rub together, let alone enough to get a hotel room," she said in defense only of their choice of location. She considered the physical act itself not nearly as scandalous as how she had to pursue Duncan after the physical conquest.

"What kind of wedding shall we have?" she asked him as the spasms of his release still ricocheted through his body. She held him captive for an answer, her long, bare legs wrapped around his solid waist under the cover of her swirling skirt.

His thick eyebrows knotted in confusion. He had thought Byrne far more experienced and worldly than the type of girl who would cling to conventional social mores, especially after so freely offering herself to him. Her insistence on marriage, her assumption rather, tugged at a thread that threatened to unravel the identity he was trying so doggedly to create.

"There has never been a happy marriage in the history of my miserable family," he blurted out. His eyes bore into hers. This was not avoidance of responsibility but inherited suspicion and dread.

Byrne took his pointed face in her hands and lifted his chin. "Well, there has never been an unhappy one in mine, so that makes up for it."

Duncan rotated his shoulders in their sockets, stretching his neck as though trying on a new skin. Then he slowly pivoted away from Byrne's embrace and drew his knees to his chest.

"Do you really want to be the first in your family to marry outside the Jewish faith?" he asked.

"Didn't you notice? After the roast beef, my father took cream in his coffee," she said. "There was butter in the cake my mother served."

Duncan drew his chin into his turtleneck sweater, not following.

"We're orthodox, but not strict," Byrne said, laughing. "Mother has already adopted you. She will just have to accept you as a changeling."

Duncan, at last, smiled. Fanny knew him for what he was. And Byrne trusted in the man he would become.

So he knew it wouldn't matter to Byrne that the ring he gave her when he formally proposed came from a box of Cracker Jacks.

"Will you do me the honor?" he asked, on bended knee.

Byrne, towering over the man she had practically insisted on marrying, burst into tears.

"When they publish my first novel," Duncan said, his voice betraying alarm, "I will buy you the biggest diamond they have at Tiffany's. Or the Star of India, whichever you prefer."

"It's not that," Byrne said, pulling him into her arms. "Don't be ridiculous."

Duncan stiffened, unsure if he should be relieved or insulted.

"Should I have asked your father for your hand first?" he asked.

"That's just it," Byrne said, sobbing again. "If we get married then we'll have to live together."

"That would be the logical assumption."

"But I can't move out. Father couldn't get by without my salary."

It was March of 1933, the same month Roosevelt took the oath of office and the state governors closed every bank in the nation. Even if he had some savings or inheritance to tap into, Duncan couldn't have cashed a single check or withdrawn a dollar from a bank.

"Then I'll move in with you. And you can add whatever money I make to the family's resources," Duncan said.

Byrne ground her mouth into his, almost violent in her need to show Duncan how much she appreciated what he was proposing. But when their lips unstuck, she still didn't say the word he wanted to hear: yes.

"It would humiliate him," she said.

"It would humiliate any man," Duncan agreed.

They sat side-by-side on a wrought iron bench, Byrne fiddling with the Cracker Jack ring, sliding it on and off her finger until Duncan clamped his hand over hers.

"We will go to New Jersey and do it there. No one has

to know but the two of us and a justice of the peace. We'll tell your parents only that we are engaged, and we'll wait until things turn around to move in together."

Byrne and Duncan married, in secret, on May 13, 1933, and six months later Michael Miller landed a job. Shortly afterward Duncan asked Michael for permission to marry his daughter and Byrne circled a classified advertisement for tall, beautiful dancers.

The entire Miller clan walked into Manhattan's city hall on December 9, 1933 – stomping wet snow from their boots and standing proudly behind Byrne and Duncan as they exchanged vows. It would be the date they would celebrate as their anniversary for nearly 60 years, the day a piano-playing dry cleaner from Hungary gave away his little gypsy to a young man from Charleston, South Carolina. Byrne never even had to change her last name to officially become the married woman she already was.

7

The Phony Marriage

BEAUFORT – 1991

THE BEAUFORT COUNTY LIBRARY was a squat, one-story building whitewashed so many times you couldn't tell if its walls were brick or concrete. It smelled of mildew and old carpet. Palmetto bugs crawled along the cracks of the foundation as if they took over during the night, after the librarians went home. Most people came inside just for the air conditioning, and not a soul paid attention to me, poring over U.S. immigration code, wondering if surfing would qualify Sonny as an eligible athlete or as providing a "unique and valuable service" to the country.

It was in the stacks of the Beaufort County Library, looking for legal paths to immigration, that I discovered how easy it was to be considered married in South Carolina. If I were his wife, instead of just his live-in girlfriend, Sonny could get a green card and begin the process of becoming a citizen. If two people of opposite gender lived together, there was no requirement for a wedding. All you had to do was call it common law. No verification was required, not even any specified period of cohabitation. You could be married without a piece of paper, without a church, without witnesses – a status as deliciously ephemeral and impermanent as a wave. It went way back, I surmised, to thinking South Carolina slave couples weren't human enough to warrant the paperwork. The writers of that law could never have imagined it might one day help a cowardly young woman get her half-Mexican boyfriend citizenship.

"The common-law argument is perfectly valid," I told Sonny that night when he got home from his shift at a bar on Bay Street. "It's just unusual."

Using the stereo's remote, he skipped from the start of one Doors song to the next. I stepped directly in front of him, blocking the signal. "I can get us a hearing, but we'll have to practice. We have to be on the same page. Rick can disappear because the real you will have a green card. It has a beautiful ring to it, doesn't it?"

"Speaking of a ring, shouldn't you wear one?" he asked me. "I mean, if we're going to fake being married it couldn't hurt."

"K-Mart's still open, isn't it?" I said.

We jumped in the pickup truck and headed to the strip mall, me carrying on like this was somehow impulsive and romantic.

We thumbed through the spinning, plastic displays of costume earrings, peered over glass cabinets stuffed with cheap watches.

"I hate the commercialism of romance," I said. "Those Zales ads make me puke. Why does the poor guy have to hand over three months' salary?"

"Because it's supposed to be forever," Sonny answered. Forever for us came to $32.95.

I fiddled with my K-Mart ring all along the drive to the immigration hearing in Charleston. Sweat beads formed on my upper lip, and an itchy rash broke out on my finger where the cheap ring rested. Sonny told me to spit on it and slide it up a little higher, until it jammed against my knuckle.

When it was finally our turn to be interviewed by the INS, I felt wooden, like my tongue was glued in place and my feet nailed to the floor. Luckily, the inspector asked Sonny the first question.

"How long have you been in this country?"

Sonny gave the answer we'd agreed upon.

"We've lived together all that time," I jumped in. "I've got a statement from our landlord in Beaufort."

"So this is a common-law marriage claim," the inspector said. "Why not just get married for real?"

"We are married for real," I said. "We hold ourselves out as man and wife. We wear each other's rings."

I resisted the temptation to show him my left hand. I exhaled through my nose, loudly. Maybe righteous indignation would cover my nervousness.

"Let me rephrase the question," the inspector asked. "Why did you not get married by a justice of the peace or a minister?"

He shouldn't have been asking me this. It was none of his business. He didn't know how many steps above a bedroom you have to hide to block out the sounds of a mother crying. He wasn't the one who held up a plastic laundry basket and said it was a pretty Valentine's present. He didn't see the jerking shadows a wrestled rifle casts on the walls of a trailer in the woods of Oregon.

Fuck you, mister, I don't owe Sonny anything.

"Religious differences," I sputtered.

This wasn't on our script. I pulled it out of thin air. Sonny stared, wide-eyed, counting on me to save him from instant deportation.

"His mother, being Mexican, is Catholic of course." I was leaping out of the curtained wings and onto a dark stage, hoping a spotlight would find me. "My father is a raging atheist. Calls Mexicans 'wetbacks' or 'beaners,' and that's if he's in a good mood. Won't step foot in a church. His mother won't accept anything less than a cathedral. What would you do?"

The inspector raised his eyebrows and a noise came from somewhere in his naval cavity. First a wheeze, then a snort and then he leaned back in his chair, erupting in laughter.

"I'll sign the paperwork," he said, getting up to shake our hands. "Just promise me one thing. Wait until one or the other of your parents is dead before you decide to have children."

Sonny decided to celebrate on the way home.

"I would like my *wife* to drive," he said, tossing me the keys. The word felt like a spider landing on my skin. "I brought a joint along just for the occasion."

I didn't argue. I wanted him to relax and forget the circumstances of our victory. By the time we got home, the mellow had worn off and he was ready to down a few beers.

"I thought you were going to punch that guy in the face, the way you looked at him," he said. "I nearly pissed my pants."

I laughed and handed him a beer.

8

The Screened Porch Stage

BEAUFORT – 1991

BEAUFORT WAS SUPPOSED to be the launching pad for our futures. Sonny would get his pilot's license in no time. If he could learn to navigate above a landscape of ribboned salt water, he really would be able to fly me anywhere, just as he had promised. I was a 25-year-old, would-be TV star, waiting for a bizarre scandal or a dramatic live shot of a hostage situation so I could move on to bigger, better-paying markets. Instead, my assignment was to interview an old man with Alzheimer's.

"What's the news hook?" I asked Suzanne, my boss. Masses of glamorous blond curls draped over her tanned arm as she handed me a clipping from the morning paper, *The Beaufort Gazette*. I scanned it, sucking out the marrow of the story. A Charleston research hospital had suspended Duncan Miller's experimental Alzheimer's treatments over ethical methodology concerns. Byrne Miller was convinced her husband had been making progress and was outraged at the possibility of backsliding.

I recognized her name. A canvas banner advertising an upcoming presentation of the Byrne Miller Dance Theatre was strung between the live oak trees at the entrance to the town's historic district. I imagined a never-ending dance recital, replete with chubby Southern daughters in fluffy tutus.

"Byrne is a respected member of the Beaufort community despite being a Yankee. That alone is newsworthy," Suzanne told me. Her deep, TV-anchor voice was warm and conspiratorial, somehow cloaking an awareness of my questioning her judgment. "The publicity might nudge the hospital board to reconsider." She smiled with the hint of a wink, and I understood in that instant how women in the South get anything they want. "Plus she's a dancer so I think you'll enjoy meeting her."

Towns so tiny that only a public television station can survive don't exactly demand journalistic objectivity. Filling airtime, while not offending the politicians who controlled the state budget, was my unofficial job description. I hadn't accepted this reality when I drove the WJWJ station van to Byrne Miller's house for the first time.

There is nothing so draining as 90 percent humidity at 10 o'clock in the morning. My hair clung to my forehead like a wet sock inside the drum of a washing machine. My sunglasses fogged up the instant I got out of the news van, and the heavy videotape recorder hanging off my right shoulder managed to snag the top button off my shirt and gather the folds of my skirt into a wrinkled bunch at mid-thigh.

"You must be the new one," the tall, lean woman said when I rapped on the front screen door of her cottage at 2400 Wilson Drive. It was a pronouncement, really, her welcome. She spoke with perfect diction and her voice resonated through her held-high head. Her words would have struck me as haughty were they not delivered through a slowly spreading smile. "Let me help you with those lights or at least the tripod. I'm not as feeble as my advanced age suggests."

Beaufort was a town of fewer than 12,000 full-time residents, so I had expected a Deep South, Miss-Miller's-School-for-Dance character: long black Lycra skirt, a strand of pearls partially hidden by the sleeves of a soft pink cardigan tied about the neck. Byrne glided through the door in a crisp white linen pantsuit cinched at the waist, a brilliant silk scarf wafting from an impossibly long neck. The hand that reached for my light stand was bare but for an exotic silver ring the size of a cameo broach – the kind that might secretly open and spill out some mystery potion or poison.

"Duncan's waiting for you out on the veranda," she said. "It's cooler there, under the ceiling fan. And he loves to watch the river. Helps him find the words."

Perhaps because Suzanne had described Duncan Miller as a novelist, I hadn't considered that the man she sent me to interview would have to hunt for words. *Great,* I thought, *this story will never make my demo reel.* My fledgling television career was going nowhere. If quitting wouldn't have meant moving back in with my parents – sullen, surfer-husband in tow – I would have lugged that skirt-scrunching, outdated video gear right back into the van with the cheesy news logo paintjob.

I was prepared for a sad story, pleas for support, even desperation. I had planned on shooting close-ups from photo albums of a life before Alzheimer's. Even the soundtrack would be tragic. *Carmina Burana* played in the background from a turntable in the corner of the living room. I looked around the house as I brought my equipment to the porch. What else would make the story sing? A Navajo rug in faded reds and browns stretched over the wood floor. *Hmm, they must have spent time out West.* Wheelchair scuff marks traced a dotted line along once white walls. *Ouch, their days of wandering the back roads are ancient history.* Homemade wooden furniture clustered around a pot-bellied woodstove. *Duncan must have lost his marbles long ago; a woodstove in this swampy sauna of a state?* I smiled to myself. The props were perfect for illustrating worthiness and drawing out empathy.

"Duncan was as good with his hands as he was with words," Byrne said, patting a thinly padded, boxy sofa. "He built this and our summer home in Connecticut too and still managed to finish six novels along the way."

I decided I would pan my camera across the leather-bound volumes of Byrne and Duncan's library, ending with a shot of all the books he'd published. But on first glance I didn't see any. *Wow, that's humble. I'd fill every shelf with my own books if I'd written any.* Instead, I slowly moved the camera's lens past titles by Thomas Mann and Jack Kerouac, lingering over the complete works of Shakespeare. It would show how much his mind once grasped. I would write a poignant script explaining how the disease robbed a person of his dignity.

"Duncan, darling," Byrne said as she stepped onto the screened-in porch, "this is Teresa, the new reporter from the television station. She's going to interview us and then film your next visit with the doctor."

I am? Did Suzanne promise a follow-up story and forget to tell me? Or is Byrne just assuming I'll oblige?

I entered behind Byrne. An old man, hunched over in a wheelchair, tilted slightly forward as his wife approached, just enough for his eyes to lock onto hers and smile. In Duncan Miller I witnessed what could not be stolen, a muscle memory so deep that lighting up at the sight of his wife was an involuntary response. In the instant before Duncan's gaze drifted over to me, he moved the viscous, sultry air between them like a breath over still waters. Byrne's face softened to receive this soundless ripple, and her eyes danced with reflected love.

Byrne leaned over Duncan, transferring his weight to the back wheels in one smooth, graceful turn. I realized it was a *pas de deux* and that Byrne danced where others simply shuffled. She brought Duncan's hand around, close enough to reach for mine, and he followed her lead.

"If – there is another visit to the doctor," Duncan whispered. There was a trace of an Oxford accent in the low tones. Long ago he must have been far away from here. The voice better matched the portrait I had passed in the hallway. A younger Duncan had posed for a photographer, wearing a striped yachting shirt, a pipe perched between smooth, thin lips. "A pleasure ... to make ... your ..."

As his sentence trailed off, I saw that smile again. The back of Byrne's hand was stroking his cheek. If it is possible to be envious of a man with Alzheimer's, in that moment I was, swept into the surging tide of the woman who cherished him. Byrne pulled up a rattan chair and watched Duncan listen to the questions I asked. When he lost the words to answer, she supplied them. He nodded and cupped her hand under his, like a king and his bride on side-by-side thrones. She translated silence.

Here was a man facing obstacles far worse than a fake social security number and wimpy waves. Yet all Duncan needed was Byrne. She, alone, was strong enough to fight the battles he could not.

If this proper-postured octogenarian could summon such willpower, so could I. All I needed to do was love Sonny as much as Byrne loved Duncan, and I would be as free as I had been chasing waves along Mexico's coastline.

9

There are gifts better treasured than repeated.

~Byrne

Taking Turns

WASHINGTON HEIGHTS – 1934

WORDS DIDN'T SETTLE on a blank page for Duncan, they whirled around his brain, as if each individual letter were flicked up like a grain of sand in a passing funnel cloud. Some days he was at the center of the vortex, curled in fetal position, anchored by the weight of his Underwood "noiseless" typewriter. The meter and intent of his thoughts touched down here and there, strings of sentences flapping and twisting behind. Other times he was sucked up and spread thin, high above what he was trying to say. He was all-knowing but as powerless as a feathery layer of ice-crystals, his thoughts cirrus clouds trailing a powerful thunderhead of emotion.

It was on those thin, cirrus days that he saw himself in the harshest light: a married man living in the apartment of his wife's parents while she sent home paychecks from Washington, D.C. Each letter he struck flew up and hit an inked ribbon, and all he could think of was Byrne's long legs kicking through the air above a stage instead. If she could have seen him pounding the Underwood's rounded keys, Byrne would have wondered if the ferocity was to punish her for the scant inches of golden leotard other men saw instead of him. But she would have been wrong. Duncan wasn't jealous, he was frustrated. His wife had found a way to capitalize on her talent and he was still at the mercy of his own.

This was to be his year, this first full year of their marriage, to stay at home and work on a career. His plan was to submit an excerpt to *The Atlantic Monthly*; the notoriety would make publishers take note.

"We'll take turns following our passions," Byrne had told him when she accepted the offer to go on tour with the Sara Mildred Strauss Dancers. "You work on your novel, and I'll make the money, and then when you're published it'll be my turn."

The burlesque act was nothing more than pantomime for Byrne. On stage she would improvise as much in her mind as with her body, pretending her movements were as ferocious and evocative as those she'd seen in Harald Kreutzberg's performances. She could mimic the great modern dance master and still be apart from herself and whole. For Duncan, the novel he was freed to write was more like a tangle of thoughts he carried with him than anything tangible. The ordeal of its unraveling made him hesitate and stumble.

"It's about the sexual love a boy has for his mother," he had tried to explain to Byrne. "What it should be, attacked by what it becomes."

Byrne had draped behind Duncan at his typewriter, kissing his neck as she peered at the page where he had typed only the title: *Sit in Dark Places*.

"Let's just tell Mother it's about a boy's love for his mother," she suggested.

Byrne knew better than to ask Duncan if his novel were autobiographical. It's not that she was afraid of the answer, she told herself. It was that she was afraid for Duncan. He still had told her nothing about the family he'd left behind in Charleston and she'd watched as her husband took to Fanny's attentions like a forgotten flower, finally watered. There was no baseline in his reactions; it was as if he'd never had another mother to compare her to. The ordinary acts of kindness that flowed from Fanny like exhaled oxygen were to Duncan revelations. He responded like an orphaned puppy, exposing his throat to the alpha female who adopted him as one of her own.

"I'll take good care of him," Fanny had told Byrne as the three of them stood at the train platform with all the other dancers bound for Washington. She kissed her daughter and then stood back for Duncan to have a final moment.

Byrne leaned in, and down, so that her high forehead could lean against Duncan's. "I'll behave, I promise," she said, already second-guessing her decision to join the tour.

Duncan pulled back, grabbing her shoulders. "Do nothing of the sort," he exclaimed. "This is your chance to be anonymous. Invent yourself anew each night. Be brazen. Be bold. Be burlesque!"

She twirled for him, coyly dipping first one shoulder, then the other. If he'd told her to ride to Washington naked she would have stripped her clothes and left them in a pile at his adoring feet.

"Come see me, if you can," she said. "If I'm awful you can slip out in the dark and I will never know."

"I don't need to buy a ticket," he replied. "All I have to do is close my eyes and I see you dance. Now get on that train. You are marvelous and I have a novel to write."

Byrne leaned from the window, waving and blowing kisses until the train's increasing momentum rippled the skin on her hands and neck. She folded herself back into the car like a newborn giraffe, settling into new savannahs. She would become as marvelous as the woman Duncan saw behind closed eyes.

IT WAS FANNY WHO saw what happened when Duncan was alone with the weight of his words. He locked himself up in Byrne's childhood bedroom but could not hide from his frustrations. The walls of the apartment shook with the reverberations of each tortured keystroke. She called his name when it was time for meals, and when he didn't emerge she slipped a note under the door, telling him to return the tray when he was finished.

It was only Michael Miller's gentle piano playing that lured Duncan out into the living room each night. Fanny would shuffle in and out of the kitchen, refilling coffees for the men and sharing the news of the day with Duncan as though he'd returned from an extended overseas trip.

In May of 1934 she told him, "They finally caught up with those hooligan bank robbers, Bonnie and Clyde."

Duncan looked up at Fanny questioningly, drawing a finger across his throat like a blade. She shook her head, imitating a machine gun instead, then laughed as Duncan fell over and twitching on the sofa.

By July she couldn't get him to snap out of his melancholy, even when news of the outside world made their lives seemed charmed by comparison. "They say it got to 117 degrees yesterday in Oklahoma. The fields are turning to dust." She waited, hoping for any kind of reaction, ready to laugh even if he asked for ice-water.

In August she informed him that Adolf Hitler had declared himself *Fuhrer* of Germany, after already becoming president and chancellor. Duncan looked at her with eyes emptier than empathetic.

"I've simply nothing to say," he apologized.

"Have you heard back from the editor of *The Atlantic Monthly?*" Fanny asked, fixing her unwavering eyes on his.

Duncan shook his head no. "It's been more than a month. Ellery Sedgwick has built his reputation on discovering new talent. Surely he didn't make Ernest Hemmingway endure this disrespectful, slow form of torture."

Fanny smoothed the collar of her son-in-law's shirt. "The same Hemingway who had already written *The Sun Also Rises?*"

Duncan let his shoulders slump. Fanny was right. The leading literary magazine of the day hadn't so much discovered Hemingway as exploited him.

"Be patient, Duncan. No one is an overnight success."

She told him then to get rid of the typewriter, that it wasn't any of her business and this suggestion would be her last, but the noise alone was enough to drive a person crazy. "Write it out by hand," she said, "there's less pressure that way, like composing a letter to yourself."

He rolled the idea around, stretching his hands so that Fanny could hold them and rub the tips of his fingers. "The order," he said, letting her soothe him, "what if it's all out of order?"

"Don't worry, Duncan," she said, "Byrne will type them for you when she comes home. She will figure out where everything belongs. That's what women do."

Byrne was, in fact, doing what most women would never dare to do. Each night she and 17 other girls spilled onto a stage in front of men eager to forget their troubles for a few minutes before the movies started. In the chorus line number, she was always near the wings, the dancers arranged from daintiest in the middle to lankiest at either end so that the height of their kicks would seem to undulate like waves.

Without her glasses, she couldn't see much past the first two rows, so she was never nervous. The theater seemed to her more like a cocoon of lights and sound. The musical score was too garish for her classically trained ears, so she listened for the undercurrents of sounds instead. The swoosh of silky stockings brushing between fleshy thighs, the rattle of the rickety light fixtures, and the squeaks and moans of the weathered boards became instruments in her symphony. She found rhythm in the random – imagined moods in the cacophony.

When the curtains closed between numbers, she didn't have to worry about complicated costume changes; she simply removed layers. The Sara Mildred Strauss Dancers walked a tight rope between titillating and tawdry. Touring companies tended to escape the attention of police decency raids shutting down their counterparts in Manhattan and Harlem halls like the Winter Garden or New Gotham. Byrne's second number involved standing on a pedestal, waggling her hips, wearing only two inches of cloth and a fake garnet glued into the recess of her bellybutton.

She culled her memory for distraction and inspiration, drawing motivation from a different literary character each night. *I am Joan of Arc,* she told herself one night, *my flesh armor enough for any battle.* Her arms stiffened into daggers, her jutting hip became a shield. The next night she abandoned fierce poses and moved with what she hoped was soft and spiraling grace. *I am Lady Godiva. Shutter all your windows and I ride for you.*

One man could not avert his eyes. Dean Goodelle was the troupe's only male dancer and probably its only trained modern dancer. His presence confused Byrne as much as it must have raised eyebrows in the audience. He was delicate and flexible, with hands more expressive and fluid than any of the girls'. He wasn't bulky enough to serve as acrobatic ballast. He didn't fill the role of muscular stunt man, catching and swinging buxom partners across the stage. He danced atop a velvet-covered dais across from Byrne's, his elongated neck and slanting nose casting shadows as otherworldly as a Balanese Wayang puppet.

It was for Dean Goodelle that Byrne truly began to dance, taking cues from his supple contortions and expressive interpretation of emotion. She was an inspired mimic, eager to stretch the limits of her current circumstances. And he saw in Byrne a talent she was only beginning to suspect.

"You should study with Polly Korchein when you get back to New York," he told her one night as they walked back to their boarding house. "She will draw you out, make something of your promise."

Byrne stood a little taller, squaring her shoulders over feet in parallel position – the stance of modern dancers.

"Is tuition expensive?" she asked.

"I will introduce you," he smiled. "Scholarships can be arranged, when this is over."

It was over sooner than Byrne expected. One night only five months into the tour, there was a telegram on the floor of her room, slipped under her door sometime during the night's performance. It was from Fanny.

"Come home," it read. "Stop. Your husband isn't eating. Stop."

Byrne swung herself onto the top bunk, rolled onto her back and flattened her palms and flexed her feet against the low ceiling. She pushed as hard as she could, grunting and straining against the unfairness of it all. This year was supposed to be Duncan's turn, not hers. She believed so completely in his promise that she had left home to make it possible for him to write. But her brilliant husband's talent was ignored while she was paid handsomely for wearing next to nothing. He was feeling so defeated that he couldn't eat while she was beginning to imagine herself an actual dancer. She pressed even harder against the low ceiling, transferring the power from her stage-toned stomach and burlesque thighs to the plain white plaster overhead, and when the ceiling did not come crumbling down, she made her decision. Plenty of other tall, beautiful dancers could take her place. There would never be another Duncan.

10

The Lizard King

Beaufort – 1991

Through my lens, the dance I'd witnessed on the screen porch of the Millers' cottage was more than a love story. It was a scene I lifted up and transposed over my own life, like crinkled tracing paper. Without Byrne, Duncan's story wouldn't have been told. Without me, Sonny would become equally invisible.

He must have seen it first, my shadow swallowing his identity. My life had purpose and praise, a degree of notoriety in the very small pond that was Beaufort. Everything he had been in Mexico was erased. He went from being the most vibrant star in his universe to nothing more than my common-law husband. I shouldn't have been surprised that our orbit, the way we circled each other in this new universe, began to wobble. That I was caught off guard was a sign of the distance I was putting between us.

"I'm throwing a party tomorrow night," Sonny announced one night, as he was getting ready for a dinner shift. "I've already cleaned the house so don't let Wipeout in. I don't want to have to clean up after a filthy dog, too."

A filthy dog? Wipeout, the puppy he had begged me for

had been reduced to a filthy dog, not even my filthy dog or yours.

"Did you hear me?" he persisted. "I'm throwing a party."

I nodded, assuming he meant his friend Dennis would be coming over. Dennis was a sweet, scruffy construction worker who had dropped out of high school and lived in a doublewide trailer with his dad. Sonny and Dennis had nothing in common, but Sonny picked friends for their devotion, for their willingness to entertain him and be entertained by him.

Dennis was both loyal and mischievous. He had knocked on our door one night while his underage girlfriend waited in the front seat of his car, sipping a beer.

"Did you guys ever play Ouija board?" Dennis asked, as casually as if he were asking us if he could borrow a cup of sugar.

"Dude, bring it in. I'm game," Sonny answered.

"No, you both gotta come with me. There's way more spooks at the graveyard."

It was a thick night in the dead of summer when the rattle of cicadas was all that stirred the air. Dennis drove us to the back of Beaufort National Cemetery on Boundary Street and hid his low-rider in a grove of live oaks.

"See, it's a full moon," he said. "We won't even need flashlights."

The low brick wall that penned in the meticulously groomed gravestones was wide enough to straddle. The wall was wide enough to balance a Ouija board and let a mid-summer night's imagination hover and propel our moonlit hands. It was wide enough to fit a Styrofoam cooler with a 12-pack of Old Milwaukee beer. And it was wide enough for a surfer who believed he was communicating with graveyard spirits to hop atop and beat his chest yelling, "I am the Lizard King!"

Through the moon-refracted haze of humidity, Dennis saw a porch light flicker across an empty lot behind the cemetery. "Shit, we better blow before somebody calls the cops."

Sonny only howled louder, lifting his chin and leaning his entire body forward as though the magnetic pull of the moon would suspend him forever.

Months later, when he told me about the awesome party he had unilaterally decided to throw, he lifted his chin the same way.

"I invited some people from your TV station, too. They seem psyched."

This was Sonny trying to pull our stars into alignment, a grand gesture of inclusion and optimism. And it terrified me.

"Who, exactly, did you invite?" I asked, hoping he wouldn't say my boss, Suzanne.

"Everyone. I know my friends bore you."

The look that passed between us dripped with implication and consequence. I blinked first.

"I'll make shrimp burgers," I said, to his back, as he left to work a dinner shift. "Everybody loves a good shrimp burger."

Even under ordinary circumstances, a 25-year-old rookie television reporter wouldn't dream of inviting the first boss of her first real job to a party at her run-down rental house furnished with yard-sale bargains. I filled my head with all the ways it could go wrong. What if the wheezing window air-conditioning unit chose that night to die? What if the six cans of Raid I sprayed each month failed to annihilate the hordes of palmetto bugs that squeezed in through every ugly strip of wood paneling? What if my 80-pound, attention-starved dog jumped up on my boss or, even more likely, nuzzled the body parts that happened to be snout-level?

Each scenario I imagined was worse than the one before it. What if Dennis or Sonny passed around a bong in front of everyone? What if the teenaged Ouija board entourage started doing tequila shots? What if the neighbors called the cops? I couldn't stop my mind from leaping to the next illogical conclusion. Our dirt yard would fill with flashing squad car lights. There'd be a rap at the door. It would be a cop I'd probably interviewed, maybe even Police Chief Jesse Altman who always helped me set up my lights when I covered trials in municipal court. Sonny would insist on answering the door, reeking of pot smoke and twitchy with confrontation.

What name would he give? His green card listed his real name, but Dennis and his work buddies had always known Sonny by the fake name on his papers: Rick. At the television station, I had introduced him only as Sonny to avoid confusion.

I avoided telling Sonny the truth as well – that mixing our two social groups would never work. I pretended to be asleep when he climbed into bed at 3 a.m. He smelled like fried seafood and beer, the air interrupted by his crooked, fist-fight broken nose as he snored. I slipped out from the covers and looked down on him. He curled in his sleep, muscles tensing through deep REM waves, and I saw in his twitching a boy I wanted to save. Back in Mexico, I had wrapped my body around his when we slept, to comfort him when the night-mares of his father's suicide returned. He wasn't the one who had changed. I had gone from his believer and champion to his judge and jury. I found a flashlight, and while Sonny slept, I wrote out a list of groceries to buy for the party.

The next evening, Dennis and a six-pack of underaged girls arrived long before Sonny said they would. *Good*, I thought, *maybe they'll get high before anyone from the station gets here.* That scenario would be better than half the crowd sneaking into our tiny bedroom during the party and huddling inside until smoke wafted under the threshold of its flimsy door. Out came the rolling papers, and soon the walls reverberated with the sounds of Jimmy Hendrix and Jim Morrison.

"Do that king of the castle thing again," Dennis's girl-friend shouted over the music. "You know, like you did that night in the cemetery?"

Sonny was balancing on the black metal frame of our futon sofa singing out "I am the Lizard King!" at exactly the moment when Ron, the technical director for the newscast, poked his head through our front door.

"Teresa?" he called out, uncertain he was at the right house.

Ron was in his late forties. His wife carried a bouquet of flowers and a bottle of white wine. They must have thought we were grownups, that Sonny had invited my co-workers to a normal dinner party. I was pulling shrimp burgers out of the broiler when Ron and his wife made their way into the kitchen.

"Can we help?" Ron asked. *Only if you're the Mad Hatter and those flowers are actually mushrooms that make me small enough to hide in Wipeout's doghouse.*

Sonny burst into the kitchen, without his shirt, and offered a surfer-style, fist bump, thumb-wrestling handshake. Ron managed a thumbs-up that morphed into a Hawaiian hang-loose before aborting the attempt and introducing his wife.

"Pat, this is ..." he turned back to Sonny. "You know I don't know your actual name, just Sonny. "

"Just Sonny, you got it, *compadre.*"

Ron laughed. "Fair enough. So, back to introductions. This is my wife Pat. Pat, Sonny is Teresa's ..."

Pauses don't get more pregnant than this one was. I pleaded inside my thoughts. *Please, Sonny, don't say hus-band. I haven't told a soul.*

"Old man," Sonny said. "I'm her old man. Good enough?"

"Hey, that's cool." Ron changed the subject. "Is that The Doors on the stereo? I haven't heard them in years."

It was connection enough for Sonny. He flashed me a see-it's-all-cool smile and led Ron and Pat into the living room. More people from the station were filing in, reporters in khaki pants and Polo shirts gawking at the collection of glassy-eyed girls with tattooed lower backs and cutoff shirts. I walked around with a tray of shrimp burgers as things became curiouser and curiouser. Sonny and Dennis were stacking empty beer cans into a pyramid, carefully lining up the ones they'd half-flattened and converted into pipes with sawed out holes in the middle. Palmetto bugs crawled around the base of the pyramid, sniffing out remnants of sugar and backwash. I rubbed the smoke from my eyes. Giant surf posters thumb-tacked to the wood paneled walls looked dingy and faded in the harsh light of the bare ceiling bulb, and the "Legalize" pennant of fuzzy felt that Sonny mounted over the stereo was shrouded in cobwebs I hadn't noticed until that moment.

I heard a metallic screech. John, the shy overnight engineer who always wore WJWJ public television programming t-shirts from the 70s, was testing the strength of our sagging plastic lawn chairs as if deciding if any of them would support his weight. He leaned against the windowsill instead.

"Who's ready for the entertainment?" Sonny asked. "I've got a black-market copy of *The Doors* movie."

Dennis's girlfriend offered Ron her seat, like he was an old man on a crowded bus. It took Dennis a full minute to follow her cue and offer his lawn chair to Pat, quietly nibbling on a shrimp burger like a terrified mouse. Another engineer from the TV station helped Sonny position an assortment of speakers, and I flitted around the room replacing empty beer cans with store-brand Cokes.

Sonny cranked up the volume, and Dennis and his girlfriend leaped to their feet for the first concert scene, waving cigarette lighters above their heads. I could see the engineer scanning the room for fire detectors. Pat had balled up a piece of paper napkin and plugged her ears.

"Gee Teresa, I wish we could stay longer," she said, after 20 torturous minutes. "I promised I'd take a friend's shift at the hospital, so we really should be going."

I could have cried. *Take me with you. I'll swab corridors, push wheelchairs, anything to be anywhere but down this rabbit hole.* Ron was staring at me, as if he was considering something.

"Damn," he said, loudly. "I forgot to tell you that Suzanne called."

"Oh." *Please no,* I thought. "Is she coming?"

"No. But she needs you to cover that county council hearing tonight."

Ron knew that county council hearings never happened on weekends, but I didn't pretend to protest.

"I guess that's what happens when you're the new girl," I said. Sonny raised his eyebrows, in silent challenge. "It's why they call it work, after all."

Ron mumbled apologies and clapped Sonny on the back before he could proffer another complicated handshake. I didn't bother to change my clothes before I slipped out behind him.

"You're not taking my truck," Sonny yelled from the doorway. "I'm not canceling this party. We're going to need more beer. It's *my* truck."

I stopped, caught in the act of escaping from my own home.

"No problem," Ron intervened. "We'll give you a lift to the station. You can just drive the news van and bring it back on Monday morning."

My exit route was clear. All I had to do was *not* react.

I had seen my mother do it: stand back with a meek smile while my father mocked her in front of neighbors or her daughters. I always thought she was weak for letting him and yet, there I was, smiling and blowing Sonny a kiss as I rode away with Ron and Pat.

I decided to call home after two hours had passed. With any luck the party would be loud enough he wouldn't hear the ring. The answering machine picked up, and I was relieved to avoid another confrontation.

"Hey it's me. It's going to be a little while before I can wrap up," I said.

I jumped when Sonny's voice came on the line, interrupting my excuses. There was laughter in the background and Sonny started to sing Jim Morrison lines from "Graveyard Poem."

"*It was the greatest night of my life.*" Sonny's voice was pure bravado, mocking and affected.

So this is why he waited to pick up the phone. He had cued up the perfect line to get back at me, from a song we used to sing together under the stars in Mexico. "*Although I still had not found a wife …*"

I could picture him, stoned, performing for Dennis and the others, pretending my absence meant nothing to him.

"*I had my friends. Right there beside me.*"

I had abandoned him, probably embarrassed him in front of his friends. I knew the lyrics. I could sing along, signal I would make it up to him.

"*And I gave empty sermons to my head,*" I recited.

I could have left the station right then and picked up a 12-pack on the way home. I stayed away until almost midnight instead. Sonny's pickup was the only vehicle parked in our yard when I drove the news van home. Wipeout was tied out in the back howling. She pawed at me, desperate to come inside. Sonny was passed out in the living room, and I tiptoed into the house and did what

I imagined Byrne would do for Duncan. I put a pillow under Sonny's head and kissed his sweaty forehead.

"I missed you, baby," he said, waking. His voice was soft and confused. "Don't ever leave me."

I was transported back to a hollowed-out scoop of Mexican sand with Sonny curled up next to me, telling me the things he had never told anyone else. How his mother had told him to lie about his father's death whenever anyone asked. How his older brother had showed him how to get high and forget it all. How he hated the Canadian girl who stole his brother away by getting pregnant, leaving Sonny in the house all alone with his mother.

I stroked Sonny's head and squeezed his hand three times. This was our *pas de deux* and I would never leave him all alone on the stage. He squeezed back four times.

"I've been thinking, *amor*," I said. "You haven't talked about flying for a long time."

"Flight school is too expensive," he said, sitting up. "I can't do shit about it until I earn more than I do as a fucking dishwasher."

"It's not your fault," I told him. This was a delicate dance; I couldn't step on his feet. "You could support us both if you had a pilot's license, right?"

"But that takes flight school," he said. "We're going in circles."

More like waltzing, actually, I thought to myself. *We're moving in little boxes, one right angle at a time.* He came forward while I stepped back, pretending to let him lead. Then I drew him one step to the side and back together.

"There's this job I could take in the mornings," I said, "before my shift starts at the TV station. It's a radio program and they need a news announcer for the morning drive. It's part-time. Starts at five and ends at nine. I could be back at the TV station by 10."

"What do you mean?" he asked.

I would work two jobs if it kept the dreamer in him alive. I would be his Byrne. I would lift him up until he took flight.

"Use your green card with your real name and sign up for flight school tomorrow," I told him. "That's what I mean."

11

Expensive clothes are like art,
possible to admire without needing to own.

~Byrne

Piano and a Bed

GREENWICH VILLAGE, NEW York – 1934

BYRNE MADE ONE LAST stop at the theater in Washington, D.C., before catching the train back to New York City. It was early afternoon, and the rest of the Sara Mildred Strauss dancers were still back at the boarding room mending tears in their fishnet hose. The house was dark. Her thoughts felt like echoes in the silent theater. She had intended to take a final bow, allowing any tears that still threatened to spill to do so in front of an empty orchestra pit instead of Duncan or her mother. But alone, without the blinding lights, the transporting crackle of recorded music or the rustle of movement in her peripheral vision, Byrne felt as out of place as she had in the back row of her first ballet class. Months of performing already seemed like a dream rendered jumbled and disorienting by morning.

She sat in the front row of seats, audience to what she was abandoning, and braced herself for regrets. But all she could picture was Duncan. His was the talent yearning for the spotlight. She told herself she could walk away from this job as easily as she had the job at the magazine; it was only money. Real dance was something Dean Goodelle or

Harald Kreutzberg did on stage. For the past few months, Byrne had simply disappeared into the lights, pretending to be someone else, somewhere else. Duncan was the one who needed recognition, the one who deserved it. Byrne vowed to reinvent herself as often as necessary to give it to him.

When she stepped off the train at Penn Station, Duncan was leaning against an elegant steel column, head bare, hat pressed against his heart. He didn't wave or run toward her. The piercing intent of his gaze was enough to part the crowds. Byrne forced herself not to shriek and run to him. She willed the second hand on the hanging clock above his head to linger and walked as deliberately as she could toward him, one high heel crossing in front of the other as though the platform were her private runway, her trembling chin high and her spine erect. It was to be their first and last reunion. She would make the moment stand still.

It was Duncan who broke first, lifting his hand to her face and tracing a diagonal line from her temple to her lips. She felt a scratch along her skin. He was holding a copper house key between his fingers.

"What's this?" she asked, taking the key from his pale, cold hands.

His blue eyes smiled a second before his lips did. "To watch the night in storms, the day in cold," he greeted her with lines from Shakespeare's *Taming of the Shrew*. "Whilst thou liest warm at home, secure and safe."

At home? The key she pulled back to examine was not familiar. Her husband wasn't taking her back to her parents' apartment in Washington Heights. He picked up her suitcase in one hand and offered her his other.

They walked, hands clasped together, 25 city blocks down Seventh Avenue, separating only when it began to rain and they had to hoist Byrne's suitcase above their heads as an umbrella.

"The wheel is come full circle. I am here," Duncan said, stopping at the corner of Seventh Avenue and Perry Street.

"And where, exactly, is here?" Byrne asked. She knew, of course, that they were deep in the heart of bohemia: Greenwich Village. It made sense that Duncan would be drawn to this gritty, pulsating part of the city. Among its artistic radicals and political refugees he would surely find an audience. If this enclave felt more natural to him, then she would gladly say goodbye to the comfort of her parents' home.

"See that restaurant?" Duncan pointed at what used to be a speakeasy. "I presume it is where Edmund Wilson got liquored up and wrote me that spineless letter. They say he's still a regular. Nothing better to do, apparently."

Byrne felt a cold drop of rain trickle down the back of her neck, and the lining of her stomach seemed to tighten.

"By the way, *The Atlantic Monthly* seems to share his view. They passed on my manuscript as well."

This was why her mother must have sent the telegram. Duncan hadn't only stopped eating; he'd stopped believing in himself. He was tormenting himself with rejection. He needed the shelter of his wife's support to recapture his confidence.

"What did the letter say?" Byrne asked. "Surely they gave a reason."

"An actual, articulated reason for rejection? No," Duncan shrugged. "But they did say I was the only one writing in the style of Thomas Mann this side of the Atlantic Ocean."

Byrne stood her ground in what was now a gentle rain, forcing her young husband to stop, turn and look at her.

"First-time novelist Duncan Miller," she said, pausing for dramatic effect, "compared to *Death-in-Venice*, Hitler-hating, Nobel-Prize-laureate Thomas Mann. In the same sentence?"

Duncan's pointed chin began to flush. He allowed the whisper of a smile to separate his pinched lips. His proud bride wasn't finished with her sidewalk proclamation.

"Mother worships Mann. She'll tell everyone at synagogue. I hope you saved the letter because I intend to have it framed."

When they crossed 14th Street, Duncan pointed east. "Five minutes that way and you're at the press that published *Tender Buttons*," he said. Then he spun Byrne around and pointed west, toward the Hudson River and the basement office of *The Little Review*, one of the leading *avant-garde* magazines of the day. "That press closed three years ago," he said, "but there's a million more to take its place. *The New Republic's* days are numbered."

They veered off the noisy main thoroughfare and zigzagged through alleys. The backs of row houses were corseted in fire escape ladders and capped with converted rooftop studios. The orderly grid of Manhattan dissolved into secluded, leafy, angled streets that Duncan seemed already to have wandered. The muscles in Byrne's body relaxed when they stopped at Morton Street, a six-block-long link between the docks along the Hudson and Washington Park. She smiled as he unwound the scarf from around his neck and tied it in a blindfold over her eyes.

"How much farther?" she asked as he led her down Morton Street. Duncan didn't answer but at regular intervals he pressed his hand to the small of her back and guided her around what must have been fire hydrants or low-hanging window planters. She would gladly have gone in circles rather than relinquish Duncan's possessive, intimate touch. The rain felt lighter on her head, as if sheltering boughs of graceful trees were arched above. She followed unspoken sounds of arrival: the creak of a wrought-iron gate, the well-oiled clunk of a heavy deadlock turning. She could hear the gentle hiss of a gas lamp over a receded doorway. He was leading her into an elegant building, she could tell by the scent of a polished wooden handrail leading up smooth marble stairs. It couldn't possibly be any place they could afford to rent. She'd sent home almost $50 a week to Duncan while she was on tour, but even if he'd saved it all, a building like this would be out of reach.

She began to pat the walls with the palms of her hands, feeling for limits to her imagination. A key clunked in an unseen lock. She stepped inside a room and Duncan pulled a door closed behind them both. She felt the inward rush of air come to a rest and settle around her ankles. She heard the faint crackle and hiss of fireplace embers. Then Duncan's lips enveloped hers and he undid the blindfold with one hand and the zipper of her dress with the other. The first thing her eyes took in was the double bed they'd received as a wedding gift from her uncles, its iron headboard awkwardly butted up against a marble fireplace.

"Beauty such as yours commands a fiery crown," he said. Byrne flexed her feet to avoid scraping the opposite wall as they tumbled onto the mattress.

Afterward, Duncan gave her a tour of their apartment, without leaving the bed. Before the Depression it had been a second floor parlor, he explained. The elegant marble fireplace was the anchor around which guests reclined on settees and chaise lounges. Now a collection of tenants shared the once grand building: writers and artists, refugee scholars from Europe teaching at the New School's University in Exile, and immigrant workers building the new overhead rail line along the West Side.

"We have our own entrance, a private bath and two whole rooms," Duncan said, "though they are close enough together that I can gaze at you from either one."

Byrne laughed and pointed to an empty space along the

far wall, next to a stove and icebox.

"Will that be the dining enclave?" she asked.

A heavy rapping at the door interrupted Duncan.

"The movers must be here. Do you happen to have five dollars on you?"

Byrne pointed at her purse and groped for the undergarments strewn across the hardwood floor. She had barely tugged her slip into place when Duncan snatched a crisp bill from her purse and swung open the door. Behind it stood a battered upright piano and a stout Italian man in overalls catching his breath.

"You didn't say anything about stairs," a second mover grumbled from the other side of the piano.

Byrne darted behind the bathroom door and eavesdropped as the three men tugged and prodded the piano up against the empty wall next to the stove. She watched through the space between door hinges. Clumsy fingers repositioning for better grip revealed the instrument's questionable pedigree. It was far from the meticulously maintained piano she had grown up with. Byrne heard Fanny's voice before she saw her mother slip into the apartment, dodging the departing movers.

"Henry Duncan Miller," began the lecture. "Don't tell me that you bought your wife an out-of-tune piano when you haven't even a table or chair to your name."

Duncan was fingering the keys, like a delighted child poking at bubbles in a bath, when Byrne stepped into view. She was five-feet-nine inches of flustered, just-ravaged dancer's body rigid with indignation. "Mother," she declared, "you can sit on a bed and you can eat off a piano bench if you have to. But if you haven't a piano, you can't make music!"

Fanny threw up her hands and groaned, then winked at Duncan and waved her daughter into her open arms.

There was so much to teach Byrne about taking care of a man, but on the day of her return to New York, Fanny made do with showing Byrne how to tend the icebox and light the stove. But Byrne's fingers were better suited to avoiding the missing keys of an old piano than striking a match. After watching her daughter go through a book of matches without success, Fanny left with strict instructions for the newlyweds to come for supper with the family every Saturday. Byrne didn't notice the newspapers Fanny had pulled from her purse until the next morning. Her mother had circled all the secretarial jobs recently advertised.

Byrne reviewed them, singling out the ad from the Hotel Taft seeking an experienced writer to be in charge of responding to its correspondence. "I could do that job," Byrne told Duncan over breakfast of black coffee and three stale biscuits she'd saved from the train ride the day before. "Writing is no different than dancing – words as well as wiggles can leave an audience begging for more."

She was more right than she realized. At the interview at the Hotel Taft, she watched as a young man was ushered out of the hiring office just ahead of her. He could have been a young star on Broadway, so handsome and apparently well-qualified that the interviewer ran after him, past Byrne and the other would-be correspondents lined up in the hallway.

"Here, you forgot the writing test," the smiling interviewer said, as if he were asking the applicant for an autograph. "It's just a formality really. It was such a pleasure to make your acquaintance."

Byrne felt no such breathless reverence at the conclusion of her interview. "Thank you. You will hear from us," were the only words ushering her into the hallway.

"But what about the writing test?" she asked, determined to leave them begging for more. She lifted her graceful hand, palm up, elbow bent coyly at the waist, settling her weight provocatively into her left hip as though she were back on the dais wearing nothing but elegant, elbow-length gloves. She tossed out a dazzling smile. "I expect the same opportunity as the other prospect."

The interviewer stammered, returned to his office and handed Byrne a sample letter to answer at home. This would be the test of her writing ability, handling a faux complaint with grace and aplomb. For Byrne, the Underwood typewriter perched on the piano bench was an old friend who simply facilitated her naturally tactful words. She filled a blank page with speed and ease. Duncan watched her fingers fly over its round keys, as transfixed as had the machine, which was to him pure torment, transformed into a grand piano.

Byrne was so confident in the brilliance of her letter of response that when she returned to the Hotel Taft to deliver it the next day, she packed a sandwich in her purse. She'd eat at her desk to make a good first impression on her new employers once they'd read her letter and offered her the job. Instead, the interviewer treated her to lunch in the hotel's restaurant and a week later Byrne turned over a full paycheck to her husband.

Duncan kissed her hand, squeezing her knuckles in his gentle fist, and told her he'd be back in an hour. She removed her navy blue, heel-cupping secretarial pumps and soaked her aching feet in the bathtub. Duncan must be scavenging for celebratory champagne, or maybe the ingredients of a romantic dinner, she thought. An hour passed and she wrapped herself in a robe and sat down at the piano. She was rusty and the notes seemed as forced as her indifference to the hour. What could be taking him so long?

She peered out of the window – the streetlamps throwing shapes into shadow and the soft greys of the sidewalk into grainy blacks. When at last she saw him, Duncan was a pair of legs teetering under a towering stack of boxes, bows and ribbons where his belt and tie should have been. It wasn't until he was inside that she saw where the boxes were from: Saks 5th Avenue.

"Duncan what have you done?" she whispered, a flush rising from the place on her chest where her hands had clutched.

"Open them and see," he replied.

Each box was layered with scented tissue paper, opening like the petals of a camellia blossom. Byrne lifted the delicate straps of a shimmering white gown that rippled to the hardwood floor in silky waves. It swirled at her feet as Duncan moved her shoulders, appraising his prize in the light glancing in from the window.

"Try it on," he said. "The salesgirl didn't have legs as spectacular as yours but I made allowances."

Byrne took a step back, toward the bathroom, but Duncan shook his head. He'd spent three hours in the dressing rooms of Saks 5th Avenue searching for a costume worthy of the goddess he considered his wife to be. This was a transformation he intended to witness, to treasure. Byrne let the robe slip off her shoulders and flicked it off to the side with pointed toes. Duncan's eyes trailed down her throat, the curve of her breast and the hollow of her waist.

She stepped into the gown, swiveling to pull it up and over the swell of her hips, pivoting so that Duncan could fasten the zipper. He wrapped one arm around her waist and bent over, nuzzling the small of her back until he had the metal slider clenched between his teeth. With gentle tugs he made his way up until his chin rested between her shoulder blades. She stepped away from him then, to measure her reflection in his expression. It was more intoxicating than any encore on a stage.

She opened the other boxes, spilling with expensive accouterments like gloves, a matching handbag and cashmere stole to cover her shoulders. She may have left the stage for Duncan but he was determined to build her a pedestal.

"Let's go out," he said. "The Brevoort is just on the other side of Washington Square Park. With you in that ensemble, we'll get the best table."

It was then that Byrne realized her barely 20-year-old husband had no concept of budget. To Duncan, decorating the woman he adored was the best use of money he could imagine. Clearly, she would have to take over their finances, find a way to salvage what little might be left of her paycheck before the rent was due. But money had no place in fairy tales. Especially not the night her handsome prince meant for his princess to float in unencumbered adoration.

"Darling this dress isn't meant for martinis, it was born for concerts," she said, eyeing the piano. Never mind its bare bushings and keys that slopped from side to side, or that the slightly sinister sharp she had to substitute for a missing key made the tendons in her neck twitch. She would extend the enchantment of the evening through any means at her disposal. "I intend to do the dress justice."

She lifted the hem of the gown and draped it like a mermaid's tail beside her on the piano bench. She tossed the sheet music aside and leaned into the worn keys with closed eyes. For Duncan's private concert, the music would be melodies she knew by heart.

He watched from the bed until the candles she had lit dissolved into pools of wax that dripped down the face of the piano. He watched the next morning as she tucked each sheet of tissue paper back into the Saks 5th Avenue boxes. She crossed the satin gloves delicately at the wrist. She folded the mermaid hem of the gown in a crisp line across the column of its skirt. Unless the salesgirl pressed her face into the fabric and breathed in the notes of the night before, she would never know the gifts had been unwrapped. It would be Byrne's own once-upon-a-time story to tell for the rest of her life.

"Don't you want to keep anything?" Duncan asked as Byrne finished tying the last bow.

Byrne held her hand across her chest. "I already have all that I need, here."

She waited for a response, sensing that he wasn't quite convinced.

"Duncan, my love, no future occasion could ever recapture what happened in this home last night," she said. "There are gifts better treasured than repeated."

12

Mermaid

ONCE UPON A TIME in a land far away from Byrne and Duncan Miller, I relied on my mother and Hans Christian Andersen for fairy tales. My mother nicknamed me her "princess" the day I was born, and the Danish writers' collection of stories she bequeathed to me when I learned to read became the closest thing to a children's Bible my atheist father allowed in our house. I didn't grow up learning stories of baby Jesus in the manger. I could recite verses of *The Emperor's New Suit* and *The Little Mermaid* instead. Those two fairy tales seemed to me perfect examples of bravery. The proud emperor paraded naked before his subjects rather than admit he'd been duped, and the little topless mermaid was willing to have her tongue ripped out to marry the prince she'd once rescued. It didn't occur to me that both were ridiculously unhealthy models of behavior and slightly exhibitionist to boot.

I realized, after a Halloween costume party with a surplus of little-girl royalty, that being a princess wasn't quite as special as being a mermaid. So I spent as much time in the water as I could. There was no room for reservation or embarrassment in my quest; I was 12 years old before my mother hinted that I shouldn't answer "mermaid" when people asked me what I wanted to be when I grew up.

"If I'm not tall enough to be a ballerina," I protested, "why can't I be a mermaid?"

"I'm not saying you can't be one," she consoled me. "But it has to be a secret. Just tell people you want to be a marine biologist when you grow up. When you do your science experiments underwater, you can turn into a mermaid and get paid for it."

My mother conveniently taught swimming lessons at the Hillsboro indoor pool so I spent hours each summer day cross-legged at the bottom of the pool, holding my breath and trying not to puff out my cheeks too much. Through the stinging, chlorinated water, I looked up at my mother's legs, treading water, and resolved never to look like I was riding a bicycle. I squeezed my legs together instead, pointing my toes and flexing at the hip to propel myself under the struggling students. Blowing tiny bubbles from my nose, I could undulate across the entire length of the pool without coming up for air. I refused to wash my hair with the special chlorine rinse my mother used because I wanted my blond hair to turn green, like the moss tangled in the illustrated Little Mermaid's locks.

I was utterly, selfishly unwilling to share my Hans Christian Andersen book with my little sister Jenny, which is perhaps why, 20 years later, she became the first legitimately married Bruce daughter. She actually had a wedding and subsequently told people she was married, and she produced children from that marriage. After Brandon was born, she moved as far away from Hillsboro, Oregon as continentally possible: Orange City, Florida. My job at the TV station in Beaufort meant that my very first nephew was now only a four-hour drive away. And Orange City is only an hour's drive from my favorite place in the known world: Weeki Wachee Springs.

For any girl with the misfortune of being born before Disney's *The Little Mermaid* spawned an industry of mermaid merchandising, Weeki Wachee was the only place you could actually see "real" mermaids. I had begged my parents to drive our camper to Florida instead of Mexico each year but never got closer to Florida than a postcard my mother found at a garage sale. It was an ad for RC Cola – the Weeki Wachee mermaids posing in glittering tails and clamshell brassieres. When my nephew's proximity gave me the excuse for a pilgrimage, all I had to do was convince Sonny to let me borrow his truck. It turned out that the best way to do that was to make him think I wanted him to come along for the ride.

"So now you think I'm a *mariposa?*" he said, using one of the tamer Mexican translations of homosexual. "Because that's the only kind of guy who goes for that shit."

"Of course not. You're absolutely right. So all I need is to borrow the truck," I told him. "It's not like you'll have to worry about guys hitting on me or anything."

I waited, like Wipeout, half expecting a hand down my throat to take away what he never meant to offer. But Sonny reached for my wrist instead and twirled my cowry shell mermaid bracelet.

"Well, I did tell someone I'd take her shift at the restaurant this weekend," he said. He laced his fingers through mine. "I'll get a ride. You go swim with your mermaids."

I didn't bother correcting him. You didn't just hand over an admission fee and swim with the Weeki Wachee mermaids. They performed live underwater shows at a half-underground, manmade cavern with air-conditioned amphitheater seating. Their secret, which I was completely okay with overlooking, was sipping air from tiny hoses at discreet intervals while languidly executing moves as complicated as those performed by Olympic synchronized swimmers.

A grown woman with a budding career in television news probably shouldn't have contemplated abandoning her secret husband and frolicking half naked in an amusement park, but being a Weeki Wachee mermaid would have made up for the lingering humiliation of a stage career that had started and ended in a rat costume. There are no height requirements to be a mermaid. Even short, muscular ones are alluring and hypnotic. In the open water, mermaids are neither auditioned nor judged and no one fences them in. They can explore any sea that beckons and out-swim any threat. It would win me no aunt-of-the-year award, but I used my nephew's innocence to indulge my private fairy tale.

At first Brandon thought the mermaids were a little creepy. "How come they don't say hi back?" he asked after pressing his fleshy little hands against the Plexiglas wall of their tank to get their attention.

I had to come up with a plausible explanation, fast. "See the bubbles?" I asked. "Inside each one are invisible words like 'hi' or 'nice to meet you.' They talk to each other. Humans just can't understand what they're saying."

He looked up at me in stubborn confusion. "Then how do *you* know?" he asked.

He had me. There was nothing to do but tell him his favorite aunt was actually a mermaid. "I wanted to be one ever since I was a little girl your age," I said, crossing my fingers behind my back.

"My age?" he protested. "I'm not a little girl."

"I know, and boys can't be mermaids anyway. But girls your age who love to swim and take lots of ballet lessons to be super graceful can turn into mermaids when they grow up."

"So are these mermaids your friends?" he asked.

I proved it when one of Weeki Wachee mermaids agreed to take a photograph with the two of us after the show. From then on, Brandon called me his Auntie Mermaid. I had hidden many identities over my lifetime: a rat in *The Nutcracker Suite*, a quiet accomplice in my father's domestic dominance, and now the common-law wife of a half-Mexican surfer. But the chance to be a mermaid, even if it was only pretend, was the one secret identity I cherished.

Hans Christian Andersen himself couldn't have created a more devoted character. I would have gladly exchanged my legs for a tail to keep Brandon's belief in my mermaid-enhood alive. I would have paraded through an emperor's kingdom stark naked to prove my belief. In Brandon I had a loyal subject and devoted audience, and I treasured the magical world he allowed me to create.

Jenny was my accomplice. She peeled the label off a tube of sunscreen and told Brandon it was special lotion that made my tail invisible. Each time we went to the beach or a pool, my trusting nephew dutifully slathered invisible tail lotion all over my legs so that no one would find out our secret. We made up mermaid Morse code to communicate underwater. We collected tiny shells for me to give to my mermaid friends for earrings and bracelets. When I sang Brandon to sleep, he begged me never to give up my voice for a prince.

I wasn't ready to give up being Auntie Mermaid when Brandon became a big brother and started questioning everything from the Easter Bunny to Santa Claus. Now there were two nephews to convince. Raiden was a second potential believer. I would simply have to increase the authenticity factor by renting a costume.

There were no mermaid costumes readily available in Beaufort even if I had been willing to risk the ridicule of renting one. So I found one in a theatrical costume shop in Washington, D.C., and had it shipped to my sister's house. The next time I visited Florida, she sneaked it into the bathroom while the boys were napping.

Apparently mermaids have longer torsos than ex-gymnasts do. The double D clamshell bra cups came up to my chin. The netting that connected the bra to the tail like an invisible leotard was as scratchy as fishnet hose. My sister laughed so hard I thought she would wake the boys.

"Just cue up the Hi-8," I told her. I had brought along a video camera to record the moment, so we'd have proof of it to guard against future doubts. "Throw that Kleenex box cover over the lens so it's camouflaged."

"Copy that," she giggled. "Tissue-cam operational."

Inserting myself into the tail was the trickiest part. Rubbery scales tend to stick to human rear-ends, and it turns out to be rather difficult to climb into an empty bathtub when your legs are cinched at the knees and ankles. I got the costume's sequined flipper caught on the boys' Batman shower curtain and Jenny had to drape it over the sink so that I would have enough open space to display my tail. Once we figured out how to roll the waistband over to take up the slack of the torso netting, I shoved aside yellow rubber ducks and Tonka trucks, then maneuvered my ribcage and right hip bone into the base of the porcelain tub. My tail barely cleared the water faucet, and I arched my side into a natural mermaid-on-the-rocks pose. I could hear my sister in the boys' room, setting the scheme into action.

"Brandon honey, it's time to wake up," she called. "Auntie Mermaid needs you to bring her a towel in the bathroom."

Seriously, that's the best you could do, Jen? The way her request sounded aloud should have been my first cue to abort the mermaid mission. What if Brandon told someone, a nurse or teacher maybe, that his aunt asks him to bring

her towels when she bathes? But it was too late. I heard
Brandon rummaging through the linen closet. He knocked
before sticking his arm through the door, draped in a Weeki
Wachee beach towel.

"I got your favorite one, Auntie Mermaid," he said.

"Bring it in B-man, I can't quite reach," I called out, cringing.

When he poked his head around the door and saw a tail
flopped over the edge of the tub he dropped the towel. His
hand froze in place like a scarecrow, fingers splayed. He was
too stunned to scream. He just backed up slowly, his eyes
pools of confusion.

"Brandon, don't be scared," I sputtered. *Please, don't
hate me for this someday.* "It's just me."

Jenny hugged him from behind.

"It's okay. We all knew she was a mermaid, right?"

Brandon still hadn't spoken a word when his little
brother shoved past the logjam at the door and careened
toward me with a toddler's headlong enthusiasm. I reached
over and swept Raiden into the tub as smoothly as someone
with her legs shoved inside a tail can manage. He laughed,
reaching for the sparkly sequins of my clamshell bra. *Whoa
there, Ray, private mermaid parts.* I removed his hands.

"Water?" he said, reaching for the faucet handles instead.
I sat up to block his access. *Sorry, buddy, it's a rented costume.*

"All done," I said, raising my palms in the universal
symbol of finished cookies and empty zip-lock bags of
Cheerios. "Brandon was just bringing me my towel so I
can dry off and get my legs back, right, B-man?"

Brandon gingerly passed me the towel from the floor
and waited outside the door until I'd changed back into
my people clothes.

"Legs!" Raiden squealed when he saw me walk out of
the bathroom. He was pointing to where my tail had been.
"Legs!"

"Duh, dummy," Brandon said, his first words since the awkward encounter in the tub. He dropped down on the carpeted floor and flopped across it on his belly. "See how she'd look if she tried to walk with her tail?"

That afternoon, Brandon conspicuously elected not to hold my hand as we walked down the beach, still unsure what to make of all that had transpired. We counted ghost crabs scurrying at our feet and pelicans plunging with prehistoric grace into the surf.

"Auntie Mermaid, look," Brandon exclaimed, pointing just ahead of a surfer attempting to ride an anemic wave. "I think I saw a tail!"

The sun seemed brighter, the sea more sparkling. He still believed. "Of course you did," I told him. "You're related to me after all."

Brandon paused, contemplating. "It's okay if you want to go play with your friend." He raised his eyebrows and nudged his head in the direction of the sighting.

"I'd rather hang out with you. And besides, she's already playing with someone."

Brandon's eyes scoured the water, landing on the surfer. "With that boy?"

"Bingo," I said, pinching his cheek. "How do you think those surfers go so fast? We pull their boards underneath the water."

He nodded in understanding and then another revelation washed across his face. "So does that mean he's her prince?"

I shrugged a maybe and walked on. Brandon kept looking back at the surfer. "Auntie Mermaid, do you have a prince back in South Carolina?" he asked at last, with all the sweetness little boys hold in their hearts.

I reached for his sweaty hand. "Why on earth would I need a prince when I have you?"

13

Every woman should have at least one affair.
It builds confidence.

~Byrne

Flowers for His Thoughts

GREENWICH VILLAGE – 1935

IT WAS MANIPULATIVE, this test of Duncan's thoughtfulness Byrne found herself analyzing on a winter's day. "If only I could take it back," she thought. But he was six long Manhattan blocks past never mind and more than that to go before she could phone him at work, which she knew she wouldn't do, not when he was still the new man at the magazine.

This was her year to follow artistic passions, and by rights she should be at the piano. There was sheet music to master, more to prove that she still could than for any practical purpose. But her hands were too fluttery for conviction, her long, bony fingers overreaching the intended keys. Gershwin felt as jangled as her conscience.

So she built a pot of soup, instead. Built, because she thought of cooking as construction, a never-ending process that sustained without ever quite satisfying. The soup, a hearty stew really, would be ready whenever the wooden spoon that stirred it could stand upright in the thick ooze. She added ingredients to a base of vegetable stock in the order they occurred to her. Celery shavings caught her eye, left over from the Waldorf salad she had assembled for Duncan the night before. Why not the bruised and forgotten apple core too, for a little sweetness? The ham bone, naked and clanking against the pot's sides, seemed to cry out for cardamom. She lifted the lid of a square tin box and drank in the scent of India. Byrne, standing in her Greenwich Village kitchen, swayed in flowing silks and braided sandals as real as the music playing in her head. If the soup had needed saffron, she would have been a Flamenco dancer from Andalusia, draped in polka dots.

It was her mother Fanny who had taught her the map of spices, and how to line the tins up sideways to cram in as many as possible. "Like a chorus line of Rockettes," Byrne had pronounced, "angled shoulder to chin for high kicks."

"Like linens on a laundry line," Fanny had corrected. "Each corner close enough to the next to share the same peg."

Byrne found any excuse to re-arrange the spices on the rack. Her father had built it for her when she moved out, a replica of the one he'd made for Fanny, but filled with new tin boxes. "Something to remind you of home," he had said, not that there was any chance she would forget her doting father. Michael Miller always brought home floppy, fist-gripped bundles of day-old flowers from the street vendor at the corner of 164th and St. Nicholas Ave. The fragrance of them had balanced out the scent of the laundry chemicals that clung to his skin and clothing from long hours at his dry cleaning business.

Byrne tried to sound casual and indifferent as she tidied up after Duncan's breakfast. "You know what our little love nest needs?" she asked her husband. "Fresh cut flowers. The light from the window needs something lovely to bathe."

Duncan turned to her, arms open. For a second, she thought he wanted her to undress again. She glanced at her wrist watch. Surely there wasn't time for a second serving of morning sex. That was when he laughed.

"Spare a moment for a man who can't manage a tie without you?" His face didn't naturally settle into helplessness. It was a forced, false expression that made her laugh.

"I can think of other ways to tie you up," she wanted to say, to sound sexy and witty. Instead, the dry cleaner's dutiful daughter looped the silky fabric through the knot he'd already loosened for her. "There. The most handsome man on Madison Avenue."

She was already regretting her passive hint about flowers, didn't remind Duncan of it as he grabbed his fedora and sucked the air out of the room. Who was she to demand a demonstration of his devotion so soon into their marriage? In the seven months between their secret marriage and the public one, the drama had been delicious. They had been forced to hide their wedding rings whenever her parents opened her bedroom door, cheerfully declaring dinner ready. After her parents were asleep, Byrne would undress for Duncan.

"You are marvelous," he had said the first time. Byrne had no way of knowing then that she was a poem he would never tire of, that his choice of words to describe her would need no further editing. She paraded for her secret husband, worrying that her mind would never dazzle him in equal measure.

Now the 25-year-old wife of a writer just starting out in the mad world of advertising, Byrne stood over the stove of the apartment they shared imagining the moment Duncan would come home from work. He would not remember the flowers. Instead, he would be bursting with the injustices of the day, how someone or other hadn't seen the genius of a tagline he had written. She already knew what he expected – that she would share his indignation, even top it with exasperated declarations of loyalty. "You're too good for them," she'd say. "They're jealous now but one day they'll be working for you."

She defended him without reservation. His head was so full of big plans and bigger ideas that he didn't have time to divulge the details with lesser intellects – or his wife. Byrne knew almost nothing of Duncan's life before they'd met in Central Park. He spoke with what she assumed to be an authentic Oxford accent, measured and musical, despite being born in Charleston. "The nanny, I suppose," had been his only attempt at an explanation. She knew there were parents, still alive, and siblings, three sisters and a brother, but none came to the wedding in Manhattan's City Hall. "I have a new family now," he had said. "Why should the past play any part in it?"

Byrne was the star in his uncharted universe, no sisters or mother to compete with or emulate. She could keep or leave her religion and answer to no one. She was free to change her identity from prospective concert pianist to Vaudeville dancer with no raised eyebrow reproaches. She would be compared to no other women in his past. "You are my beginning," Duncan told her and she vowed never to pry.

Instead, she held out a hand for him to leap into her past. Duncan loved lounging in their bed, listening to stories of the many men who'd tried to win her heart. "Is it normal for a man to not have a jealous bone in his body?" she had asked him once.

He rolled her into missionary position and pecked at her check. "So it's normal that you want?"

"I'd be bored to death," she answered, before wrapping her long legs around his waist.

Long before Duncan, there had been the Hungarians – older than Byrne but always in a group so as never to alarm her protective parents. They hungered for the earthy company of a long-legged girl on their rigorous hikes through the Hudson Valley; the late 1920s were a giddy time for Byrne. "They must have lusted after you," Duncan teased, "forbidden, unripe fruit that you were."

"No, I was just tall and could keep up with any man," Byrne insisted. The foreigners had seemed to Byrne to have a sophisticated, European sense of balance – physical exertion bordering on competitiveness during the day, cultural immersion in Manhattan by night. Byrne escorted the Hungarians to operas at the Met and dinners at Delmonico's. The evenings always ended with dancing in glamorous nightclubs.

Later came Jeff, the lawyer who had fancied Byrne to be the elegant cufflinks of a successful corporate costume.

"He dreamed of dinner parties with me at the piano," Byrne told Duncan. "He thought I had just enough of an education to know that his was superior."

He proposed and Byrne accepted, with misgivings. "Too flashy," she had said of the two-carat diamond engagement ring he gave her, and turned it so the stone dug into her closed hand. On the day they were to marry, her wary uncles presented Byrne with a check. "Use this to go on a six-month cruise, alone," they pleaded. "If you still want to go through with marrying him when you return, you'll have our blessing."

It was the beginning of the Great Depression and Byrne postponed the wedding. She didn't think she had to tell Jeff that she tore up the uncles' check. She assumed that her integrity was understood. It was not. Jeff took the ring back while he waited for her to come to her senses. "You can wear it after we're married," he told Byrne. "I won't have you bought off again."

The ring on the hand that closed the door of the tiny apartment years later was much smaller. Byrne turned each of three locks with a different key. Greenwich Village was more colorful than secure. When she stepped out on the sidewalk, she wrapped a long scarf around her elegant neck, her thin arms winding around her head like a stunted *port-de-bras* in ballet class. She abandoned the winding of it halfway – letting the ends fly out behind her like Isadora Duncan. "No – you follow. I'll lead," she told the wind-lifted scarf, smiling at her own impudence.

The walk to the Polly Korschein dance studio was long enough to replay the request for flowers a hundred times in her head. Duncan would think it plebian, at best – far better to have asked for a slice of the moon. Worse, he would imagine a lifetime of demanded reassurances when *he* needed none. He trusted in her love without banal insecurity; why couldn't she?

By the time she arrived at the dance studio, she had stretched the thought beyond the point of fixation, where the rest of the world fell away and she saw nothing except the hand before her face. One part ammonia, four parts water and her clenched wad of *Daily News* dissolved the splatterings of other dancers' exertions. Byrne earned her tuition scholarship by arriving early to mop the wood floor and clean the long mirror. She started at the top left corner of the mirror, washing it from left to right as methodically as reading a column of newsprint. Byrne lost herself in her own reflection, sinewy and scraped clear of any mystery.

"That's it!" she said aloud, her revelation suddenly so obvious. Duncan saw her clearly; she had shared every step of the life that led to him. His past was closed, its mysteries unsolved. She needed flowers because she didn't know what made him dance.

As the other dancers arrived for class, Byrne joined in. The warm up still felt awkward to her, the clenched inertia of modern dance technique so different than the strutting poses she had mastered for the burlesque stage. Without the lights and cacophony of recorded music, she was stuck with the weight of her body and her thoughts. There was nowhere for her mind to wander, not with Polly Korschein teaching class. The beat of each warm-up exercise was counted aloud, the tone of Korschein's voice matching the staccato slapping of the rhythm on her thigh as she examined the dancers lying face-up on the floor.

"Extend one, two, three," she drilled, the hand still marking time. Byrne lifted her legs from the floor, trying to arrive at the height of the movement on the count of three and not before, which would be cheating.

"Hold four, five, six," Korschein called out. Byrne cramped with the strain and the palms of her hands pushed against the floor to distract her.

"And release seven, eight."

Byrne was pressing her lips together, exhaling through her nose, when what to do about Duncan suddenly came to her. Her legs went limp. Her husband was not an extension of her body, a limb she could learn to control. She would know him only in the joy of release.

After the two-hour class, she ached from the exertion, still sweating as she started the walk back to 54 Morton Street. But she was decided. After class tomorrow, when Duncan had forgotten all about the flowers and wouldn't read anything into it, she would buy her own.

"I thought you might need a warm bath," Duncan said as she unbundled herself in front of the fireplace. "Go ahead, it's already drawn."

She guiltily pulled her eyes from the naked, flowerless windowsill to his upturned face. How could she be disappointed? A bath was infinitely more thoughtful than insisted flowers.

"Care to join me?" she asked, to mask her blushing thoughts.

"No, you need to stretch out, soak those long legs of yours," he said. "Besides, there isn't room."

She could see an uncertain, flickering light under the closed door of the bathroom, knew that he had lined the lip of the porcelain tub with candles even before she smelled the waxy wonder of it. The draft of the door's opening sent a dozen flames stretching sideways from their wicks like the torsos of dancers in a Martha Graham class.

Byrne gasped. Floating in the place of bubbles were the mounded petals of a hundred yellow roses.

14

Master Class

THE MARTHA GRAHAM DANCE Company coming to town constituted big news in a place as small as Beaufort. The TV station was one of only three buildings with an elevator in the town. There wasn't enough news or staff to produce a live newscast at both six and 11 o'clock like normal TV stations, so our engineer just recorded our half-hour newscast as it aired each evening and replayed it verbatim five hours later. Bad weather remained expected, local election ballots still uncounted, football games forever about to begin. If news happened over the weekend, WJWJ viewers didn't see it until Monday.

Not that anyone minded. Grocery stores shut down by nine each night, and merchants on Bay Street took Sundays off. Yet, unfathomably, the woman I'd met covering her husband's experimental Alzheimer's treatment was bringing the world-renowned Martha Graham Dancers to town. And I'd been assigned to cover it.

"How does Byrne do it?" I asked my boss, Suzanne, when she handed me the press release. "Martha Graham is the Picasso of modern dance."

Suzanne smiled. "What's even more newsworthy is talking the company into teaching Graham technique to uncoordinated middle school students."

Billy, the station's cameraman, couldn't pass up the chance to show that he knew much more about the subject than I did.

"It may be news to you, Teresa," he said, through a mouth full of almost-finished candy bar. "But this isn't the backwoods. Byrne's big time. She rakes in grant money and makes all dancers teach in the schools. Doesn't matter how famous they are. She says jump, they say yes ma'am, how high?"

He licked chocolate off each of his fingers as he listed the names of companies who'd performed for the Byrne Miller Dance Theatre. "Paul Taylor, Mummenschanz, Eliza Monte, take your pick."

"And how do you know all this?" I asked. Billy was hardly a typical modern dance aficionado. He was large enough to flip my desk over if he sat down hard on its corner, and he kept a police scanner next to his bed at night. He was also my ride to work every morning.

"I'm her lighting director," he said. "Haven't missed a performance since I moved to Beaufort. Grab a tape. If we time it right, we can get an interview before the dancers go into rehearsal."

By the time Billy and I arrived at the middle school, the Martha Graham dancers had turned the gymnasium into a rehearsal hall. The bleachers were folded up against the walls, and it reeked of hormones and sweaty basketball games. Teenagers – creatures that I'd discovered normally swarm around a video camera like a tipped-over vending machine – sat cross-legged in front of Byrne.

She was leaning into a tall conga drum, explaining how a phrase is broken into counts of eight. Billy began to set up the video equipment, breathing loudly, already working up a sweat.

"Put your hand over your heart and close your eyes," Byrne told the students. "Listen to the beat, that's the tempo."

At first a few boys giggled and squirmed, but Byrne didn't react. She kept beating a rhythm on the drum and even Billy began to move more gracefully. She commanded the room with eyes closed and chin lifted, a feathered bird's nest of white hair encircling her face. The company dancers arranged their muscular bodies at the base of her drum, lying head to toe. Then, as Byrne played, they began to demonstrate. First just their feet moved, flexing and releasing at the ankle. Then shoulders pulsed and arms extended, lengthening the line of the spine. Chins strained and torsos pulled away from the hardwood floor, as if by a magnet hovering above.

The kids began to copy the movements, matching the rhythm. Before their brains caught up, they were lifting their upper bodies off the floor, contracting and releasing muscles to the pulse of Byrne's drum. A few dancers rose, dispersing themselves among the students to support a neck here, position a leg there.

"Do you know how hard that is?" I whispered to Billy. "She's got them doing Graham contractions without saying a word."

After the class, I hooked up a microphone to interview Byrne Miller. She started speaking before I'd even asked a question.

"Martha Graham was the first one who felt that dance had to come from your inner body, not just your arms and your legs," Byrne began.

It dawned on me that Byrne wasn't being rude. She was accustomed to Billy playing the role of both cameraman and reporter. I motioned for her to look at me, not into the camera lens.

"She was the symbol of modern dance throughout the world," Byrne continued, adjusting her eye line to meet mine without missing a beat. "She touched people even if they never saw her perform."

I bent my head forward, the only cue Byrne needed to continue.

"Even photographs of this woman dancing are so marvelous and other-worldly that they move anyone who sees them."

As she spoke, I realized Byrne was describing the same effect she had on Beaufort. Her sheer magnetism could persuade people who normally cast shrimp nets and drove pickups into attending cutting-edge modern dance concerts. I could see how she had lured Billy away from his police scanner to serve as an unpaid lighting director – she was already transforming me into her personal publicist. Her eyes sparkled with enthusiasm. She flirted with the camera, and I could feel Billy's chest puffing next to me. If Byrne Miller sold heroin Beaufort would be full of addicts. When the interview was over, which was to say when Byrne decided I had enough material to work with, she reversed roles and asked me a question.

"Why don't you take the master class tonight with the company? It starts after your newscast is over."

How does she know I dance, let alone well enough to take a professional class?

"I've been watching you move for the last 20 minutes," she said, as if I had spoken out loud. "You've had years of training, and it shows in every breath you take."

"Actually she used to be some kind of rhythm gymnast. Not a dancer," Billy interrupted.

I glared at him, certain that I was blushing from head to foot.

"What did I do?" he said, sweaty palms upturned. "I saw your resume before you got hired. It was on Suzanne's desk."

I glanced at Byrne, wondering if this blurted disclosure would change her opinion of my capabilities. After all, I had turned down the ballet scholarship, broken my back instead of making the Olympic team. Dance was a private balm for my soul, not something I had offered up for judgment since that audition 12 years earlier.

"Well that explains your calves," she said, winking. "I'll see you at seven."

I wanted to sweep my arms through a *port de bras* and bend into the deepest *curtsy* at her feet. In Byrne's eyes I was an undiscovered talent, worthy of dancing side by side with Martha Graham's company. She didn't care about my past failures or present floundering, and I bowed to my new queen. To Sonny I would say it was just a class after work, nothing special. Byrne's invitation was a treasure he would not take from me.

Five hours later I was pressing my pelvis against a hardwood floor, certain that the sun streaming through windows high above was a spotlight held in position by the gods of dance. Byrne had selected the perfect place for the Martha Graham dancers to conduct their master class. About a dozen students waited inside a wooden building that was once a dance hall in the Gullah part of town: the Silver Slipper Club.

The floor sagged in spots worn smooth from jiving soles and jitterbugging heels. The un-insulated walls let secrets slip out into the night, like notes from a long-ago blues singer. It was the kind of place where reputations were ruined and restraint cast off like shrimp nets into murky Beaufort waters. Of course Byrne would ask her followers to dance here. In the Martha Graham Company master class, there were no classical poses, balances or fluttering across the floor on tip toes. Graham's was a vocabulary at home in the Silver Slipper: violent spasms, trembling and falls to the floor. She called her signature contractions the physical manifestation of grief, but to me, pressed against the floorboards of a Gullah dance hall, they were birthing pains of belonging.

Class started on the floor, the dancers all looking up at the exposed beam rafters of the ceiling instead of at each other in the mirror. I was grateful for the anonymity but I couldn't even see the teacher. It was disorienting, and I had to fight the urge to copy the movements of dancers lying next to me.

When I raised my neck and torso into a Graham contraction off the floor, I could see two women on either side. One had a gray ponytail trailing down a scooped-neck ballet leotard and I recognized her as Lisa, the wife of a brainy professor I'd interviewed several times. She was struggling to hold the position, shoulders awkwardly raised up to her ears and a few beats behind the demonstrators. Still, she looked to be the age of my mother, who would never even attempt this position.

On my left was a tall, younger woman cheerfully cheating, balancing her weight on an outstretched hand. She looked at me and grinned, impishly proud of her solution to a ridiculously difficult exercise.

The movements were unfamiliar yet somehow natural, the exact opposite of every ballet class gymnasts take as part of training. When the demonstrators rippled through the class with gentle corrections, they separated my turned-out feet and placed them in parallel position. Suddenly there was more power underneath my thighs, a primal pushing-off point for my jumps. Instead of leaping through the air with primly pointed toes, I exploded with flexed feet and angular arms. And with every sharp twist of the neck, I could see

Byrne in the corner, eyes fixed on me, patterning the steps with her hands. It was as if she were dancing with me.

Sixteen counts of choreography became 32, 64, and then whole movements of music filled up with glides and spirals. There were falls and recoveries from one side of the hall to the other, rushing advances from the back wall to the front. In the corners, layers of discarded clothes began to pile up next to handbags and water bottles, cast off as the dance expanded. One after another, students collapsed onto their piles of clothes, conceding to spectator status, cheering on those still standing. The class, billed as 90 minutes, swelled into two-and-a-half hours. Finally, Byrne moved into the center of the Silver Slipper and began the chorus of applause. For the dancers, she clapped, for the students, for the spirit in the room and the sultry air that bound us all together one night in a Gullah dance hall.

Outside it was cooler, but still wringing with humidity, when I draped myself over the railing on the front steps of the Silver Slipper. I could hear Byrne inside, going over the schedule for the next day's performance with the dancers and one by one, the women who took the master class gave each other sweaty hugs and got into their air-conditioned cars.

Lisa-the-professor's-wife waved at me from behind her steering wheel. "See you at the concert," she called out. Her accent was thick with the heavy consonants and long vowels of Swiss or German ancestry. Yet her voice was somehow lilting and light in the afterglow of dance. Then there were only two of us left, panting on the steps of the Silver Slipper Club, not willing to break the spell and go home.

"I'm Teresa," I said, reaching out to shake the hand of the woman I'd caught cheating in the warm-up.

"I'm Lillian," she answered. "How long have you been with the company?"

I stared at her, wondering if she was joking. Then she

asked how I liked Beaufort so far, and I realized that she actually thought I was one of the Martha Graham dancers.

"I love it, especially when people give me far more credit than I'm due," I answered. "By tomorrow, I'll barely be able to walk. I'm actually just a reporter who used to be a dancer, but thanks anyway."

"I knew you looked familiar," she said. "WJWJ, right? Byrne's always on the news. That's where I've seen you."

This was more familiar ground; I was getting used to being recognized. I checked my watch, wondering if Sonny had forgotten to come pick me up.

"I'm waiting for my husband, too," Lillian said, her smile gone. "I almost wish he'd never come."

"*Too*," she'd said, as though we shared a sinking dread of miserable husbands. I stiffened, replaying the conversation for any slip I might have made. *Was it my body language, or did this woman always leap to conclusions?* Either way, I felt exposed. I suddenly hoped Sonny never got my answering machine message about the dance class, that he wouldn't peel into this gravel parking lot and announce, with his usual glare, that I answered to him. I wanted to savor the flavors of my other self, the one who moved so freely she could be mistaken for a professional dancer.

And then I looked at Lillian. The mischievous enthusiasm I'd seen on her face during the class had washed away, like a message written on sand too close to encroaching waves. She was biting her lower lip and slouching, inches less than the tall, vibrant woman she'd just been. I could feel her wishing she could rewind her words and be alone with whatever impulse drove them from her lips. Just a few minutes before, she had been part of the swell of support and joy inside the Silver Slipper, and I couldn't let that slip away.

"You were great in there you know," I said. "Nobody can take that away. Not even an asshole."

By the time a tear made its way down Lillian's cheek, there was a smile there to swallow it.

"Is it that obvious?" she asked. "Do I have 'pushing 40 and about to be divorced' written all over my face?"

I didn't answer, afraid that anything I'd say to comfort her, to share the misery, might be equally true of me.

"Byrne is the only one who really understands what I've been going through," she said.

I must have looked like I wasn't following because Lillian launched into explanation.

"I'm one of Byrne's collected daughters. Lisa is one too. We're scattered around the world, wherever she's danced."

I didn't have to ask what Lillian meant by collected daughters. I was beginning to know the silky feel of Byrne's favor, the web she wove that made me feel more charming, witty and talented than I did with anyone else. It was the other part of Lillian's confession that confused me.

"Byrne Miller gives you advice about divorce?" I asked. "But she and Duncan have the perfect marriage."

Lillian laughed. "Byrne never gives out-and-out advice, just little stories from her life that somehow make you see things in a new light."

This rang true. The first thing Byrne had ever said to me was that she was not as feeble as her advanced age would suggest. Perhaps she was not as straightforward either.

"What she wants for me is to find my own Duncan. But she doesn't think I should leave my husband until I have a few affairs under my belt. For practice, I guess."

If it was possible to sweat even more profusely, I started to. "Go out and have affairs?" I repeated. "Cheat on your husband – as in 'try before you buy'?"

Lillian nodded, like this suggestion might be offered up by Ann Landers.

"Maybe she meant it figuratively," I said, as gently as

I could. I could imagine Byrne inventing quippy mantras she might call something like womenisms – equal parts feminism and witticism. But I was still wrestling with the idea of a woman as wildly successful in love as Byrne Miller ever advocating infidelity. She moved her husband's wheelchair like they were a duet dancing on stage. I'd seen how she held his hand, finished his sentences. Collected daughter or not, Lillian must have misunderstood.

15

Monogamy is overrated.

Honesty is imperative.

~Byrne

The Combination

GREENWICH VILLAGE – 1937

Even uttering the word "copy" made Duncan's throat constrict and his mouth feel too small for his tongue. "It's perfect in an unintentionally forthright sort of way," he confided in Byrne. "A writer creates words but an ad man is only an imitation of a writer, a copier."

There was no way for Byrne to pull him off these thoughts with counter arguments or comparisons. That Duncan was clever enough to concoct witty slogans or persuasive enough to sell products was no solace to a man who still hadn't finished his first novel. *Sit in Dark Places* might as well have described his ambition, festering alongside the bright light of the day job that to the outside world defined him. He took no pride in the milestones that other men would have celebrated – raises, a bigger office, client requests that he be assigned to their account.

The only benefit or solace he allowed himself was the open admiration of women. Just as Fanny and Byrne had been drawn to Duncan's charm and intensity, so too were secretaries, receptionists and even the models whose job it was to illustrate or decorate his work. Mr. Miller, in the eyes of these eager young women, had the spark without the swagger. He noticed even the tiniest detail that their bosses, boyfriends and husbands didn't. He remembered their names, asked after their interests, even knew what colors would look best next to their skin. Four years of marriage to an older woman had made him expert in the art of observation and encouragement.

Byrne, not quite 30, was three years past a successful, if brief, burlesque career. On stage she had shed any inhibitions about her body and replaced them with honest self-appraisal. She still had jutting breasts and gams you could see from the back of a theater but her back did more than connect the parts Vaudeville audiences paid to see. It braced her every movement, supported her elongated spine and elevated her expressive head. Her arms no longer dangled from her shoulders like fireplace pokers, and her flat stomach was the center of her strength and balance. Her legs, always long, were no longer gangly. They commanded a presence, even among serious modern dancers like Dean Goodelle, but she was still a scholarship student under the teacher he had introduced her to, not a paid member of any professional dance company. She was beginning to think she never would be, until an unexpected announcement after a particularly brutal technique class.

"There is to be a master class with my good friend and mentor," Polly Korschein told her class as the dancers warmed down. Her eyes bored in on Byrne, her oldest and least experienced student. "Let there be no doubt, Harald Kreutzberg is the master. Please be worthy subjects."

It was not her teacher's reputation Byrne was determined to uphold when she walked into the master class. It was her own. Kreutzberg was the German dancer she'd mooned over from the balcony of a movie theater in her teens, the revolutionary performer who'd inspired the only love letters she'd ever written. In the years since then, Kreutzberg's controversial style was transforming modern dance in America, severing any ties it had to ballet or Broadway. His influence was so intense that a young Mexican who saw him dance, José Limón, gave up painting to study dance instead.

Byrne meant to be marvelous, to transcend whatever choreography Kreutzberg offered and imbue it with purpose and passion. She wore a long-sleeved black leotard with pointed sleeves that fastened around her middle fingers instead of breaking the arm's line at the wrist. Her flesh-colored dance skirt was asymmetrical, slit to the thigh in the front and swooping past her left ankle. She had dressed for the master class in front of the fireplace, and when she began to wrap a flat silk scarf around her smoothed-back hair, Duncan tugged it away.

"Hold nothing back, my love," he said. "Every part of you is too stunning to subdue."

She had the unconditional support of a younger husband, the self-confidence of years of training, and full control over an imposing body. So Byrne had no idea why it felt as though she would throw up.

Kreutzberg can't possibly know I wrote those wretched letters, she told herself. It was only a class, after all, not an audition or an interview, and stage fright was something she left behind in Washington. She leaned over her bare feet, gripping the floor in parallel position exactly the width of her hips, her thighs in second position *plié*. Ten minutes remained before class began. A musician was setting up drums, adjusting the tension of their skins, while dancers bounced and shook their limbs, like puppets, loosening up.

Byrne stood up too fast. The rehearsal room dimmed with what seemed like a buzzing noise before coming into focus again. She dropped her head back and opened her mouth in an exaggerated yawn to stretch the muscles of her neck. *Maybe my ears need to pop. My equilibrium is off.* Her hands felt clammy as she flexed her wrists for a forearm stretch. *I should get a glass of water. There's still time.* Then Kreutzberg made his entrance, black cape sweeping behind angular shoulders.

Byrne had intended to find a spot in the front row, better to see and be seen. But in the collective inhale of students at the arrival of their master, she shuffled to the back, next to a *barre* she could grab if the room continued to spin. Kreutzberg didn't speak; he just began to hop from one leg to the other. Byrne and all the other students realized the class had begun and mimicked his movement – side to side like children desperate for a bathroom. The drummer found a syncopated beat and leaned into his congas, watching the teacher even more intently than the dancers, anticipating changes in his rhythm.

Kreutzberg added a tilt of the head, tentative and twitching, and his movements were suddenly reminiscent of a gazelle before a hunt. He added an arm swing, bent 90 degrees at the elbow, hands clenched, and a room full of dancers became skiers dodging unseen dangers down a steep slope. He dropped to the floor and they were assassin's victims, suddenly stilled. He lunged forward with a primal roar and they were a phalanx of sound and fury.

Byrne abandoned herself to improvisation, forgetting all about silly love letters and sweaty hands. The room became a tunnel, all light focused on the powerful, muscular man at the front – leaping and falling, spiraling down and springing up, gathering in and exploding out. She was too absorbed in following the choreography to pay attention to her churning stomach. But when the class was over, the adrenaline abandoned her and she couldn't hang around long enough even to curtsy for Kreutzberg, let alone talk to him like other dancers were. She raced to the nearest bathroom, fighting back waves of nausea. If only she had tied her hair back with the silken scarf, maybe then she wouldn't have been rinsing vomit out of it in the sink, wondering what was wrong with her.

When the vomiting continued the next morning, and the next, Byrne realized she was pregnant. She looked in the mirror and pulled her hair away from her long, sinewy neck. "It's over," she told herself. "There are no pregnant dancers."

The face that stared back at her was blanched and disbelieving, but the warm calm that settled in her stomach was relief. A role was being handed to her. She could quit without being a quitter. She could define herself as someone other than a dancer, instead of almost or not yet. It was liberating. Byrne realized she had been trapped by her own sense of destiny: fail to become a marvelous dancer and be unworthy of her talented husband or succeed and overshadow him. Duncan's artistic struggle was enough drama for one marriage, and if she stopped dancing now, there would never be future comparisons. Being a mother would anchor her, bind her to Duncan in the here and now.

Toni Alison Miller was born in June 1938. It was the beginning of Byrne's 15-year hiatus from dance, a career paused in pursuit of being as dedicated a mother as Fanny had been to her.

"It wasn't as if I was setting the dance world on fire anyway," she admitted to Duncan. "Maybe our daughter will."

Byrne and Duncan went from eating supper with Fanny and Michael only on Saturdays to twice or three times a week. It wasn't that Duncan's salary couldn't support his growing family. Byrne simply needed more help with Alison than he was capable of. He was putting in long hours at the office, working his way up from copywriting to overseeing magazine advertisements, still working on his manuscript in the quiet nooks of Greenwich Village bars and hotel lobbies at night. Byrne worried about him spending so much time alone, battling words that wouldn't come, but she understood his search for the perfect setting. He couldn't get any writing done at their Morton Street apartment. Alison was colicky, perpetually ricocheting from sleep to screaming.

It took all of Byrne's Fanny Brice facial expressions to distract Alison, all of her dance training to find new ways to rock and swing her needy daughter. Jane's birth, three years later, upended whatever balance Byrne thought she had created. Alison demanded even more attention, flipping between delight and despair like a switch. At grandmother Fanny's apartment in Washington Heights, there were distractions, like a reliably loud Electrolux vacuum cleaner that overpowered even Alison's worst wailing. Extralucky, Byrne nicknamed it.

When Duncan would walk into Fanny and Michael's apartment mid-week, briefcase full of ad copy, he was greeted by the sight of Alison on Fanny's hip as his mother-in-law vacuumed Persian rugs. His daughter demanded physical contact in exchange for silence. As a child, he'd never held such currency, such power. The Miller family's devotion to Alison was a constant contrast to his own childhood, and it left him unsettled and unsure of how to act. When he watched baby Jane on Michael's lap as his father-in-law pounded the keys of the upright piano, Duncan saw an implicit trust he'd never known and couldn't fathom how to earn. It was only when he saw his exhausted wife stretched out on the settee, snoring through the cacophony, that he knew exactly what to do.

"You are beautiful even in repose," he'd mutter, kissing her forehead so she'd wake for dinner.

Byrne had never felt as beautiful as Duncan declared her to be, and even less so after having two babies. Her lower back ached from constantly carrying Alison on her hip, even after her younger sister began to toddle on her own two feet. The dowdy apron she tied around her waist was stuffed with tantrum distractions: rustling candy wrappers, a squeaky clown's horn, finger puppets and a tambourine. She jiggled Alison on her knee, gently patting her daughter's back like the drums that had once accompanied classes at Polly Korschein's studio. It seemed like a lifetime ago, modern dance now an ancient, wistful part of her history.

It was the inner quiet of dance that she craved – the centered calm that came with concentration. She missed the luxury of pursuing her own perfection, practicing turns without getting dizzy by fixing her gaze in the mirror and snapping her head around to that same spot before her body caught up.

Preoccupied mothers have no such tricks to keep their balance, and it was months before Byrne realized that Duncan had hired a model from one of his tobacco advertisements to be his personal secretary. It was wonderful news, of course, a sign of upward mobility if not the literary acclaim that still eluded him. Her name was Margaret or Marjorie or something – Byrne hadn't really paid attention. Duncan's world seemed less and less connected to hers, or rather to the all-consuming vortex that was Alison.

"Go meet him for lunch then if you're feeling invisible," Fanny had told her. "I'll watch the girls." Surely other wives visited their husbands during the business day, but Byrne couldn't see any evidence of them in the imposing lobby of Duncan's building. The seventh floor receptionist asked if she had made an appointment and Byrne laughed, a little too loudly. She was still collecting herself when Marjorie or Margaret or whatever her name was emerged to escort Byrne to Duncan's office.

Byrne saw the fashionable pencil skirt first, grazing shapely calves and pinching a tiny waist. Then she noticed the freshly powdered nose and perfectly blotted lips. Duncan's secretary could have stepped out of a mail-order catalog – airbrushed perfection with a voice to match. She spoke in a cultivated half-whisper, as if Byrne's very presence was some sort of an intrusion.

"I'll let Mr. Miller know you're here," she said, clicking her manicured red fingernails along the edge of a desk. That was when Byrne first noticed the scent, a familiar note of lavender that lingered in the stillness of the air between them. She stiffened as she realized Duncan's shirts smelled of this woman's perfume. Her mind raced through explanations. *Of course it does. They work in close proximity. It doesn't mean anything.* Still, Byrne made up some excuse about the time, how she hadn't noticed how late it was. Could the girl just let Duncan know that Fanny looked forward to seeing him at dinner.

Weeks later, when Duncan told her he'd taken up pipe smoking, she pushed aside the little voice that told her it might be to cover up the scent of lavender.

"No wonder they let you have a secretary," she said, plucking the pipe from his lips and provocatively pursing it between her own. "It lends such a distinguished air, don't you think?" Duncan smiled and reached for her, and for once she didn't make him wait until she was sure the girls were asleep. She swept the sheets clear of folded socks, crayons and tossed-aside hair ribbons and they tumbled into a bed that smelled of the family they were. It was only in the afterglow of reconnection that Byrne dared to ask Duncan how the writing was going.

"Maggie's going to type out my manuscript," Duncan said. "She's really very fast."

It's Maggie now? Byrne hadn't noticed when the secretary's name became so familiar. She turned her head so Duncan wouldn't see the rapid blinking back of tears.

She had always been Duncan's believer, the one sharing turns with him in dream chasing. Now that she was no longer dancing, Byrne defined herself as Duncan's muse, the one who tended to his inspiration and made sense out of chaos. A wife should figure out where everything belongs, that's what Fanny always said; not some secretary who happened to be a model and who probably smoked the same brand of tobacco that she likely packed Duncan's pipe with every morning.

Byrne gladly would have traded places with Maggie. Her mornings were filled with potty training a reluctant Alison and chasing after Jane before she crawled on top of the piano, reaching for the open window. "Me out?" she asked, turning to look at Byrne and wobbling dangerously close to the ledge. She was talking already, mostly copying the words that expressed the frustrations of her older sister. Me, mine, no, now, ow – what Jane lacked in syllables she made up for in repetition.

The constant stream of vocal demands desensitized Byrne. She hardly noticed words that didn't come with built-in shrieks, like exclamation points. Which was probably how the word "Maggie" had seemed to sneak into her household. Duncan began to mention his secretary's nickname with casual regularity. Maggie was coming in to the office on Saturday to help with the manuscript. Maggie had an extra ticket to a ball at Webster Hall. Maggie's purse was stolen on the subway. She lived only a few blocks out of the way. It was safer just to walk her home.

It was when Maggie became part of a particular one-syllable word – *we* – that Byrne knew she had to take action. "*We* impressed the hell out of that moronic executive… *We* celebrated with drinks at the Brevoort… *We're* backed up at work; tell the girls I'll see them in the morning." Byrne couldn't allow another woman, however innocent and helpful, to share in the *we* that belonged to her, that defined her marriage. *We* was only one short step away from *us*, and *us* was one syllable Byrne vowed to keep for herself.

"You know, Duncan," she tossed out one morning with all the off-handedness she could summon, "with all the extra time you put in at the office, your poor Maggie probably doesn't eat supper until much too late."

"She hasn't complained," Duncan said, his tone almost ashamed of having never thought of it himself.

"Of course not. She admires you and she wants to keep her job," Byrne continued.

"It's not intentional. She knows I would never let her go," Duncan sputtered.

"There's only one thing to do. We must simply insist she take her suppers with us. It's the least you can do," Byrne said.

Duncan stroked his goatee and nodded. "I suppose I could ask."

It took only four days before Maggie's curiosity got the better of her. She arrived on Duncan's arm, clutching a bouquet of flowers in her free hand. She was even more frighteningly lovely than she had seemed at the office, with thick artificial eyelashes and gloves dyed a deep chocolate color to match her ankle-strap pumps and satin handbag.

"How thoughtful of you," Byrne said through air kisses. "I love flowers. I'm sure Duncan's told you of the time he filled our bathtub with rose petals."

Duncan's secretary looked down at her offering of daffodils and blushed as she shook her head no.

"Well, never mind," Byrne said through a patronizing smile. "These will perk right up with some water." There was no need to share with Maggie the entire truth of the bathtub flower story: how Duncan had petulantly demanded the petals remain in their watery grave until they'd turned into a smelly sludge.

Maggie fussed with the flowers still drooping in her hand "Well, anyway, here they are," she said, handing them to her host.

Byrne had rehearsed her performance as thoroughly as a Sara Mildred Strauss number. Normally she didn't wear high heels but she wanted to look slightly down her nose at Maggie all night. The costume she selected was glamorously figure flattering but carefully camouflaged to appear effortless and casual. She let the braided belt of her dress drape low on her waist as if she hadn't bothered to cinch it all the way, and tendrils of hair spilled from a loose chignon that emphasized her elegant neck. She even smudged a puff of pastry flour where an apron might have been tied, had she not secretly asked her mother to prepare one of Duncan's favorite desserts: hazelnut baklava.

The girls, who normally fought over their father when he came home in time for dinner, were already asleep in bed, exhausted after the top-to-bottom apartment cleaning Byrne had turned into an all-afternoon game to wear them out.

"What a lovely home," Maggie managed as she squeezed past Byrne's breasts, which practically blocked the entrance hallway. "Oh, a piano. Do you play? I'm taking lessons. I'm probably not very good. But then again I have fast fingers. Duncan always says so. I mean Mr. Miller. Right, Mr. Miller?"

It was impossible to tell whether Maggie was intentionally insinuating the intimacy Byrne already suspected or if she was worried she'd blown her chance to upstage her boss's stay-at-home wife. Either way, Byrne realized that all she'd have to do was guide Maggie to the edge of the pit she would surely dig, given enough time.

"Wine," Byrne said as though the thought just occurred to her. "What we all need is a nice glass of cabernet before supper." That Maggie spilled that wine down her starched white secretarial blouse was just pure luck. How was Byrne to know that she couldn't complete a thought without awkward and graceless hand gestures? Maggie's normally flawless face blotched with hives of embarrassment, and Duncan had to walk her home wearing the scratchiest baggy cardigan Byrne could loan her.

Byrne called Maggie at work the next day, making sure she would come for a rain-check supper and promising to serve only white wine. It would go perfectly with the flaky lamb and eggplant moussaka Fanny had agreed to make for Byrne's second attempt.

"So Margaret, Duncan tells me your apartment is right next to the New School. Have you ever thought of taking classes?" Byrne asked, serving her a sloppy slice of moussaka.

"Goodness, no. My father says that place is a haven for communists and their sympathizers. My name would be mud."

Duncan nearly choked on a chunk of eggplant, and Byrne handed him a freshly pressed napkin.

"Well, your father gave you a perfectly lovely first name instead," Byrne said, patting her hand. "Queen Margaret is my favorite character in *Richard III.*"

Maggie paused, mid-forkful of moussaka, confused. "Is he the one who chopped off all his wives' heads?"

"Close enough," Byrne smiled. "Margaret might actually have preferred it."

Duncan closed his eyes, digging for the quote. "I do find more pain in banishment than death?" He opened them, looking into the twinkling eyes of his wife.

Byrne piled another slice of moussaka onto Maggie's plate and finished the line for Duncan. "The sorrow that

I have, by right is yours, and all the pleasures you usurp are mine."

Maggie dabbed the corners of her painted lips with her napkin. "The Ink Spots, right? I'm always trying to get them to change the radio station in the lunchroom. All the other girls like Frank Sinatra, but I've got nothing against the coloreds."

Duncan dropped his napkin and scooted his chair a few inches away from Maggie before bending over to retrieve it.

"Of course you don't," Byrne reassured Maggie. "Maybe tomorrow night you can play us some of your favorites on the piano. You did say you play, right? Duncan loves a performance, especially after a long day at work."

The girl beamed at Duncan, sodden chunks of pastry dough clumped between the ridges of her perfect teeth.

Duncan rose from his chair. "What a lovely thought, but we daren't wake the girls," he said.

"I'm sure they'd love to meet Margaret," Byrne said. "They get so bored with only their mother's playing."

"Actually, Maggie and I have almost finished that project," Duncan sputtered. "There shouldn't be much need for working late."

"Well, Margaret, consider our home yours," Byrne said, collecting Maggie's coat from the bed. "You've been delightful company and such a help to Duncan."

She was still drying the dishes when Duncan returned from walking Maggie home.

"Isn't that Fanny's casserole dish?" he asked, pointing to the rectangular glass baking pan now emptied of the flaky moussaka.

Byrne debated the dangers of protesting too much.

"She loaned it to me," she quickly compromised. "We don't have anything big enough for three."

Duncan stared at the dish in his wife's hands, weighing

her explanation against the evidence of the evening.

"What are you looking at?" Byrne interrupted. "Did I miss an ink spot?"

Duncan threw his head back and laughed and Byrne knew then that she would never have to entertain the secretary again.

"Of all the attributes a woman could possess," Duncan said as he folded his wife into his arms, "yours are the unique combination I could never live without."

16

Do Not Affect To Be So Delicate

BEAUFORT – 1991

I SUSPECTED THE REASON Byrne Miller drew me close in the first steps of our dance together was simply because she loved an audience. Why else would she invite me over to her house to gossip about the Martha Graham dance performance? It certainly wasn't my history that intrigued her. She'd seen me dance, yes, but she didn't know I had broken my back trying to make the Olympics and somehow ended up with a common-law husband from Mexico.

I had every intention of keeping my secrets as I walked up the brick path to her cottage on the Beaufort River. Chubby Carolina wrens chirped greetings from the base of a palmetto tree in her front yard. Wipeout strained against her leash when squirrels scampered up a 100-year-old live oak. Byrne didn't hear the commotion. She was absorbed in trimming a rose bush at the base of the stairs. I didn't figure Byrne for a pruner.

"Only this bush," she said. "We go at it regularly, she and I, but she never seems to realize it's only for her own good. Rather like technique drills in dance class, don't you think?"

Apart from the roses, Byrne's garden was a study in abandon, wild with azaleas and shrouded with Spanish moss.

"The azaleas I leave to their own devices," Byrne said. "They're utterly indecent already, showoffs, just like me."

The air smelled of salt and bolting cilantro. There was movement to it, lifted and waved by a sea breeze. Wipeout twirled in front of Byrne, swirling her feathery tail for attention.

"Oh, hello there. Who is your beautiful friend?" Byrne asked.

I told her then of how Wipeout was born in Mexico and spent the first months of her life carried to and from a sandy beach by teenage surfers. How when Sonny first saw Wipeout, she had been cupped in the hands of a street-corner vendor and he had to have her. All his life, he'd said, he wanted a dog just like her.

"And how long would that be?" Byrne asked.

"Oh, we're the same age," I said, not adding that I felt years older than Sonny by the time we had reached South Carolina, more like his mother than his lover.

"Let me show you the river side of the house," Byrne said, letting it slide.

We walked around back and I saw Duncan napping in his wheelchair on the porch, the thinnest of screens filtering mosquitoes from the fragrant air.

"He's had a rough morning," Byrne told me in hushed voice. "Confused and frustrated with confusion."

She led me down a narrow dirt path between a tangle of wisteria and confederate jasmine. Wipeout bounded ahead, sliding on the thin veneer of pine straw and fallen oak leaves. The path led down a bank about 15 feet to the bottom before splaying out into a skirt of broken oyster shells and old bricks at the water's edge.

"Duncan loves being close to the water," Byrne said.

"That's why we moved here. That, and the fact that my daughter Janie was posted at the Marine Corps Air Station before the divorce. She was killed earlier this year, out West, by a drunk driver. That's the radar tower, across the river."

There was a daughter? Byrne had known a loss like the one that crippled my family? I grew up never mentioning the death of my little brother, knowing only how far my father ran from it, so I had no idea how to respond to Byrne. It felt oddly trusting and generous, her telling me when we barely knew each other, yet casual – a footnote rather than devastation. Somehow she'd managed to move on with her life and welcome me into it.

Willowy spartina grass stretched in every direction. I was tangled in the very roots of the marsh, witness to the rising waters, speechless. We could have been standing in a primeval swamp, until an FA18 fighter jet screamed overhead.

"Wow, you're right in the flight path," I shouted. There was a sign at the entrance to the air station on Beaufort's Highway 21, declaring "The noise you hear is the sound of freedom."

She laughed, too loud, the way a person does when happy for distraction.

"Some days it's like living in a war zone. It's rather ironic, actually, these jets flying over this particular house. I protested Vietnam, marched on Washington, handed out communist leaflets, everything."

I imagined a daughter who joined the Marines, maybe to declare her independence from a larger-than-life mother. Byrne followed this daughter all the way to South Carolina only to have her taken away too soon. Brackish water lapped at my feet and tiny crabs scattered in every direction.

Wipeout's ears perked up. A silver-haired woman, barely five feet tall, peered at us from the bluff that connected all the waterfront cottages.

"Greetings, neighbor," Byrne called out in a sing-song voice, waving vigorously.

The woman scurried away, like one of the crabs into some hidden hole. Byrne started to laugh again.

"I've known that woman since 1969, when we moved here from Santa Fe," she said. "I'd heard all about Southern hospitality. I thought for sure she would drop by and welcome us to the neighborhood."

"Didn't she?" I asked.

"Seems news that we're Jewish arrived before we did. Yankee Jews, even worse. Days went by without a peep. I finally decided to turn the tables. I baked a wonderful pie and walked it over. That teeny little tutu of a woman poked her head out and said, 'We may be neighbors, but we're not neighborly.' She hasn't spoken to me since."

"Did she accept the pie?" I asked.

"Never has returned the plate," Byrne said. "Bless her heart."

We went inside and Byrne pulled out the Graham dancers' glossy program. She thought they should have rearranged the order of the dances, better to pull the audience along to a crescendo. I remembered nothing of the architecture of the performance. My eyes had been glued to feet and arms, the steps and positions delicacies I had tasted in the master class. The sheer athleticism spoke as much to me as the artistry, and when I showed Byrne the positions I was still replaying in my head, she couldn't help herself. She turned my chin a few degrees, showed me how to lift my arms through the moves instead of rushing to the final poses. Physical contact that would have felt impersonal in a dance class was oddly intimate here. I caught a reflection in the window, a courtesan and her tender teacher.

"You know what would have made the concert perfect?" Byrne asked. She moved into the kitchen and uncorked a bottle of Beaujolais Village as I sat down. "If I could have erased the audience."

She poured two goblets of wine, upending the bottle with a practiced flourish.

"You must promise not to tell, but the real reason I bring these companies to Beaufort is purely selfish. I want to see them. My secret fantasy is to have whatever brilliant company I desire perform a concert for me, alone, in a marvelous theater. Even the orchestra would have to be hidden. I'm an unrepentant snob with a whim of iron."

I offered a toast – to Duncan's taste for snobby women – and Byrne let loose a laugh from deep in her gut. There were secrets in her unladylike bellow, womenisms she might one day share.

"Duncan always did have immaculate taste. When we were living in New York, he was an advertising man – one of the clever ones who came up with the witty slogans. He was surrounded by beautiful models, far more beautiful than I."

"It didn't drive you crazy?" I asked.

"I never tried to compete for his attention. I admired the women around him as much as he did. It didn't bother me if he slept with them when he had the opportunity, because I knew something they did not."

I choked on my wine. She couldn't be talking about the sweet octogenarian gurgling in his sleep on the porch, cheating on her.

"Which was ..." I egged her on, pouring a glass of wine. *Maybe Lillian got the affair part right.*

"Which is," she corrected me, "that whatever combination of attributes I possess is the unique combination he can never live without. It doesn't matter if he admires one or another trivial quality in someone else – I know with utter certainty that he loves the complexity that is me."

I thought of me, sitting next to Sonny on the aborted ride to Hunting Island State Park. How I'd botched it. Byrne would have known exactly how many times to squeeze Duncan's hand. She knew exactly how to make anyone who met him fall in love with their love story, especially me. I worked at a PBS television station with a loyal following. Duncan was dying. Thousands of people watched the stories I put on the air each night, and Byrne knew this could only help her cause. She was sharing a bottle of wine with me not to deconstruct a dance performance but to build a partnership. She was recruiting me through our shared language of dance into something more tragic, more real, than anything on a dance stage or television screen. Her public battle to save her husband's health might have looked futile and tragic to those who watched it unfold on WJWJ, but to me Byrne seemed to have a perfect love and a perfect life. The worse mine got, the more I wanted to escape into hers.

My pathway to this fantasy was Duncan. It felt strange thinking of someone old enough to be my great grandfather in romantic terms, like a crush. Perhaps it was the drama of his predicament that drew me to him. He relied on Byrne for literally every breath, yet he gave me the sense that, just by listening, I was helping too. Being around Duncan made it feel like there was still time for Sonny to become the man he was meant to be, that clearly it took years of unconditional love from a woman like Byrne. I felt sorry for Sonny, bound to him by deaths we each endured. But I admired Duncan.

"Life is hard to bear," he started to say weeks later, when the nurses tried to find a solid vein to draw blood. I was on assignment with the Millers in Charleston. I'd rationalized covering a blood draw as newsworthy because so many of the Millers' friends in Beaufort had donated plasma for the halted research: the county's chief librarian, a high-school French teacher and members of the Byrne Miller Dance Theatre board of directors. Yes, it was routine lab work, I'd told Suzanne, but important background footage in case the hospital agreed to begin Duncan's experimental Alzheimer's treatments again. Squeamish, I could barely watch, even through the viewfinder of my video camera. But there was Byrne's hand, reaching out to hold his.

"But do not affect to be so delicate!" Byrne said.

Her voice was loud, bouncing off the white tiled walls. I looked up from the viewfinder, shocked at her lack of sympathy. The veins of the husband she cherished were collapsing in front of us, and she was telling him to suck it up and be a man about it?

"We are all of us fine sumpter asses," she continued, drawing each word out as if for emphasis.

I turned off the camera, not wanting to film what seemed like the first cruel thing I'd ever heard her say to him. And then I looked over at Duncan. He was mouthing the words along with her. He took a deep breath as the nurse began to draw a thin line of blood into a syringe. When he exhaled, it was to complete Byrne's sentence.

"…and assesses," he said. Beaming.

Yes, I thought to myself, it will be a long time before I understand the power between these two people, or how to build a love like theirs. It was so unlike the only other marriage I'd witnessed up close and over time. My father needed my mother for someone to tower over. Duncan respected Byrne as much as he adored her. During that same taping in Charleston, after interviewing his doctor, I asked Duncan for an on-camera reaction.

"Byrne is far more eloquent," he said. He gazed at her face as she spoke, for him, and when she finished he swept his trembling arm through the air as if bowing before her.

"Marvelous," he said, each syllable a shallow exhale.

On the long ride back to Beaufort in the WJWJ news van, Byrne told me she met Duncan at a writers gathering in Manhattan.

"His intellect dwarfed mine, and I still can't fathom why he would fall for me," she said. "I've never written more than a good letter, and he has invented six entire worlds through his novels."

I glanced at the rearview mirror between us. Duncan's chin was nestled in a pillow Byrne had strapped under the seat belt across his chest, knowing the 90-minute drive would be difficult for him. He looked as comfortable as a pricked and prodded man in his eighties could, fast asleep and drooling.

"Well, you must have caught up in the intellectual category somewhere along the line," I said. "What was that you were quoting back in the hospital – Shakespeare?"

"Oh no, that was just a bit of Nietzsche I adore. Delicious, don't you think, considering how indelicate I can be?"

I had no idea who Nietzsche was.

"Yes, but I'm not sure I understand the summer asses part," I said.

"I suppose it is a bit archaic. Sumpter asses are beasts of burden. We are capable of bearing so much more than we pretend."

Pretend to bear?

"But you've already endured so much," I blurted out. I was thinking of her daughter's death, the anti-Semitism she encountered in the South and now Duncan's torturous descent into silence. How much more could either one of them possibly be expected to bear? I saw that she was looking in the rear view mirror, smiling.

"It may not be obvious but I am the luckiest woman in the world. Not a morning has passed in almost 60 years where he has not watched me dress and told me I am marvelous."

17

There will always be a woman more beautiful,
witty or willing. Trust that your unique combination of
attributes is what the right man cannot live without.

~Byrne

Alison

GREENWICH VILLAGE – 1943

THERE'S BOUND TO BE jealousy, Byrne's neighbors told her. No cherished, first-born daughter gives up the title of baby of the household without a fight. Byrne would politely nod and smile, as if Alison weren't at that very moment squeezing the garter belt of her pantyhose, scraping her thigh with chewed-rough fingernails. If she held her higher, letting her nuzzle the soft spot of her neck where her draping hair made a little cave, Alison's fingers might wrap around her bra straps instead.

They were well-meaning, these second-generation immigrant mothers who peered into the pram where Jane gurgled and cooed. They shouted over Alison's incoherent moaning. Some of them even dared to stroke her hair or hand her treats, as if she were a terrified puppy.

If only Alison were simply jealous of her little sister, Byrne thought. Pulling hair, stealing toys, even throwing temper tantrums would surely be easier. The shrill peaks and morose valleys of Alison's moods mirrored Byrne's nerves: sliced open and quivering one minute, drained and deadened the next. If anything, Jane could sometimes calm her older sister by distraction. A sudden move, a loud burp, a buckling of the knees that sent her sprawling would jolt Alison out of the world that enveloped her. She could be sweet then, even consoling to her little sister. But it never lasted. The despair always returned.

"I think it's noise that torments her," Byrne tried to explain to Duncan. "She holds her hands over her ears when there's thunder in the distance, or a streetcar."

They watched as Alison sat under the piano, cross-legged, in a pile of shredded paper. She held up a brown paper grocery bag and tore it into three strips, crunching each one into a ball the size of her fist. The scratchy, crackling noise bounced around the walls of the tiny apartment.

Duncan sat on the piano bench and leaned over his self-consoling daughter. "I despise loud noises, too. Daddy understands."

But Duncan wasn't the one who watched other kids Alison's age playing with their siblings at the playground. He wasn't the one who sat on a cold bench to study their reactions and catalog typical responses. Byrne was.

One observation, in particular, had scraped a cold, hollow space in her gut. She had taken the girls to the playground and watched as a little boy chased after his sister. Everything the girl said, the boy copied. Every time she raised her voice, he yelled even louder. Finally she held her hands over her ears and marched off to the seesaw, yelling in a sing-song voice. "I can't hear you. Go away, I can't hear a word you say."

Alison stood on the other side of the seesaw, back turned to the rest of the children. The palms of her hands flattened her ear lobes, blocking out the world. She was talking too, louder than the little girl with the annoying brother, but she was shouting over voices no one else could hear.

"Take her to a hearing specialist," Duncan whispered when Byrne told him, not wanting Alison to overhear the tearful conversation. "And if they don't know what is wrong with her, we'll find another doctor."

Byrne's shoulders shook and her thin frame convulsed with sobs. She spoke to her daughter every day. She knew there was no problem with Alison's hearing, but Duncan was still flailing to reassure his wife.

"Byrne, my love. We live in the most medically advanced metropolis in the known universe. Someone will know how to make it stop."

One doctor did, but his diagnosis stopped Byrne's heart. "Think of it as a form of childhood hysteria" the man wearing a starched white smock told her. His voice was colorless, his tone carefully antiseptic. "The word schizophrenia comes from the Greek. Phrenia meaning brain. Splitting of the brain."

Byrne's brain refused the definition. It was her heart that split when she watched her little girl strapped to a gurney, two metal plates pressed on either side of her shaved head. "Electroconvulsive therapy, ECT" the specialists at Bellevue hospital called it. But Byrne and Duncan knew it as shock treatment. "Her condition is otherwise incurable."

Incurable, they pulled Duncan aside to explain, and most likely inherited from what was known as a "schizophrenogenic" mother. ECT was much safer and more effective than camphor injections into the diseased brain, especially if there were other children in the household. Electrically induced seizures would inhibit violence and self-destructive tendencies later in life. Duncan signed the necessary papers with trembling hands, a writer who would have erased every word on the page if he could.

"She won't remember anything," the doctors assured Byrne. She wasn't allowed to watch the treatment. Bone fractures often resulted from the violent spasms thrashing through little bodies. Byrne didn't need to watch. She would never forget. Her own muscles trembled and contracted, twitching with the guilt and rage of a blamed mother. She had no support groups to consult with, no family history to prepare her for the searing pain of Alison's alteration. It was convenient, the short-term memory loss created by 220 volts steadily pulsing through a child's brain. Patients woke erased of the erasing, making anesthesia unnecessary.

Alison emerged a shaken, vague, disoriented girl and Byrne a woman who felt she had betrayed her child. The crying stopped, for a while, but when it returned, there weren't enough shredded paper grocery bags in the world to drown out the noises in Alison's head. Byrne tried to trust the doctors, needed to believe their prognosis. But each subsequent round of shock treatment seemed to rob Alison of observable emotions and replace them instead with absences – she was disinterested in speech, incapable of interaction. Even her little sister's tears and tumbles were invisible to Alison.

Byrne swept back into Bellevue with a dancer's walk led from angry hips. "What more can be done?" she demanded.

"It is time to institutionalize the patient," the doctors told her. It was easier for them to remove Alison's gender, her age, even her name from the conversation.

For Byrne it was a body blow on a dark stage. Institutionalize: the consonants were like crashing cymbals in a discordant orchestra. She reached for a *barre* that wasn't there, off balance. She struggled not to fall, gripped her feet in second position parallel, knees bent in *demi-plié*. Her core instinctively curled into a Martha Graham contraction. She exhaled, hands flexed at the end of hyperextended arms. She was pushing away the word, the palms of her hands telling the doctor no, he could not take away her wounded daughter.

In Duncan the doctors sensed a willingness to consider the options – limited as they were. The patient's mother was herself suspect, clearly too emotional and prone to outbursts. Duncan, not being the parent questioning his culpability, listened to the evidence presented. He reviewed the charts of Alison's brainwaves and asked questions of the doctors. They barraged him with the medical rationale of the day. Hospitalization at this early stage might shorten her suffering. Alison would be eligible for Bellevue's new public school for emotionally disturbed children. Jane would be afforded a peace and quiet that might prevent her from succumbing to the same disease.

It was more than Byrne could bear. "Speak again of taking my child away from me," she threatened, a cobra about to strike, "and I will attach those ECT wires to your testicles."

And so began the longest solo performance of Byrne's life. She set about "curing" Alison at home, with or without the approval of doctors. It would be a new role, experimental and unproven, and she faced it with as much courage as others she'd been equally unprepared for.

She would simply have to teach Alison the boundaries and reactions normal children intuited. She would forcibly engage her daughter's attention with colors, patterns, sounds and movements. She would demand reactions and reject withdrawal. She would be mother and coach, consoler and dictator. Alison would go to normal schools, when she was ready, never an institution. Until then, there were regimens to follow, articles to read, researchers to consult, doctors to audition – activities all scheduled and tracked on a blackboard hung below the spice rack in their tiny kitchen.

Duncan acquiesced more than contributed. The demands of work, and the torment of the novel, drained him of energy to spare for Alison. He soothed his daughter when he could, but retreated from the day-to-day intimacies that took up all of Byrne's focus. It was in bed at night, when the girls were asleep, that Byrne recounted the day's struggles and defeats. Underpants defiantly pulled up over tights and dresses. Eggs dropped one after another onto the keys of the piano. Words known for years replaced with baby talk.

Duncan pulled Byrne into the curve of his torso and listened. He rubbed her shoulders and listened. He stroked her hair and listened. When her pillow was wet with tears, he gave her his own. This was their connection now, not Shakespeare or poetry or dance or writing. Instead of inspiring each other, they consoled each other.

It was not enough for Duncan. One day, returning from a scheduled visit to Alison's psychologist, Byrne saw that the top sheet of their bed wasn't folded the way she'd left it that morning. She pulled back the blanket. The indentations in the mattress were not her own. She lifted her pillow to her nose. It was too fluffy and did not smell of her skin, her sweat or her tears.

Feeling drained from her hands and feet. Her arms felt numb, draped over the pillow instead of holding it. Her legs were sandbags – slit open and spilling grains of sorrow over the slippers Duncan left tucked under the bed. Her spine crumbled and she shriveled to the floor. This had to be payback for what she'd allowed the doctors to do to Alison. Her weakness had been swallowed by another's and there was nothing left but to rely on a dancer's distance. *The body is simply an instrument,* she instructed herself. Lift the head. Roll onto the side. Draw up the knees. Push onto the tailbone. Align the vertebrae. Wait for the curtain to rise and go through the motions.

"It isn't that you found solace in another woman," she calmly told Duncan that night after the girls were asleep. "Or even that you did it in our bed, while I was attending to our daughter."

Duncan's tearless eyes told Byrne what words could not. They were angry at having been found out, at having hurt her. But they were neither pleading nor promising. They were a beaten blue, no longer sparkling.

"What I cannot forgive is that you tried to cover it up," she said, peeling his cold hands from hers. "You have never lied to me before and there can never be distrust between us."

Duncan cried then. First came silent, convulsive sobs for himself and for what he knew he might lose: the trust and love of his two daughters, the respect of the mother-in-law who accepted him and replaced the broken family that nearly destroyed him. Then came flowing regret for what he'd done to Byrne, the shock and betrayal he had added to her already weary shoulders. But when the tears finally stopped, he couldn't swear to sexual fidelity.

"I need for someone not to know," he told Byrne and she knew that he meant about Alison. "There has to be another layer of air to breathe, a place to float away and forget."

He wanted an arrangement, an escape hatch from the broken child he could not fix. "You want an open marriage," Byrne finished his thought, "to return to me a whole man."

Duncan nodded, clinging to her. "You know that you are the unique combination I can never live without."

Byrne closed her eyes and let his body lean into hers, unburdened. "Life is hard to bear," she said.

"But do not affect to be so delicate," Duncan mumbled in response. "We are all of us fine sumpter asses and assesses."

It was settled then and they clung to each other, clothed but naked in mutual anguish. What had once been unthinkable in their fairy-tale love story was now out in the open, bruised and painfully honest.

"We cannot be everything to each other, at least not until Alison is cured," Byrne said, finally. "We will learn to look the other way, to accommodate each other's needs from time to time. But never, ever lie to me again."

Duncan kissed her wedding ring. He would not always be on stage with her, but theirs was a love that would last long after the curtain fell.

18

Flying Lessons

BEAUFORT – 1992

GETTING UP AT FOUR on a summer morning to read the news for a top-40 radio shift feels more humid than heroic. *Do not affect to be so delicate,* Byrne Miller had said, and her sacrifices for Duncan made my taking on a second job to pay for Sonny's flight school seem paltry by comparison. But the night air in Beaufort was something close to tar. A window air conditioning unit shuddered all night through our tiny rental house, and the bare front window that I'd check for signs of daybreak dripped with condensation in the dark.

I left each weekday morning like a swamp hunter, out to bring down an extra paycheck in exchange for pilot lessons. *We are all beasts of burden,* wasn't that how Byrne described a sumpter ass, or was it a summer ass? I was too sleepy to mince words or meanings; it was all I could manage to find the key for the pickup parked on the grass outside.

How had my father managed to get up so early all his life? When I was in high school, it had been my job to pack his lunch pail every night before I went to bed. He left to drive to the dispatch office at three in the morning, only to drive a 16-wheeler all day and then drive back to our trailer in the Oregon woods at night. To make extra money, he did long hauls every other weekend, flying out to used truck auctions in places like Laramie, Wyoming, and driving back whatever flatbed his boss had won a bid on. Those regional flights on tiny planes, over the rivers and mountains of the Pacific Northwest, must have been what inspired my father to take flight lessons. It was the one dream he had in common with the man still sound asleep in the house behind me.

"This is Mark Robertson with the soft sounds of KISS-FM, easing you into another good morning with the lovely Teresa Bruce from WJWJ-TV," the middle-aged disc jockey began our broadcast. "Right after these messages from our sponsors we'll be back with this morning's celebrity pop quiz. I'll give you a hint. Teresa will have no idea what the answer is."

I slithered out of my house each morning in flip-flops and wearing no makeup, blaming the hour. Mark Robertson somehow managed to trim his tidy beard, maneuver a braided belt through the loops of khaki chinos and clean the lenses of his wire-framed eyeglasses. He peered through those spotless glasses to verify that the body slouched in the seat opposite his microphone in the KISS-FM radio broadcast booth was indeed alive.

I held up six pages of copy I'd ripped from the AP wire machine. "I thought you hired me to read this," I grumbled. "It's called the news. People need to know it."

The on-air light flashed red again, and Mark leaned into his microphone to avoid the sputtering sound human breath makes when it forms letters like P's and S's. I slouched so far away from the mic it was never a problem.

"We're back and here's this morning's first name-the-name game. Okay Teresa, which former star of *Private Benjamin*

– the movie, probably before your time – is co-starring with Meryl Streep in *Death Becomes Her*?"

"How would I possibly know?" I wasn't trying to be obstinate. I was raised inside a gym. Pop culture was something only girls who weren't trying to make the Olympics knew anything about.

"Okay here's a clue. She laughs a lot. You might try it sometime."

"I would. If you were funnier."

Mark hit a button that cued up the sound effect of a cymbal crash. Ba-doom-boom. He was smiling.

"*Touché*. Okay last clue before we open the phones to listeners. We're looking for the name of the woman famously *not* married to Kurt Russell."

My head jerked up. *I never mentioned being married. Or not. Does he suspect something? Does everyone know about Sonny?*

"What is that supposed to mean?" I barked. Mark pulled away from his microphone. "I mean, who is Kirk Russert? That's what I meant to say."

"Kurt with a T, Russell with two L's," he moaned, correcting me. "It's hopeless, listeners. She's going to need your help. First caller with the correct answer wins two free tickets to the opening night of *Death Becomes Her*."

Between news segments, I daydreamed of how our lives would start to soar now that Sonny was in flight. He had exams to study for and touch-and-go landings to practice at the Lady's Island Airport, the county airstrip that cut through a soggy wetland slightly below sea level. I preferred what the locals called it: Frogmore International. It's where rich golfers landed for getaway weekends. They parked their Lear jets next to a lumbering C-130 reconfigured as the county's mosquito-control plane.

The first few months of Sonny's ascension brought a flurry of purpose between us again. We built a desk out of plywood for spreading out navigation maps and charts. We rented every movie with a pilot in it – from *Airplane* to *North by Northwest*. We put up a dry-erase board to keep track of lesson schedules, and I took his logbook to the radio station to make photocopies in case anything ever happened to the pages that proved his progress.

"He says I'm a natural," Sonny told me, after his fifth flight hour with a certified instructor. It was like being in southern Mexico again, watching him ride the waves. He held his chin differently, a little to the left and cocked. His shoulders seemed broader. "If we can come up with a little more cash, he'll tutor me, one-on-one, through ground school."

Ground school was what worried us both. That's the part of flight training involving reading, memorizing and math, none of which had mattered to Sonny in his half-hearted Mexican public education. School in Puerto Angel was just a building without air conditioning that he'd stop in on when there weren't any waves. And only 10 years with an English-speaking father might not have given him enough vocabulary. I'd seen ground school textbooks when my father had stayed up late at night, studying for his private pilot's license. They were manuals of monotony, filled with multisyllabic words and diagrams of dense detail. I'd made flashcards to help my father memorize the material. I'd never seen him so nervous as the day he took his ground school exams, or so elated as when he passed.

What if Sonny failed? I couldn't let him. I put off the repairs of my VW's engine a few more months, asked my grandmother if she'd wait a little longer to be repaid for the truck. Sonny needed those private ground school lessons. Mark Robertson would have to tolerate a sleepy sidekick. Without KISS-FM, Sonny would be stranded.

I will fly you anywhere, he had told me on the beach in Mexico. It seemed like a lifetime ago, but it was coming true. After a required number of flight hours in the company of a certified instructor, every would-be pilot had to execute cross-country solos. These three-legged trips had to total 150 miles, correctly entered and verified in a logbook. The student was responsible for selecting the route, filing the flight plans with the FAA and communicating with any air traffic control officials along the way. The solo part meant only that the cross-country flights had to be without an instructor, not necessarily alone.

"I want you by my side," Sonny told me. "It won't cost extra and, babe, you have to see how beautiful it is up there, above it all."

My father had never offered to take my mother along on his cross-country solos; it was an accomplishment he kept to himself. I remember the telegram he sent to my grandparents in South Africa when he landed, triumphant.

"The Bruces have soared with the eagles," it said, magnanimously, as if we'd all taken part. That's how my father saw himself, as the sum total of his family. So I should have been touched, even honored, that Sonny wanted to share this milestone with me. I would never have the skill to surf alongside Sonny. This flight would be as close as I could come to being one with him, to dreaming his dreams. But I was terrified. My palms began to sweat at the thought of being trapped in a small plane with Sonny.

He waited until he knew I had a free weekend, one without dance concerts or charity golf tournaments to cover. I would have to be like Byrne, show some faith in the man I claimed to love. So I strapped myself into the cracked-leather instructor's seat of a Cessna 152 as Sonny began his pre-flight check at Frogmore International. I fiddled with the headset he handed me. It looked like it belonged in a Soviet-era aircraft. More like two green cans connected by duct tape than the sleek device I used at the radio station.

Nothing about this flight would be familiar or comforting. Even seated shoulder to shoulder, I felt nothing like a co-pilot. But I knew Sonny needed me to trust him.

"Ignition off," I heard him say aloud. *Shouldn't it be on?* I willed myself to remain silent, unquestioning. I could hear the soles of his lace-less running shoes suctioning off the hot sticky tarmac, then his voice again. "Check."

Who is he talking to? I looked around to see if someone could hear him, but we were alone under the blazing sun. I realized Sonny had memorized a ritual, taken literally the only books he'd ever voluntarily studied.

This deliberate precision was something I'd never seen in him. He walked in a circle around the plane, running his hands along the leading edge of the wings, checking bolts, wiggling the flaps and then wiping the grease off his hands before he checked off the list on his clipboard.

Sonny climbed inside the cockpit and started to fill out more forms.

"What's your weight?" he asked.

I didn't answer. Dancers and former gymnasts are loath to part with such delicate details.

"Don't make me guess," he said, pretending to back away from a stickup, hands raised. "I can't afford to piss you off."

He was right. He couldn't. I was paying for this plane and this cross-country solo, and I hated that it meant he censored even his sense of humor. We were equally the guilty and the wronged.

"I have to know the exact numbers for my calculations," he said, the smile gone.

"Put down 115," I told him. It matched the same 10-pound lie on my driver's license.

I cupped the headphones over my ears but still the sound of the propellers starting up rattled me. Once we were airborne the engine was incredibly loud. The headphones seemed to focus the clattering roar directly into my brain pan. It was so loud I couldn't hear Sonny through the headsets he kept fiddling with. I could almost pretend I was alone, looking down over breathtaking sea island vistas. Alabaster beaches were bleached boneyards of erosion with uprooted, wind-peeled trees. Tidal rivers twisted and encircled islands with names sweeter sung than said: Polawana, Wadmalaw, Warsaw crying out to Half Moon, Distant, Lady's. Sanded lifts of land were smothered in mud slicks, scraped with oyster banks and split by inlets, points and necks.

Until that flight I had no idea how low the Lowcountry really was. From the air, the magnificent live oaks were simply ground cover – lumps of leaves and branches without dimension. When Sonny veered to the north and we paralleled the coast, I didn't dare breathe. A deep inhalation would surely cause the waters to displace the land, overflow the shallow lips of sand and oyster rakes. How close to drowning I had been, unaware.

Sonny figured out how to connect his headset to mine and the solitude was broken. It was getting hot inside the tiny cockpit and sweat trickled down my neck.

"Can you recognize any landmarks?" he asked. There was an edge to his voice, a nervous sharpness that usually came before defensiveness.

"What do you mean?" *Unbelievable. He's lost already.* I looked down again and realized that every ribboning creek looked like the one before. We were flying above a flat jigsaw puzzle. Without the ocean, there were no solid edges.

"Never mind, there's a water tower," he said.

I took no comfort in Sonny dutifully recording our position on a chart. The air rising from the earth was hot and bumpy, and the drone of the engines gave me a headache.

"How are you doing?" Sonny asked.

I tried to smile, but he saw the dullness in my eyes.

"Don't tell me you're afraid," he said.

This wasn't helping. I wanted him to keep his eyes on his instruments. Instead he was imagining insults.

"Great," he muttered. "You don't think I can do this. You think I'm too stupid."

I felt sick. I closed my eyes and stopped speaking to him. I pictured myself on my kayak, paddling along one of the cool rivers far below. Wipeout would be on the bow, paws stretched out in trust and contentment. I willed myself to breathe slower, not to take the bait.

"You try it. It's not as easy as you think," Sonny told me. "Put your hands on the yoke and feel what it's like."

He pointed at the U-shaped steering wheel in front of me, the one an instructor usually sat behind. Touching it was the last thing I wanted to do. My palms flowed with sweat.

"I'd rather not," I said. "You're doing a great job."

"You fucking, condescending bitch."

This was another test. If I chose not to engage, it would be the same as failing. He would feel insulted.

"If you start bawling, I swear Teresa, I will let go."

I gripped the hard plastic handles in front of me. My hands shook. "Are you satisfied now?" I shouted.

His hands flew to the headphones cuffed to his ears – I'd forgotten that we were connected by microphones. My shouted reply probably deafened him. I braced for retaliation and it came in a sickening lurch. I looked at Sonny and he stared at me, hands defiantly folded across his chest.

"Keep the nose steady," he ordered.

My feet stamped around, searching for a brake pedal to stop the plane. It must have been 100 degrees inside the cockpit, and I was losing peripheral vision.

I knew this feeling. It was what had always come over me before I fainted as a kid, when the walls began to spin.

With childhood epilepsy it's called an aura, like an invisible force field that shorts out your brain's circuitry. Whenever I felt one coming on, I had a second or two at most to crouch down and protect my head from the collapse about to happen. But in the cockpit of a Cessna 152 next to Sonny, I couldn't put my head between my knees to make it stop. The control column was in the way.

"Sonny, listen to me," I told him. *Keep your voice calm,* I told myself. *Breathe.* "I'm sorry I shouted, but I'm about to pass out."

"It's called a stall. Keep the nose up," he said. "You're so smart, Miss Master's Degree, you fly the plane yourself."

We began to tilt into a downward spiral and my hands released the yoke in terror. I covered my eyes and sucked air through my nose. *Maybe I'll faint before we crash,* I hoped. It was my last cogent thought. What came next were the ephemeral manifestations of panic. One association careened into the next like blobs of paint sliding into each other on a tilted palette. I know now that panic runs through with colors, like hypnotic campfire flames. Red comes first – the blinding, burning heat of fear. White appears suddenly – not like a flash but like oxygen leaving the room, an absence of pigment equal to the lack of air to breathe. Blue enters like a drowning surge, pouring into gaping mouth, flared nostrils and squeezed shut eyes. Finally it all goes black – a silence that seems like death but in this case was actually just the erasure of all engine noise.

It seemed like black hours before Sonny took control again. I threw my headset to the floor and pulled my knees up to my chest for the rest of the flight. Thin, sticky vomit trickled down between my breasts like drool. The engine roaring was my rage, the turbulence my helplessness. The plane was as hot as hell should be, and I was already in its outer circle when Sonny pointed out the first airport registered on his flight plan.

We were somewhere north of Charleston and my salvation was a landing strip stretched out between rows of scraggly pine forest. The muscles in Sonny's neck clenched in concentration as he set the plane down, wings dipping slightly before he corrected. He taxied to an open space near the tiny terminal and it took every ounce of self-control to wait until the engine stopped before I unbuckled my seat belt. My pants were dark with pooled urine and my shirt soaked through with sour sweat.

Sonny was busy tying down the plane when I began to walk toward a small cluster of buildings.

"Wait up," he called and when I didn't, he ran after me and grabbed my arm.

"Where are you going? We're not done. This is just a lunch stop."

I wrenched my arm free and kept walking. There was a small trailer ahead with a sign for rental cars.

"You stop for lunch," I told him. "I'm renting a car and driving myself home."

"Don't do this to me, *amor*," he began. "I need you with me in case anything happens."

I stopped, letting a shudder of realization work itself from my neck down my spine. He wanted me to be with him so if anything went wrong we would both suffer equally. This was love to him, tormented and bruised by forces I couldn't control. Part of Sonny wanted an admirer, like I had been in Mexico. A darker part of him wanted someone to hurt.

"Look. I'm sorry I made you take the controls," he said. "I just wanted to know that you believe in me." His eyes were daggers of need and rage. "Well, do you?"

"I can't get in that plane again," I told him. I wouldn't become my mother, wrestling over a loaded hunting rifle in the living room of a single-wide trailer. "I will have a seizure and you'll have to do an emergency landing. I'll feel better when I'm behind a wheel, on solid asphalt."

Sonny knew it was only partially true, but there were too many people around to make a scene. This was his new identity, the life where nobody knew his past. The tables were turned. I was the one who could drag him down.

Good, I thought, remembering all the times I'd held my breath and hoped he wouldn't embarrass me. *See what it's like to be at the mercy of an unbalanced mind.*

"I'll call you from the next airport," he said. "If you leave now you'll be home by then."

"Oh, I'm leaving now," I told him, but when he lifted off I knew I wouldn't go back to a home shared with him. *Please just release him,* I found myself begging the sky above. I didn't care if he stalled the engine over a farmer's field or plunged into a tidal river as long as I didn't have to make a decision. It wouldn't be my fault, an accident in flight. I could start over and pretend I'd never met him.

On the long drive back to Beaufort, I was far from a small-town TV star, unrecognizable as the woman who could hold her own with Martha Graham dancers. I was a trailer-park girl dragged back down to the world where women didn't talk back or trust their husbands with secrets. To the world where little girls kept the peace even if it meant selling out their mothers' courage. My eyes didn't register the beauty of the Carolina slash pine forests and tannic, black-water swamps. I was peering around the corner of my childhood living room in Oregon again, trying to see what my father was yelling about.

Maybe he's mad at the head-up-his-ass-dispatcher, I had told myself then, a 13-year-old intimately familiar with all the ways my father described his oppressors. *Or that pussy-whipped union rep he hates.* It hadn't mattered who or why, when I saw my mother lurch toward my father with the hunting rifle.

Suddenly, 13 years later it was clear. On the back roads of a state 3,000 miles away from that living room, I realized my mother never intended to shoot my father that night. She was just trying to make him say it wasn't her fault. That he hated his life. That I won the ballet scholarship. That she kept secrets from him. That my little brother wandered off when she turned her back for just a minute. That his tiny, crushed body couldn't be revived. My mother couldn't shoot my father that night because she couldn't quit him.

I couldn't turn out just like her.

19

The Turning Tide

IT WAS APPROACHING TWILIGHT when I dragged my plastic kayak to the Pigeon Point public boat landing and waded out into the brackish water of the Beaufort River. Wipeout swam beside me, front paws clawing at the stern in vain attempts to clamber aboard. Cast net shrimpers, waiting to back their jon boat trailers into the water, stared gape-mouthed as I muscled 80 pounds of wet dog into the kayak without flipping.

"Stay," I told her after she was aboard. I tapped the space between my legs where I wanted her to sit. She settled on her belly, paws stretched forward toward the bow like a sphinx. We were free, swept into the gentle current swirling around the peninsula.

Up ahead I saw bottlenose dolphins and I paddled toward them, wondering what Wipeout would do. She was once the kind of dog who wagged her tail at strangers, presenting her head to be stroked. Now she was afraid to take a treat from an open hand. What if she caught a glimpse of dorsal fin? She had utterly no comprehension of the mass lurking out of sight below. The dolphins were only a boat-length away and there was no way to get Wipeout back on the kayak if she swam out after them.

"That's a good girl," I whispered, wedging her hind quarters between my ankles just in case. "Stay here with me."

It was suddenly silent and still. Wipeout stopped panting and the surface of the water melted into a wide, glassy ring around the boat. I felt the wake of a tail fluke pass underneath at the same time that I heard the sound. A puff of misty blow came from the water to my left, spraying both of us. Skimming the surface was one curious eye, black with mystery and gone so fast it could have been a wink. Wipeout put her head down on her paws, not looking back to see my reaction. She was unwilling to relinquish her vantage point, the place where she could see what might be coming next. I let the kayak drift into the marsh, between stands of exposed spartina grass. We were hidden then, below a golden horizon, floating over undulating dolphins.

The cool, enticing river was cradled in primal ooze the color of a bad bruise. If I stepped off the kayak and into these pluff mud banks, I would sink to my thighs in it. Every pore in my skin would clench to shut out the inky slime but it would be too late. It would suction the flip-flops right off my feet. Still, it was tempting. For a moment there would be a giddy descent into childhood puddles and wiggling toes, a place of peace like I knew before the Olympic battles between my parents, before the days of scholarships and expectations, before Sonny. But that sweet slide would never last. I would feel something sharp slicing across the soles of my bare feet. With every thrash, buried oyster shells would carve deeper, and I would bleed into the mud until the tide lifted me free. I stayed, huddled behind a dog who didn't dare bark at dolphins.

Across the river, I watched a raft of dead marsh-grass bob along the surface. It was riding the middle movement of an outgoing tide. That's when the current, powering beneath the murky surface, gains momentum before its final burst and the slack that follows. When I was ready, I paddled over to the inlet where a tidal cut flowed into the Beaufort River. While Wipeout balanced on the bow, I could feel the water level drop – still and glassy. It was only a temporary calm, like the apologies Sonny would offer. I knew the river would reverse direction and fill back up again with muddy truth.

Byrne lived somewhere along this winding creek. To my right was the same view of the military base she had shown me from her landing. I paddled on, searching for familiar live oaks or the porch where Duncan found his words. The blades of my paddle sliced through the water, my angry muscles fighting against the current. I had to find the house where Byrne had told me all it took was a whim of iron, that we are all beasts of burden.

Finally I saw a sloping bank that reached for the waterline like a dancer's finger. It was overgrown with salt water cedar and choked in confederate jasmine and honeysuckle vine, but I found a space to pull up my kayak.

"Byrne, are you home?" I called out from 12 feet below her house. "It's me, Teresa."

Wipeout bounded ahead of me, peeing at the base of a laurel oak as I crested the bank. Duncan couldn't quite make out what was happening. I could see him squinting through the screen from his wheelchair.

"Hi, Duncan," I said. "Sorry to startle you."

My skin felt itchy under my neoprene suit. I was suddenly embarrassed to be here, but Wipeout was already nudging the screen with her nose.

"We were just paddling past." It sounded deceitfully implausible, even to my own ears, yet I could think of nothing else. "I hopped out to see if this was the right house."

He broke out into a slow smile and lifted his left thumb and forefinger from the arm of his wheelchair in greeting. Byrne joined him on the porch. Her shoulder-to-fingertip wave was a *grand jeté* compared to Duncan's, welcoming me inside. Duncan was already nodding back to sleep when Byrne drew two wicker chairs together as if she had been expecting me. I didn't know what I planned to say to her, how she could help me make Sonny disappear.

The tide must have turned while I wasn't watching. The kind of woman who let her common-law husband get away with almost killing her was the kind of woman who belonged in a house with a dog chained out back and junk cars up on blocks. She wasn't the kind of woman who belonged in master classes with the rising stars of modern dance. She wasn't the kind of woman Byrne showed off like a daughter. She wasn't the kind of woman I wanted to be.

Duncan stirred and Byrne drew his wheelchair over to join the conversation. He looked dazed, unsure of who I was or why an 80-pound, wet dog was sharing his porch.

"Duncan, isn't this a marvelous costume our Teresa's wearing?" Byrne said. "Like a leotard, only waterproof. She paddled over on her kayak for a visit. With Wipeout as bow decoration."

I felt like a petulant debutante being presented for her first season. I slowly turned in a faux promenade and bowed. Duncan tried to clap his hands, an effort so soundless Wipeout didn't flinch.

"Back in 1969 when we first moved here, the Byrne Miller Dance Theatre was a performance group," Byrne said. "And if I ever needed a man to lift one of my female dancers, I could count on Duncan to volunteer. He's a natural."

Duncan was scanning the river again, thoughts wide and long ago. Byrne kissed him on the head and stroked his cheek with the back of her hand.

"You've made his day," she said. "It does a man good to flirt, right, darling?"

"Ummm," he agreed and closed his eyes.

It was unfair to burst into Byrne's world and call it a lie, to tell her that when I tried to be like her I almost ended up wrapped around the steering column of a crashed plane. The truth was I knew more of the gap between her public and private life than she knew of the gap in mine. She'd told me about her daughter Jane, how happy she had been with the sweet man she married after divorcing the Marine. And how that happiness was shattered by the drunk driver who had killed her on a Colorado highway.

But I hadn't told her about my brother's death or how I also leaped over his absence. I couldn't explain how magical her marriage seemed to me, how the one I resulted from was filled with cover-ups and resentment. She didn't know that I didn't love Sonny nearly as much as she loved Duncan or I'd have married him by now – for real. She didn't know that I'd resolved to leave him, that the certainty of it had settled in my pelvis and thighs on the long drive back from the airport. Sonny would have to fly solo, alone and without me. I wasn't strong enough to heal both my wounds and his. I was too delicate.

The womenisms Byrne shared with me of a 60-year love that never knew jealousy or blame were not mine to copy. I had to learn to listen to Byrne's stories for what they meant to her, for how they let her glide over pain and disappointment with grace and style. Stories like Duncan the devoted husband, Duncan the writer who could not live without her unique combination of attributes. The truth might well be darker, the whole of Duncan less triumphant than the parts. Behind all the confidence and charisma Byrne presented to her audiences, me included, off stage she was a woman in her eighties, who didn't want to be alone.

She needed happily ever after as much as I did. The love she treasured was dying a little every day, and even though I was angry, I resolved not to point out that her emperor was naked.

20

Anonymity has its own rewards.
You can be trashy and no one will ever know.

~Byrne

Silence and Melancholy

CREAM HILL, CONNECTICUT – 1948

SILENCE IS BOTH PRISON and freedom, but neither
Duncan nor Byrne knew its divided truth the day it was
decided the family should leave Manhattan. Duncan was
the initial decider, the one who screamed out for a silence
he believed would transport the words trapped in his head
and loose the novel breached there.

"We need a quiet place to spread out and be still," he
told Byrne. He had removed his polished Oxfords and
pointed them toe-first toward the threshold of their tiny
apartment, crouching down to wipe traces of slush from
the welt. He stayed in that position, next to a towel rolled
lengthwise to block the draft, as if listening for an intruder. He swiveled in his socks and came to a seat on the
floor, his back against the heavy wooden door, shoulders
relaxing.

"Ahh, my love, could you bring me the jug of Chianti to
celebrate? The decibel level is already dissipating."

"What, exactly, do you mean?" Byrne asked, wanting
to trust the smile turning up the corners of his mouth but
suspecting an answer that might not warrant it.

"My resignation this afternoon was met with a re-sounding silence," he said, cocking his ear as if he were at the bottom of the Grand Canyon, listening for an echo. "I wish you could have been there to not hear it with me."

Byrne froze the muscles in her face into an expression she hoped betrayed no doubt. What did it matter whether he resigned of his own accord or had been asked? She kept her eyebrows lifted but not arched, and unstuck her lips from tightly pressed together. It was not entirely unexpected, his quitting Madison Avenue without discussion or alternative. Byrne had been bracing herself for it ever since she embarked on repairing Alison's mind. Her eldest daughter was seven years old now, after the shock treatments not as ebullient and conversational as other girls her age, but improved enough to attend regular school. Duncan, meanwhile, spent more time searching for the time and place to write than actually writing. He had gone through several secretaries since Maggie left him. Byrne typed the latest revision of *Sit in Dark Places* herself, surreptitiously correcting punctuation, learning to calibrate sentences crossed out and re-crossed out until their original intent was better finger-traced from the indentations behind each hand-scrawled page.

She sent out sample chapters with cover letters quoting the line from Duncan's *Atlantic Monthly* rejection letter. She promised each "to whom it may concern" that his publishing house could take credit for discovering the next Thomas Mann. Each prospective agent could be the genius responsible for launching a literary career. But every month that passed without acknowledgment, let alone encouragement, twisted at the knife already plunged into Duncan's confidence. Byrne could not be the one to yank it out all at once. What might gush out would drown her too.

"You leave the agency after all this time and not one word from the executives?" Byrne said, watching to see if Duncan's smirk dissipated as he shook his head. It did not and she swiveled to the floor in front of him and held his hands in hers. "They were mistakenly stunned. What should have dropped their jaws is the talent they've ignored for years."

It was how she'd learned to dance with Duncan, by anticipating his changes in rhythm and positioning herself to soften his falls. His unpredictability was in itself predictable, and the dancer in Byrne loved leaping and twisting to keep up with him. Even in their open marriage, Duncan was so much more arresting than the dutiful, repressed fathers she met at school functions, so much more human than the stream of smug doctors examining Alison for signs of backsliding. If Duncan never obligated himself to the ordinary expectations of life, it meant that Byrne was equally unfettered. If he wanted to start over, fresh and quiet as new snow, she would be a tall evergreen providing him shelter.

"You're right, we should celebrate," she said, "Chianti won't do. I've been saving a bottle of California Mondavi for a special occasion. Come, let's draw a bath and toast to a change of scenery."

Her nonchalance gave her mind time to race with the consequences of uprooting: the girls' schooling, Alison's medical appointments and, for herself, the possibility of never dancing again. But ahead of all the details was the central, unspoken question. Where would they live? Byrne perched on the edge of the porcelain tub and with one hand swirled bubbles through the warm bath water. With the other she stroked the hair on Duncan's head. He had not thought this through – she was certain of that much of her husband's nature.

"Cream Hill," Byrne whispered.

Duncan cocked his head and a trail of bubbles slithered

down his cheek.

Byrne wiped it away. "It was the perfect place to grow strawberries. Why not to grow a novel?"

Of all the places she might have suggested, Cream Hill was a near and tender possibility. Duncan's eyes smiled even before the hard line of his lips softened. He knew by heart the stories of Byrne's childhood summers in Cream Hill, picking strawberries with her Aunt Cornelia. Byrne knew that upstate Connecticut would be close enough for Fanny and Michael to visit yet far enough from Madison Avenue for Duncan never to see his own, un-credited advertising copy in the pages of a magazine. The air would be cool in Cream Hill, the soil moist. Standing on it with bare feet would dampen the cries of the city he was fleeing. He would not be distracted there; his talent could breathe and expand. They would take turns again.

"I could teach dance while you write," she told Duncan. "There is unlikely to be anyone with my training and experience for miles and miles."

"There will never be anyone like you anywhere," Duncan said, pulling her into the tub with him. "Let us at least take a train to Cream Hill to survey our chances."

Fanny came along on the initial scouting trip. "You haven't seen it since you were a little girl," she reminded Byrne, patting her daughter's hand. "It isn't as if Cornelia is still waiting there to scoop you into her arms."

When they arrived neither one of them recognized the 40 acres. Where any strawberry rows remained they were choked with horseweed and crabgrass. It was a fairy tale forgotten; only the distant profiles of surrounding mountain ranges looked familiar. Aunt Cornelia's property had fallen into disrepair and there was no running water or electricity. The only substantial structure was a six-by-nine-foot chicken coop.

"Surely you can't expect the girls to roost in there," Fanny said.

"We'll buy bolts of weatherproof canvas, the kind they use for sails," Byrne said, tugging at one of the sturdy four-by-four posts that framed the head-high chicken coop.

Duncan grinned at Byrne and suddenly she was a tall, beautiful girl standing on a metal folding chair again, improvising the steps to a new life. "The structure is here already. All we need to do is wrap it a few times and it'll become a giant tent. Girls, what do you think? We'll be on safari, only in the mountains, and Grandmama and Grandpapa can stay as long as they'd like."

"Let's not get ahead of ourselves," Fanny laughed. "This grandmama might need to begin with a day trip. And a Sherpa to bring along some creature comforts."

Alison squatted and used her long, skinny fingers to draw squiggly lines between piles of dried chicken droppings in the dirt. The hem of her dress dragged across the detritus.

"Mommy," Jane started to whine. "I don't want to sleep with chickens. I want to go home." She didn't know that in another month someone else would be living in the Greenwich Village apartment. The Millers couldn't afford to keep renting it without Duncan's salary. Until his novel sold, they would have to survive on savings. Byrne felt the walls of reality closing around her, even in the open air of Cream Hill, so she told herself what she always did to facilitate a mental escape. *Just close the door to this room and walk into another.*

Byrne turned away from her daughter scratching in the dirt and set her sights on an enormous white oak tree in the distance. There was a ladder at its base. Byrne scooped up Jane in her arms and strutted toward it. "Then you girls can live up there!" she called out, pointing up at its leafy

limbs to the bones of a forgotten tree house. Alison wiped
her dusty hands on her skirt and chased after her mother.
When Fanny and Duncan caught up, Byrne was already
telling her daughters about the life they would have under
the canopy of Mother Nature.

"We'll close it in," she said, "and put in a glass window
on the eastern side, so the rising sun will fill it with light
and heat."

Even Fanny couldn't help smiling. Her granddaughters
flitted around their mother like hummingbirds sipping
nectar from her iridescent imagination. "You can lower
down a bucket for food at mealtimes. You'll have privacy
– no adults allowed."

Alison climbed halfway up the tree house ladder and
flung herself off it, as certain that her father would catch
her as a bird expects the wind.

"We shall love it here," Duncan said, twirling his trusting daughter. "I will start a new book."

Byrne joined in. "We'll plant strawberries and eat
them with clotted cream from a cow we'll name Bessie or
Buttercup."

Duncan put Alison down and looked at Fanny as
though he might twirl his mother-in-law next. "When
winter comes, we'll find someplace closer to the city. But
until then, the Millers will go native."

Native turned out to be a good deal more civilized than
Fanny feared. When she visited Cream Hill two months
later, the girls were sharing a mattress in a solid, one-room
tree house with a cedar shake roof above their heads and a
coiled, oval rag rug under their bare feet. They stored their
hair clips and ponytail holders in abandoned bird nests
and used a system of pulleys and ropes for hoisting dolls
and books aloft. Their freshly scrubbed clothes fluttered
from easy-to-reach branches.

"There's room up here for you, too," they begged, but Fanny opted for a cot inside the canvas tent that encircled what had once been the chicken coop.

Byrne had transformed the base of the enormous oak tree into a combination pantry and cupboard. Her father's wooden spice rack was nailed to its wide trunk and pots and pans hung along the lowest boughs. Fanny watched in amazement as her daughter poached eggs and roasted a chicken in the open-air remains of a sturdy stone fireplace.

"We discovered it when we were clearing out the undergrowth," Byrne explained. "Eventually this fireplace will be the cornerstone of a proper house and we'll be able to live here year-round. Until then we'll spend winters in Cos Cob or Stamford, wherever I find the most students."

That first summer in Cream Hill, specially selected branches of white pine propped open the tent during the day, drawing in cooling breezes. In the fall, when the temperatures dropped, the stone fireplace warmed Duncan's feet while he worked on his manuscript and whittled a walking stick from the bough of a cherry tree. There were no interruptions from the outside world in Cream Hill, not even a telephone.

At first, Byrne had fretted over their lack of communication with the outside world. What if Fanny and Michael were late arriving, say, if their monthly train trip to visit their granddaughters were delayed?

"Then we will learn of their arrival when the natural order so dictates," was Duncan's reply. "*Que sera, sera.*"

In truth, no phone at all was better than one which would have rung infrequently. The sudden intrusion of it would have ricocheted through the utterly silent retreat Duncan had created for himself. Intentionally cut off from the world he had left behind, he was not reminded of the lack of responses to the chapters of the new novel he occasionally sent to publishers in New York. When he did remember to be outraged, Byrne was there to hold it up to a different light.

"No news might only mean they are leaving you alone to finish," she said.

Silence became the measure of a day's success, not whether he'd rounded out a character or unraveled an untidy sentence. Byrne gave up on trying to draw out details of his progress. "It's called *Shhhh* – about a boy who craves silence. He invents a machine to kill the perpetrators of noise," was all that Duncan offered.

Roosters who crowed too loudly were summarily sacrificed in the Millers' country household. Not even the children bothered him now. His daughters preferred the outdoors and the predictable confines of their canopied quarters over their father's random rantings.

It worried Fanny though, their isolation. "I had rather hoped your seeds would grow into a comfortable garden, but you have sown wildflowers instead," she said to Byrne as they looked up at the girls through the leafless tree one late autumn weekend.

"Bright and wild?" Byrne prompted.

"Absolutely beautiful," Fanny responded, wrapping her arm around Byrne's waist. "But it does seem as though Alison talks to herself more than ever."

Byrne squirmed for a little space between herself and perceived judgment. "Imaginary friends can be better than real ones."

"They are certainly an improvement upon none at all," Fanny said. "Just don't let her slip away simply because it is less complicated than to intervene."

Byrne tried to remain an implanted part of Alison's brain, while still allowing her schizophrenic daughter the space to define herself. The collection of stray dogs that made their way to the base of the oak tree in Cream Hill was proof, to Byrne, that Alison's brain was healing. Her quiet, withdrawn daughter was capable of empathy and patience. She was able to sense the loneliness and potential in other wounded creatures.

The dire medical predictions of violence and jealousy never surfaced. She was fiercely protective of Jane, even proud of her little sister's cheeky cunning. Alison's bursts of non-cohesive speech and sullen, long silences were within the boundaries of children excused from social expectations for lesser reasons. In rural Connecticut, Alison could pass. She was, at first glance, not so different than the loners, the timid or the simply preoccupied.

Byrne sent notes up the tree house pulley, along with her daughters' bucketed meals. Might they entertain a visitor willing to scale the leafy heights? Alison, being the eldest, would magnanimously grant permission and the three of them would play and chatter far out of Duncan's earshot.

Alison was reading every library book she could borrow about how to train dogs, and Jane wanted horse-riding lessons. "Neither of my darlings wants to take dance classes from her mother?" Byrne asked, one night, as she brushed the tangles from their hair. She pressed her nose against their sweaty skulls and breathed in top notes of tree sap and decaying bark.

Jane only giggled and squirmed away, but Alison took the hairbrush from her mother's hand. "We don't need lessons, Mother," she whispered. "We dance all the time. With the tree."

"What do you mean?" Byrne asked.

"Can't you hear the birds?" Alison murmured. "They sing the music."

Byrne could rationalize her daughter's imaginary friends and dismiss Alison's odd behaviors in the context of the entire family's unconventional existence. But a dancing tree resurrected images of gurneys, head braces and wires that bucked and thrashed through her conscience. It portended relapse, the undoing of a glued-together mind that might not quite have dried.

"I'd like to hear them too," Byrne said, cloaking her worry in cheery enthusiasm. "May I sleep up here with you tonight?"

That night at least, she could watch over Alison, keep her near and close. The girls snuggled into their mattress like overlapping chicks in a nest, but Byrne, the mother bird, felt like a gangly intruder. The tree became precipitously taller once the sun went down, its branches ominous with shadow. She, who was normally so tall and noticeable, was suddenly camouflaged in dusky foliage, reduced to just another beating heartbeat in an invisible world of them. Byrne could not relax enough to sleep. She was accustomed to the silence of her life below with Duncan, not the "who? who?" of owls so close it seemed they expected Byrne to answer. A tardy raccoon heading out to forage sniffed and shuffled all the way down the oak tree's trunk so close she might have stroked its moonlit pelt. Her girls were not alone up high above the solid ground. Alison and Jane were part of something she was not.

Byrne closed her eyes. The sound of the wind came up before she recognized what it was: a soft fluttering and rustling of leaves on the oak tree's outermost reaches. It was enveloping and disorienting all at once, direction replaced by intimacy. She felt the tree sway, rocking the tree house with it much as an elegant, gentle man might waltz with his partner. Byrne stretched out, face up, atop the coiled rag rug and adjusted her pelvis so that the small of her back was supported. She unfurled her fists so that every bone in her hands made contact.

"It *is* like dancing," she muttered as the wind made barely perceptible adjustments to her position. What had seemed delusional was instead a revelation. Alison had found a partner her mother simply hadn't seen.

21

The Lonely Nomad

LAKE ATITLAN, GUATEMALA – 1974

I DID NOT KNOW at seven years old that most Americans we met camping on the shores of Lake Atitlan were prescient hippies happy to be far away from President Nixon and his Watergate scandal back in the States. I did not know that "Mary Jane" meant anything other than little-girl shoes. I did not know why all the barefoot grownups with fuzz on their faces and braids in their hair responded with V'd fingers when my father introduced me and Jenny as his little "3A draft exemptions."

So I had no reason to doubt the woman who told me she had a crystal ball inside her tent. She looked like a gypsy to me, or maybe the pretty lady in *I Dream of Jeannie*, but with long black hair instead of blond. She wore three skirts at the same time, with bangles on her ankles and up and down her arms. When she called out to me, I quickly rubbed the tears from my face and tried to stick stray hairs back into my ponytail.

"Don't be so blue," she said. "I can tell your future, if you let me."

The gypsy lady had a tent all to herself. She looked

younger than my mother. I met her the day I was certain that all my friends had forgotten about me and that I would never meet any others. How could I? We stayed in campsites for a day or two at most, just long enough for Mom to find a Laundromat to wash our clothes while Dad fixed whatever wheel or axle was creaking, crumbling or cracking under the weight of our homemade camper.

I was learning Spanish but not fast enough to keep up with the torrent of words that gushed from the mouths of local children who chased our camper and crowded around whenever we stopped. It seemed to me that most of the time, all they wanted was something I was wearing or playing with, which my mother made me give up because I was the oldest.

"Look, that little girl is probably your age," my mother would tell me, pointing to the scruffiest child she could find. "She wants to be friends but she doesn't even have shoes. Don't you think you should share?"

I always did, but I never got a friend out of the deal – not when we would just pack everything up and drive away again. My second grade classmates back at Banks Elementary in Oregon sent letters to the U.S. Embassy in Mexico City, but I could tell it was only because the teacher made them. How else could I account for every one saying almost the same thing? "Dear Teri. I hope you are having fun. Do you have a sombrero? Are tacos good?"

I cried the day I got the letters, not because they were mostly the same but because I couldn't remember the faces of the kids in my class anymore. That's what happens when you're a seven-year-old nomad set adrift in a strange world by parents still grieving the death of your little brother. By the time we got to Guatemala, it had been 37 days since we drove away from our trailer in the woods, 37 days since I kissed my granny's wet cheek and 37 days since I waved goodbye to our dog, Simba. I was counting the gone-forever days on my fingers as I walked along the shore of Lake Atitlan.

Jenny had wanted to come on my walk with me but I wouldn't let her. Strangers would stop to coo and admire her blond curls and blue eyes, and besides, she was terrible at skipping flat rocks over the water and making up names for the volcanoes that ringed the lake. That's what I did when I wanted to remember the friends I was forgetting. I didn't even know I was crying until the gypsy lady invited me into her tent.

"Your parents seem really cool," she said, unzipping the flap that kept sand from blowing in.

"They're not," I told her. "They'd rather have a boy than me. Like they used to."

The gypsy lady didn't ask what I meant, and I wouldn't have told her anyway. Our family never talked about what happened to John John. I remembered him, sometimes, like whenever the ice cream carts along Mexico's beaches hawked orange sherbet – that was his favorite, swirled in with vanilla in little paper cups with flat wooden spoons. I remembered him in Puerto Angel, when my mother had hung up two red stockings in our camper at Christmas instead of three. But most of the time my brother was just another blurry face, one I'd never see again.

"Can you really tell the future?" I asked the gypsy lady. "I don't see a crystal ball in here." Her tent had smelly little sticks that looked like Fourth of July sparklers making piles of ash on the pillows where they balanced. I saw wine bottles with candles poking out of them and lots of books but nothing that looked like it had special powers.

The gypsy lady took my hands in hers and her bracelets made a tinkling sound as they jangled down to her wrists.

"That's because it's invisible," she said. "Stuff is always getting ripped off around here. You can never be too careful."

I nodded. She was right. Someone had already stolen

the steps to our camper and now we had to use a tree stump to climb down. A crystal ball was way too valuable to be in plain sight.

"I'm looking inside it now," she said, spreading her fingers around a sphere of empty space between us.

She stretched out her neck to move her chin closer to the invisible ball, lifted her hands above her head to get a good look at it from below and then closed one eye like she was inspecting my rounded future through a microscope.

"What's it say?" I whispered.

"It doesn't say anything," she corrected me. "It shows the future."

"Does it show if I will ever have another friend?" I asked.

"Oh, yes," she said, smiling. "Many friends. In fact, each time you move to a new country or start a new school, you will find more friends, even closer friends than the ones you used to have. You're a very lucky girl to get so many chances."

Chances, she called them, and from that day forward I let my luckiness swell up inside me like a secret. Jenny could have her cute blond curls – I had a power far more valuable. Mom could make me give away all my dolls and I wouldn't cry – she didn't know what the crystal ball had shown the gypsy lady. I would have so many friends I wouldn't need to remember the ones I forgot.

Where once I had been an unwilling passenger in my parents' escape, the gypsy lady made me feel like a stowaway, discovering new worlds. I left her tent jackpot happy, certain of my specialness. The implications of the crystal ball's prediction rippled far from the shores of Lake Atitlan. Most seven-year-old girls were stuck with the friends who rode the same school bus every day – friends who heard what happened to little brothers and whispered about strange parents who never came to open houses or school plays. Each friend I met after Guatemala would know only the me I was when I arrived, the new and different me. The gypsy lady's crystal ball was right. I was lucky to have so many chances, more than even she could have imagined.

Even after we returned to the United States, my father refused to put down roots. I never went to the same school for longer than two years at a time. We moved whenever the rent went up, whenever jobs were lost and found, whenever my father dreamed up another scheme to "beat the system" or "get out of the rat race."

The gypsy lady's words protected me long after I stopped believing in crystal balls. I made her prediction come true because I had no other choice, not with a father who never stopped running away from his dead son. After each up-rooting, it took me less and less time to decide which person I had just met would become my new best friend, better than the last one. Because I knew no place was permanent, I overlooked no opportunities. I was as good at spotting a kindred spirit as my father was at finding a new place to park his family and keep our wounds hidden.

It had seemed Lake-Atitlan-gypsy-lady-lucky when, just after completing grad school, I met Sonny. I had been in geographic limbo when I saw Sonny surfing the waves of Puerto Angel. He belonged there and I wanted desperately to belong with him. But that was long before a phony marriage, the stifled resentment of unequal lives, and the silence of a stalled plane above the salt marshes of South Carolina.

If that crystal ball had any power left, I would need it for the next move more than ever – the one away from the house I shared with Sonny.

22

No woman can be everything to a man.
To try is beyond valiant.

It's stupid.

—Byrne

Making Music

Cos Cob, Connecticut – 1950

THE UP-SHUTTERED TREE HOUSE in Cream Hill was
already receding from center stage in Byrne's mind as the
Millers drove away from its first winter, the grey stunted daylight no longer holding it in sharp focus. The oak
tree seemed content to wait for its curtain to fall, to settle
into the creaks and shivers of the snowy season. Alison
had insisted that they hide the ladder instead of leaving it
propped against the trunk. "I want it to be lonely," she said.

"Don't you mean you want it to be left alone?" Byrne asked.

"Leave me alone," Alison said, churlish and fighting back
tears. She climbed over the back seat of the station wagon
and sat with the dogs, refusing to face forward and watch
where they were going.

Byrne's heart lurched for her uprooted daughter, but
still she was relieved to see Cream Hill in the rearview
mirror. The coming of colder months was foreboding, but
worse even than the weather would be Duncan pacing
inside their tented chicken coop, unable to play out his
words in the open fields and woods. He was still stum-
bling with the weight of the second novel, and if they were

to finish building a permanent house and keep shoes on the girls' feet, it would have to be with money she earned teaching dance.

There was another reason Byrne's heart could push aside the guilt of dragging Alison away from her dancing tree house and feathered friends. His name was Gerd. He was an orchestra conductor, new to Connecticut after fleeing Hitler's Germany.

"He isn't Jewish," Byrne told Duncan, "but he comes from a family of intellectuals, even more threatening."

His English was halting, unused since he had left the study of it behind in primary school. But Byrne didn't need words to communicate with Gerd; they could speak through music. There was a piano in one of the ballet studios that hired her to teach, and he was the most overqualified accompanist of little dancers in the history of New England.

He played for Duncan once, when the triangle between them was still penciled thin and tentative. He sat for his unacknowledged audition in front of the piano Byrne and Duncan had shuffled from Greenwich Village to Cream Hill and finally to Cos Cob, in Fairfax County. Byrne settled on the sofa next to her husband, measuring his acceptance of her choice with every indrawn breath. Duncan closed his eyes and swayed to the haunting concert of a displaced man, beside Byrne and apart from her. The piano's missing keys and minor chords that substituted for them seemed fated for Gerd's plaintive, melancholic playing. When the last note rang out, there was vibration in the otherwise still room. The silence was finally broken by Duncan's thunderous applause.

"Would that every refugee bring so much beauty to the undeserving," Duncan said, thanking Gerd. He kissed his cheek, then his wife's and retired to the bedroom in their rented house, allowing Byrne to drive her discovery back to his dormitory room at the YMCA.

She would have predicted her first affair would be for the sake of words, an escape from Duncan's need for silence. She imagined long wandering conversations about anything other than Alison. But Gerd simply played for Byrne. He flung notes to her from behind the upright piano of a stark ballet room, standing as his fingers pounded so that he could watch the choreography she made of them. If his notes were heavy and thick, she was wild with movement, hands sharp and beseeching, legs flexed and fighting off the pull of him. Staccato notes mirrored back to him the release of repetition – thrusting flicks of her feet, snapping twists of her head.

Byrne was the march of a band through his bombed out streets, liberating his longing. If the meter of his playing were filled with pauses and retards, she would match them with hesitation and relinquishment. The floor didn't rise to meet her; she fell to it, accepting the bruises and the ache of it. When he was slow and lingering, she was her most receptive, time dangling between her steps like a scarf caught in wind he couldn't see. But he knew she was there. Every afternoon after class he clung to her, in dark supply closets, under the steps leading up to offices, in the long back seat of her car.

He tired of playing piano for little ballerinas long before he tired of Byrne, but Connecticut lacked no orchestra conductors. Soon, Gerd couldn't even afford his dismal room at the YMCA. "For this I left everything I loved, everything I was?" he asked Byrne one night as she dropped him off after class. The nights were stretched long with the piercing blue that signals the end of autumn, and Byrne feared that in the coming months she would lose Gerd to an even darker depression. Her husband understood. Now that they were closer to the city, he'd taken part-time work in advertising again, as much to stave off claustrophobia as to augment Byrne's earnings.

It was Duncan who suggested Gerd winter with them, but Byrne was wary of Alison's reaction. Would the presence of another man, one so clearly enamored with her mother, confuse or frighten her? There had been so much disruption and reconfiguration in her daughter's world already. Would a gloomy stranger tip her precarious balance?

"Alison, darling, this is Gerd, my dear friend. He hasn't a place to call home. We thought he might like to share ours."

Alison's violet eyes sized up the tall, thin German standing before her. Gerd dropped his hands to his sides, palms open, as if to show the thin, suspicious girl he was hiding nothing. She walked around him silently, examining the conductor in the rotating light of the open door, then the window, then in the reflected flickers of the fireplace. She took in his weathered boots with frayed laces, the extra hole in the belt he had pierced to keep his pants from falling off his thinning frame. She saw the way the hair on the back of his head was pillow flattened, as if he stared each night straight up at a sky void of stars.

She is sizing up his wounds, Byrne thought to herself. *She divides all the creatures of the world into those that have been hurt and those that could hurt her.*

Finally, Alison stopped circling and smiled at Gerd, her thin red lips relaxing over the crooked teeth of early adolescence. He was just another stray, someone to fix and send on his way.

Her grandmother, visiting for the weekend, was not so easily won over. "It is not natural," Fanny had pulled Byrne aside to whisper, although she too found Gerd's music transporting. "Duncan should be more jealous than accommodating."

"Why?" Byrne had replied. "Didn't you aid and abet me in the same maneuver back when we lived in Greenwich Village?"

Fanny sighed then, and smiled, remembering the eggplant moussaka and hazelnut baklava that had turned the tables and taught Byrne and Duncan to treasure what they shared together. She even managed to muster some enthusiasm when Byrne announced that she would be starting a sinfonietta. "For Gerd to direct, of course."

Duncan had smiled then, conspiratorially. "We'll bring the music to our man, and by extension to the *hoi polloi*."

Michael Miller spoke up next, rubbing the greying moustache above his upper lip in concentration. "Doctor Fein has a weekend place in Stamford, doesn't he, Fanny?"

Doctor Benjamin Fein had been the family physician since Byrne and Sherman were babies. Fanny's face lit up. "Yes, and he's a fine violinist. Byrne, you may be onto something."

"Once musicians of a certain caliber discover that Gerd is conducting here in America, they will line up for auditions," Byrne gushed. "It won't cost us anything to get started. I'll get the Manhattan public music library to loan us scores."

Gerd looked around the room into the faces of a family willing to recreate the lost world of a virtual stranger. He struggled for the words to thank them.

"You would do this for me?" he asked Byrne, eyes wide with an appreciation that in one evening had left physical need behind and dared for permanence and position in a new world.

Byrne bowed, right-angled at the waist, no old-fashioned courtsy for her newest challenge. She was a thoroughly modern woman entering the peak of her powers. Duncan would have his writing, Gerd his music and Alison her mind – she would accept nothing less.

"Byrne, my darling, yours is a whim of iron," Duncan declared, and the seven of them feasted on Byrne's promises.

Decades later, she tried to put it all on paper, to preserve for posterity that which began with Alison's permission.

Her scattered notes faltered for exact dates, skipped over years like the pages of a score turned too fast. They jumped between towns in lower Connecticut and rural, upstate New York with the syncopation of artistic vagrants. Each entry began with incomplete sentences, like headlines of a forgotten story.

> *Gerd's melancholy persisted. He and Lydia moved back to NY.*

Lydia, a character never properly introduced or explained, had apparently taken Gerd away from Byrne.

> *The group became the Greenwich Sinfonietta.*

Greenwich was miles from Cos Cob, where Byrne had created the sinfonietta. Still, she remained loyal to the man she wanted to save.

> *Because of Gerd's excellent musicianship and interest in new music, our little sinfonietta players, most of whom played with the top orchestras in NYC, performed with us for nothing.*

Byrne was graceful but proprietary, still claiming the group as her own. Perhaps that's why Gerd eventually left even the music behind.

> *Our new conductor, whose wife was our first cellist, was not as brilliant as Gerd, but he was good and with most of our players so high caliber, a solid success.*

Byrne held her head high with determination—momentum preferable to giving up. So too, it was, for Duncan. When he wasn't earning commissions selling ads to an assortment of magazines and trade publications, he shut himself away, putting words on pages, uncertain anyone other than Byrne would ever read them. He still hadn't finished his second novel, let alone found a publisher. He could have put his own disappointment first, demanded from his wife more than what she'd freely given Gerd. But he understood.

"A wise woman once told me that no woman can be everything to a man," he said. "That you try and try still again is beyond valiant."

"It's stupid," Byrne said, so relieved to admit it aloud that she started to laugh. Duncan took her hand, pressed it to his heart and said all that she needed to hear.

"Isn't it the truthfulness of friendship that reignites the passion?"

23

Breaking Away

WIPEOUT REFUSED TO get out of the rental car when I pulled up into our driveway after the kayak ride. She smelled of salt water and sulfur marsh gas and busied herself slurping at the spaces between her back claws. Instead of leaping into the back seat when we left Byrne's house she had shoved past the steering wheel and squatted on the passenger seat beside me. When we reached the house we shared with Sonny, she crawled under the dashboard and hunkered down.

"It's okay girl," I told her. "It looks like Sonny isn't home yet anyway." Instead, Dennis was waiting in our front yard. He was nervous about something, fidgeting with the peace sign charm dangling from a leather strap around his neck – a gift from Sonny. They called each other *"compadres."* Whatever this was about, it was hard for him.

"Teresa, if I tell you something, will you promise not to say anything to Sonny?" he asked.

My teeth ached from grinding them all day. The watertight sleeve of my wetsuit embedded the cowry shells of my mermaid bracelet into my wrist, and the layer of sweat trapped against my skin was slimy and cold. My spine

200

felt like a knotted climbing rope. I was dreading Sonny's inevitable retaliation for leaving him at the airstrip and didn't have the energy to deal with Dennis. But he would be a buffer if Sonny came back while I was clearing out, so I nodded and invited his *compadre* in.

"Can you give me a hand with this zipper?" I said. "This thing will start growing mold if I don't get out of it and dry off."

Dennis tugged at the zipper as if he were poking a stick at a snake.

"I'll just wait in the TV room," he said.

I pulled the bedroom door closed between us. The wet-suit was already bunched around my waist. "What did you want to tell me? I can hear you fine." *Make it quick. I've got a lot to do.*

It wasn't until I emerged from the bedroom in shorts and a t-shirt that Dennis could spit it out. Even then, he looked everywhere but in my eyes.

"There's this waitress at one of the restaurants. She hangs around us a lot," he began.

"You mean Jody?" I asked. She was pretty and melo-dramatic, always breaking up with her boyfriend and then chasing him all over town until he took her back. Sonny often told me I should wear short skirts and sexy sandals, like Jody, instead of the suits and matching heels I bought for work. Dennis was scraping the skin on his neck with the peace sign like a gambler's tell.

"He's with Jody?" I couldn't help rolling my eyes.

"How did you know?" Dennis sputtered. "I mean, I guess so. If he's not here."

The man who'd almost crashed his plane with me in it was right now seeking comfort in the arms of a waitress. *Figures.* Dennis paced in front of the futon, wringing his un-tucked, dirty t-shirt with his fists, but all I felt was a rush of relief. I squeezed my knees and stared down at the shag carpet, hoping Dennis would tell me that Sonny was in love with Jody. It would make for an easier escape. But Dennis wasn't about to spill any more information than he already had.

"Don't worry," I reassured Dennis. "I already heard about it."

"It's just that he's so mad at something. Did you guys have a fight?" he asked.

"Something happened in the plane this morning," I told him.

Dennis stared up at the popcorn ceiling paint as if its random pattern held the secret to extricating himself from the middle of his best friend's business.

"Well, no matter what people are saying, he didn't actually sleep with her that other time," he finally said.

There was another time? I told myself to stay calm, to act like I'd heard this all before.

"I mean, he slept in the same bed with her, but they didn't go all the way."

Go all the way? I hadn't heard that phrase since junior high. Dennis was clearly miserable. He wanted me to forgive his best friend for something he was too dense to realize I never would have discovered. I rubbed the tender skin on my wrist underneath my mermaid bracelet, stalling. My mind raced to all the nights Sonny could have said he was working late, and I would have believed him, even told him not to worry about me.

"Next time you visit your sister in Florida, maybe you should take him with you," Dennis offered. This Ouiji-board-believer was giving me advice about how to keep my man from straying – the man I was about to leave.

"Jody called it off at the last minute that time," he said. "She respects you."

That time I took my nephew to Weeki Wachee? The trip he had made so easy, come to think of it? While I had been holding Brandon's hand, telling him that mermaids helped surfers ride the waves, Sonny was back in Beaufort trying to ride a waitress. I couldn't stop the laugh that shot out from me like a surfboard in a foamy wipeout. Even a thigh-flashing waitress determined to make her boyfriend jealous wouldn't take my common-law husband away from me.

I told Dennis to go home, that everything was fine, and started emptying my closet. I was still filling suitcases with the suits and blouses I wore on television when Sonny burst through the screen door. He didn't close it behind him. I could hear Wipeout barking through the open windows of the rental car, warning me.

"What the fuck is going on here?" he asked.

It felt good watching shock register on Sonny's face, until the moment he threw his logbook at my head. I checked for blood then closed the suitcase I was filling.

"Do that again and I'll call the police," I said. He balled up his fists, straining against a rising rage. "I'm staying with friends. I want you to get out of my house by the end of the month. I'm leaving, Sonny. I told you that at the airport. It's over."

I hadn't seen Wipeout leap through the car window and into the house when she heard the thunk of the logbook against my head. She wasn't so much barking at Sonny as yelping in confusion at the tension between us.

"Shut the fuck up!" Sonny screamed at Wipeout. "Who do you think you're barking at?"

She took two steps back, snarling. She crouched, a warning winding up in her hindquarters, but she wasn't quick enough. Sonny's foot lashed out at her gut. She yipped, the bravado gone. He was still kicking at her as she ran outside to the safety of her doghouse.

A white curtain of adrenaline blinded me, and I roared, lunging after the sound and smell of Sonny. I got him around the waist and we fell together – a tangle of knees, elbows and chins in a cloud of backyard dirt. Then he grabbed my hair with one hand and pulled me up and back inside the house.

"Your house. Is that what you said?" he yelled, when no one outside could hear. "Everything is yours because you're a TV star and I'm a loser, is that what you think? Well, fuck you! We're married now, and you don't own a fucking thing that isn't mine, too."

He shoved me to the bedroom. "See that bed? Belongs to both of us." I ducked under his arm and ran. He caught up to me just as I reached the front door.

"I'm sorry," I begged, backing away from his clenched fists. He was crying but kept coming at me. He slammed my shoulders against the wall. I ducked again to squirm away, but he grabbed my arms and spun me around. I bit my tongue as my cheek hit the door.

"I didn't mean it," I said. The words clamped down on a bloody tongue. I felt him grab my left hand behind my back like he was going to twist it up to my shoulder blade. I made a fist and he circled my wrist and yanked my arm to the side. I felt the nub of the light switch next to the door and flicked it on and off, hoping someone outside would notice. Sonny's belly heaved against the small of my back and his breath was hot on my neck. I was still clenching when he pulled back and then slammed the weight of his body and mine through a strip of fake wood paneling. I couldn't tell if it was the searing pain or the sight of blood from my mouth smearing down the wall, but blackness began to press in from the corner of my eyes. The last sound I heard was the tinkle of cowry shells dropping to the floor.

I woke up in the pickup on the way to Beaufort Memorial Hospital. Something was throbbing, and I looked down to find a swollen hand the size of a catcher's mitt and no mermaid bracelet. Several tiny bones were broken, the X-rays later said.

"How did this happen?" the ER physician on duty whispered in my ear. "I sent your husband, or whatever, to the cafeteria. Do we need to call the police?"

"No," I told him. "It was just an accident."

I could hear my internal ultimatums slipping. I had gone from rationalizing that everything would be better *if* Sonny had his own wheels, to *if* I loved him as much as Byrne loved Duncan, to *if* he went to flight school. None of them brought him a happily ever after, or me.

It really was an accident, I repeated. I wasn't lying. *I never meant to end up here. It won't happen again.*

24

It is the truthfulness of friendship that reignites the passion.

~Byrne

The House of Byrne

DARIEN, CONNECTICUT – 1954

THE TRANSFORMATION HAD begun after a few bleak winters in lower Connecticut. "There is something we need to discuss," Duncan had said.

Her husband didn't usually announce a conversation, and Byrne's back stiffened as though she was expected to perform a response without knowing the steps. She gathered two wine glasses with unsure hands, her mind racing through possibilities. Duncan's tone seemed ominous and brooding. Gerd had already passed through their lives; she knew it couldn't be that. Alison was away at school, but her physical absence was easier for Duncan to live with than her presence, empty of emotional connection. Byrne and Duncan got regular reports from her school, milestones by which to reassure themselves that Alison was, at least, progressing from grade to grade with no medical intervention.

Maybe Duncan feels his obligations to family are met, Byrne thought to herself. *Maybe our arrangement no longer suits him.* She relaxed only when Duncan opened a bottle of Charles Krug Burgundy. In her husband's mind, at least, whatever it was that needed discussing deserved a wine they reserved for celebrations.

"While both my novels continue to languish in obscurity," Duncan said as he filled their glasses, "it appears my promotional work is very much admired by the Magazine Advertising Bureau in Manhattan. And since we may soon have not one but two daughters to put through college, I think it high time that we trade turns."

It was as if Duncan needed a graceful exit from his self-imposed silence and the all-consuming book about a boy who killed for it. Planning advertising campaigns and directing promotions would require cocktails, conversations and presentations. In return for putting aside his writing, Duncan would have heads nodding yes to his ideas.

"You mean you want to take a job in New York and me to take up dance again?" Byrne asked. "Duncan, I am almost 45 years old."

"And Martha Graham is what, in her sixties?" Duncan challenged. "Surely the collective value of one's life experience is worth as much to art as it is to commerce?"

He was right, Byrne would admit years later, but it was easier finding a place to study dance in southern Connecticut than it was to reintroduce her body to the rigors of performance. She discovered that an emerging star of modern dance, Lucas Hoving, had joined the faculty of the Artists of Silvermine Guild in the nearby town of Norwalk and had assembled a community dance theater of sorts. Byrne auditioned for a part in Hoving's staging of *The House of Bernarda Alba*, based on the play by Federico Garcia Lorca.

Her earlier training certainly qualified her for the amateur group, but even with the intervening years of teaching dance, her body was less flexible than it had been in her burlesque days. Her tendons clutched at the back of her thighs when she folded over at the waist and tried to rest her cheek on her shins. The hips that had boosted two babies high enough to feed carrots to carriage horses in Central Park ached after only the beginning *barre* portion of a ballet class. Jumps and leaps along the length of a stage left her gasping for breath, muscles cramping.

"Nothing a long hot bath with soaking salts won't cure," she told Duncan, who loved to sit on the edge of the tub and listen to his wife's description of the classes.

"And this Hoving man," Duncan asked once. "I thought you said he dances with José Limón?"

"He does," Byrne said. "Our little Silvermine Guild is just his cushion, a paycheck between tours. He's playing Iago in the Moor's *Pavane*."

"To great acclaim in all the reviews," Duncan acknowledged. "The dark, young Mexican's brilliant interpretation of *Othello*. It's the most modern of modern dance, so I've read. So why the Dutchman's insistence on those wretched, old-fashioned *barre* exercises that torment you so?"

Byrne stood up, sore but towering in her nakedness. She bent her knees in a *demi-plié* and pushed off into a nimble *pas de chat* past Duncan, out of the tub. "For the legs, my love. Lucas finds the assumption that modern dancers who study ballet are heretics simply ridiculous." She wrapped her body in a towel and her voice in an imitation of her teacher's thick Dutch accent. "Wiss-out de leg strength from ze *plié*, we jump only down, ne-vairh up."

At the final dress rehearsal for *The House of Bernarda Alba*, Byrne pulled the black mourning hood farther back on her head, exposing her hairline. She wrapped the costume's silken cloak so tight around her jutting breasts that there would be no mistaking she was merely a dancer playing the part of a much-older widow. She pounded Duncan's whittled cherry walking stick on the stage floor with muscled biceps, the strength of her movement saying the cane too, was merely a prop. In the story, the grieving Bernarda Alba enforces an eight-year period of mourning, ruining her daughters' chances of seducing the one man, never seen on stage, who has become their collective love interest.

"Bairh-nah," Lucas had said back at the cast announcement. His accent made even the butchering of her name sound beautiful. "You, my darling, will be the woman all who watch will hate. The one who traps her daughters in a house of sorrow and tries to control their minds."

Byrne had lifted her chin that night and nodded, head tilted a little to the left in polite acknowledgement of her teacher's selection, wondering what Lucas would think if he ever met Alison. Byrne had controlled her daughter's mind as long as she could, but both her girls were in New England boarding schools now, as distant from her renewed life of dance as Duncan was.

Lucas had stepped closer to her, his languid fingertips brushing along her throat before stopping to cup her chin. "Even your name, Baihr-nah, sounds American for Bernarda Alba. I must hide you from the critics in New York or another man will surely steal you from me for the stage."

He kissed her then, the kind of showy kiss meant to convey to the assembly of dancers watching that he was still faithful to his wife, the celebrated modern dancer Lavina Nielsen. She was part of the small, politely clapping audience, having just accepted the part of the widow's lusty youngest daughter.

The web of real-life love triangles dividing Lucas Hoving's collection of part-time dancers and students was sticky with secrets, far from the honest arrangement between Byrne and Duncan. Byrne knew when she put her husband on the commuter train to Manhattan each week, that Duncan would avail himself of beautiful models and aspiring copywriters. Casual sex was part of the Madison Avenue culture, and Duncan viewed it as a compensating factor that helped make the work interesting. But it was back to Connecticut and Byrne that he eagerly returned, with stories not of conquests but amusements and adventures. He was a different man when he wasn't working on a novel, less self-absorbed and tormented by doubt.

The weight of artistic expectations had transferred to Byrne. Rehearsals in the dead of winter tested the brittleness of her aging bones. The Silvermine studio in Norwalk was heated with only a pot-bellied stove in the far corner and the collective exertion of straining dancers.

"Jump again, and higher this time," Lucas would exhort, his breath fog suspended like a *jeté* in front of his soft, translucent lips. "And Bairh-nuh, please, do something with your hands. They are the tongue of the arm, no? Speak with them. For me?"

After months of protest, Byrne's body began to obey her will again. She knew to allow herself more time than the younger students to warm up each day. She learned how to space the progressions of demanding movements so that her hamstrings were loose and resilient when she called upon them to kick her long legs. She propelled herself across the floor with every muscle of her core engaged, protecting the brittle back and neck.

"Better Bairh-nah," Lucas encouraged. "But you only finish and begin. Give me beauty in the space between. Make a picture for me to remember before the movement ends."

Lucas began to use Byrne's body to demonstrate correct positions. Arms that had hoisted buckets of books to daughters in tree houses could remain extended for hours in a cold dance studio while he elaborated and explained a movement. Byrne could control the strain of it with the raw strength of her broad shoulders, coupled with a mother's patience. Her rough elbows softened the lines of her arms into elegant, powerful arcs that Lucas gently stroked as he spoke. More difficult than holding the position was not reacting, not allowing the ripples of physical awareness to manifest themselves until student and teacher were alone and unobserved.

In those private moments she was his partner, an equal physical force and match in wit and intellect. In class she knew her limits. The hardest days were when Lucas smiled and reached for smaller women to demonstrate lifts. All Byrne could do was watch as his hands wrapped around waists and thighs not her own. Her mind tried to create a distance from her heart, knowing Lucas was simply placing his hands where he had to. The pivot points of lifts are nearest to the woman's center of gravity, her safety depends on relinquishing to his grip what she normally girds.

But Byrne could not separate the man from the movement. Lucas's thighs parted in deep *plie*, he tossed back his shock of pale blond hair and effortlessly gave these lithe and compact women flight. It was a connection she would never share with her lover. She could improve by leaps and bounds, star in one of his productions, but Byrne Miller would always be too tall for Lucas Hoving to partner.

It was easier, in some ways, when he began to invite luminaries of the modern dance world to give master classes at the Silvermine Studio. Lucas became just another student then, transported by the power and passion of the modern masters. Some, like the young Alvin Ailey, were still harnessing their own strength, experimenting with new vocabularies of movement.

"You should have seen this beautiful young man move," Byrne breathlessly told Duncan. "He doesn't look old enough to vote."

"Isn't he the same Alvin in the Truman Capote musical?" Duncan said. "*House of Flowers*, if I recall correctly, about a house of prostitution."

Byrne giggled. "There is something provocative about him. That much I can attest to. I felt like a mule next to him. He has the legs of a leopard."

Merce Cunningham, Pearl Primus, even the pioneering Charles Weidman taught master classes for Lucas Hoving. Cast members of Broadway shows and every modern dance company in New York took the train from Manhattan for a chance to sample different, experimental techniques. Lucas would greet them all with ease and familiarity, erasing boundaries between ballet and modern, theater and dance. Byrne stood her ground in these master classes, surrounded by dancers half her age.

"They all seem in such a hurry," she confided in Duncan. "I just can't fling my body into these positions like they do or I'd tear a muscle. I'd need your walking stick then for more than a prop."

"You are an artist, dear, not an athlete."

There came a point in every master class when she believed Duncan's words. While younger dancers surged past her in the technique drills, she earned her place when it was time for choreography. It was as if her ears were bigger than theirs and she could hear what the movements were trying to say. When Merce Cunningham asked the class to move through space, without music, the ballet-trained students were anchorless and drifting but Byrne understood silence. She allowed it to lift and amplify her movements.

When Pearl Primus stood in front of a class and straddled powerful legs, flung back her head and lifted one flexed hand to an unseen sun above and the other to a distant horizon 90 degrees from its zenith, Byrne didn't just mirror the image. She interpreted it, knowing intuitively how and when to thrust one hip in front of the other, taking the pose from abandon to outrage.

Which was why, when Lucas began to break away from José Limón and create choreography for what would eventually become his own company, he wanted Byrne by his side.

"Dancers come and go," he said. "I need you to be my memory, to save what I create so I can resurrect it when the time is right."

He wanted her to write it down, to capture his movements on paper so that he was free to continue creating. He swept his feet along the floor. For a second, Byrne thought he meant for her to mimic his movements, the makings of a new combination. But he was using his bare feet to draw two vertical columns on the floorboards, with hash marks for the measures of music he hummed.

"I will start by teaching you the Laban," he said. "They have been recording ballets like this since I was with Jooss in Germany."

Byrne had heard of labanotation, how it attempted to archive choreography like a musical score. She had spent the first 20 years of her life studying classical piano. How much different could reading dance be from learning sheet music?

"You start at the bottom and follow your eyes to the top, for one thing," Lucas said, laughing. It was a conspiratorial laugh, one that invited her in like a warm shower. "The center line is the center of the body. You will be that center line of my body. Here, stand behind me."

He reached behind and drew Byrne close, until her chin rested on his collarbone and her breasts pressed against his shoulder blades. He leaned back into her, until his high, firm buttocks nestled in her pelvis and their two bodies were molded together like strips of clay.

"Now we begin," he said. "Lucas and Bairh-nuh as one."

He hummed music he heard in his head and she could

feel the vibration of it in the cavity of her chest. Then he began to sway.

"Some dancers start from the outside and get smaller and smaller," he said. "But for me every dance starts with breath, deep inside."

At first she let Lucas lead, reacting to his movements like a marionette.

"No Bairh-nuh, to write it down, to remember every element of me you have to feel my movement with your own body, the same way and same time I do," he insisted.

The afternoon's sun had abandoned them, slipping from a diagonal streak through the windows to a low slice of light at their interlaced feet, before Byrne got the hang of it. She closed her eyes and anticipated his releases and contractions, imprinting the intention of her lover's every muscle.

"Now, you are ready to make the record of this combination," Lucas said, peeling his body away from her skin. A 16-count combination, something he could have demonstrated in a few minutes, something she could have photographed with 16 frames of 35mm film, had taken them three hours.

Byrne smiled with the certainty of a treasured woman. "I know where every foot goes, every hand position, every inhale, every exhale. I can do this for you, Lucas."

"I know. This is why I asked."

Her first attempts at recreating the 16 counts of Lucas's creation were like trying to break a secret code. Lined notebook paper, turned horizontally, was too narrow to fit all the nuances she had committed to memory. So she taped together strips of colored construction paper and fastened them to a wall in her living room with sticky putty.

"What is this?" Duncan asked, setting his briefcase down in front of it. "Are you planning an amphibious assault on some unsuspecting country?"

She deconstructed it for Duncan, demonstrating the movement corresponding to each arrow or stroke mark notated within the colored lines.

"Eventually he wants me to write a book, filled with all the dances he creates so that anyone, anywhere, can re-create them."

Duncan stood in the center of the room, staring at the woman creating the written record of another man's life.

"Remarkable," he said. "My un-publishable books are not enough. Your spirit truly cannot be broken."

The words stung her conscience in a way that openly acknowledged affairs did not. She never intended for her husband to feel that she had given up on his dream. Duncan drove himself to fits of solitude when he tried to put his thoughts on paper. He needed more than a translator, which was what she was to Lucas. Nor could she simply gather words for Duncan to shape, as she had brought music and musicians to Gerd. Duncan's story was trapped inside his head and there was no notation system in the world to extract it.

She put it out of her mind and stepped into another room, one she shared with Lucas. In this room she floated between the physical and the imagined. She was so entangled in Lucas's dreams that they became her own. Months went by in a blur of purpose and adrenaline; she felt like she was an extension of his body and his mind. Nothing had ever succeeded so well in distracting her from worrying about Alison. Byrne had to tape notes on the walls not yet covered to remind herself to send macaroons in March for Passover and challah bread in September for Rosh Hashanah.

She was almost a full year into the book of labanotated choreography when Lucas came to her house one afternoon to survey the progress. Construction paper strips delineating the dances now covered her entire living room. The tempo, size and direction of every movement was contained in rows of tiny blocks, arrows, hash marks and arcs. She had created a womb of abstract symbols from four ordinary walls. It was almost ready to transfer to a printer's galley.

"I realize it looks more like a diagram than a painting," Byrne began. "But when it's all typed up, maybe we can play with the graphic layout, like e.e. cummings. It will be beautiful because the dances are."

"Bairh-nah," he said, clutching handfuls of wispy hair. "It is all wrong."

Byrne rocked back into her heels and *plied* to keep her knees from hyper-extending.

"Have I made a mistake?" she asked. "I've gone over it a hundred times."

Lucas held up the back of his palm as if to shield his eyes from his own creation.

"Oh, Bairh-nah. I no longer can teach that way. I have a new technique. I can't work like this."

He began to tear the strips of Byrne's labanotation from the walls, crumpling them up like a child suddenly embarrassed of his toys.

If he had told her of a new lover it would have been gentler than this. Byrne flattened her body against one of the covered walls, spreading her arms and long legs as if she could protect what they had created together. But the frenzy of destruction continued, and she watched, helplessly, as he stripped the walls.

"I will not be reduced to markings on a page," he said, the ideas still forming as he spoke. "Students have to learn what is their natural way of moving. First they explore it and then they work against it – to discover another aspect of themselves."

"What do you mean?" Byrne asked, releasing the wall and reaching to the floor to salvage pieces of her discarded life.

"Exactly," Lucas said, grabbing her hands until she stood upright again. "What does it mean? Seeing all this, this noise and clutter, brings you back to the basic things. When you try to break down technique in order to communicate, then you are forced to ask 'what is this movement really about?'"

Noise and clutter. Of all the words to describe what she meant to him, Lucas chose those two. Byrne's back skidded along the wall to the floor. The air drained from her lungs, and she couldn't look at Lucas anymore, couldn't bear to see the reflection of her defeat in his eyes. Duncan's whittled cherry walking stick, propped up in a corner where two dance-papered walls had joined, clattered to the wood floor.

She reached for it, straining for the strength to stand. She couldn't let Lucas into this room in her mind, the room of her humiliation. The cane from Cream Hill was the steadying force she needed, Duncan the resilience and fury. She hoisted the cane her husband carved high above her head and pivoted, making sure Lucas saw the entire movement. She was fluid and beautiful in the space between the first pose and the last. The picture Lucas would remember was the transition itself, when Duncan's walking stick became a javelin in her hand. Her forearms were capable of impaling it through him. But she kept moving, twirling the cane through her fingers until the tip of it pointed at the door. She kept it there, arm never quivering from the weight of it, and stamped the floor with her foot. He left and only then did she let it drop to the floor.

It was Duncan who tended to Byrne's shredded confidence, who helped her change her view of what had happened from betrayal to illumination.

"Maybe it had to be this way, darling," he consoled her. "It is a sign that you are meant for more than interpreting the work of others."

Byrne was as bereft as the widow Bernarda Alba, reduced to sitting center stage in mourning as the students of Lucas's new way of teaching danced around her. In his staging of the Lorca play, there were five daughters, all flirting with the same man who remains off stage. Offstage, in real life, waves of distrust and jealousy set dancer against dancer, and the man who had once made Byrne feel irreplaceable simply moved on.

Eventually Byrne did the same, joining another company headed by the woman who founded the dance department of the New York School for the Performing Arts. In Elizabeth Rockwell, Byrne found a kindred spirit, a woman who had also re-invented herself after her two daughters were grown. The difference was that Elizabeth Rockwell started her own company, something that Duncan believed Byrne could also accomplish.

"You've created a *sinfoinetta* for one man and an entire language for another. What about your own voice?" he asked.

They were summering at Cream Hill again. The "proper house," as Fanny called it, was finished: a two-floor, four-room structure with space enough for the girls and their grandparents to sleep inside. But Alison and Jane refused to trade the leafy tree house of their childhood for the confines of civilization, if the rustic house could be called any more civilized than theirs. The washroom in the "proper house" had no running water. Byrne and Duncan left it open, tiled with simple squares of pale ceramic. It looked more like a still life with pots and pitchers than a place to bathe, but the light streaming through it was long, blue and dreamy.

Duncan raised buckets of water from a well down the hill and heated it on the stove, then watched as Byrne undressed. He poured warmed water by the pitcher-full over her long neck, down her bare goose-bumped arms and between her smooth white breasts. She filled chamber pots with soapy water and sat gracefully in and over them, knees tilted off to the side like a Tahitian maiden in a Gauguin painting.

One day Duncan brought a Kodak Pony 135 camera, black with a satin chrome top, into the washroom while Byrne bathed.

"Do you intend to preserve my nakedness in perpetuity?" she asked as he focused the lens.

Duncan looked up with a smile that made his eyebrows come to a point. "Would you rather I attempt to labanotate it?" he asked.

She laughed then, able to let the defeats of her past roll over her strong, dancer's back and drain away beneath her.

"You are marvelous," Duncan said, as he snapped a photograph.

Byrne Miller at Cream Hill, circa 1955.

Duncan Miller.
(Photograph courtesy Scott and Rebecca Hartley)

Fanny Miller.*

Byrne Miller's maternal family portrait.*

Byrne, photographed for newspaper article about Lucas Hoving's Silvermine Guild of Artists in Connecticut, 1955.
(Courtesy of Judean and Joe Drescher.)

Top left: Byrne with Lucas Hoving, rehearsing "The House of Bernarda Alba," circa 1955.*

Lower left: Byrne, center, in a Calypso number, circa 1955.*

Above: Byrne, at age 57, in the pose that became the logo for the Byrne Miller Dance Theatre.*

Jane Miller.
(Courtesy of Scott and Rebecca Hartley)

Duncan at Cream Hill, circa 1971.

Duncan and Alison leaving for St. Thomas, circa 1964.

Alison Miller.

Byrne in St. Thomas, circa 1964.

Ben in Byrne's dance
class in Santa Fe,
circa 1967.*

Newspaper photo of Byrne teaching dance class in Santa Fe, circa 1968.*

Byrne leading rehearsal for "The Walls Between" in Santa Fe.*

Byrne Miller Dance Theatre production of "Once Upon An Island," circa 1970.*

Members of the Byrne Miller Dance Theatre rehearsing
Byrne's choreography in Beaufort, circa 1970.*

Duncan rehearsing with members of the Byrne Miller Dance Theatre in Beaufort, circa 1970.*

Byrne in Santa Fe, circa 1968.*

(Courtesy of Lisa Lepionka)

Newspaper photo of Teresa Bruce at ballet barre in Hillsboro, Oregon, 1979.

Above: Teresa in 1984, before suffering a broken back.

Left: Newspaper photo of Teresa at 1982 National Sports Festival.

"Auntie Mermaid" in Orange City, Florida.

Teresa on the set of WJWJ news, Beaufort, 1995.

Wipeout at Hunting Island State Park beach, 1995.

Teresa interviewing Byrne at Helena House, 2000.

Byrne teaching movement therapy to
special needs students in Beaufort, 1991.*

Byrne accepting Elizabeth
O'Neill Verner Award, 1989.*

Teresa, second from left, watching Byrne at her 87th birthday party, 1996.

Byrne at the center of a collected family portrait on her 87th birthday. Ben sits one row in front of Byrne, just below Teresa. Lisa stands in the row behind Byrne to the left and Mary and Lillian are at bottom right of the frame. Son-in-law Scott is seated just above them.

25

Wipeout

I HAD LIVED AMONG the tidal rivers of Beaufort long
enough to know that falling overboard does not have to
end in drowning. There is a natural buoyancy to brackish
water that its dark, opaque depths do not reveal at first.
Rafts of dead marsh grass give it away. They always float
in the direction of the flowing tide, and there are twisted
miles to go before the rivers open to the ocean sound and
surrender to the Gulf Stream. Twice a day the waters reverse course and flood the marshy inlets once again. All
that is lost returns. Water looks all the same along the
surface, wide and choppy, but currents are strongest in the
deep, middle channel. The pull of it slows along pluff mud
riverbanks, and it is possible to angle out of danger, cross
to safer shores on a long diagonal. Still, the geometry of
survival is not always the shortest distance between two
points.

I returned to the house when I was certain Sonny was
at work. Ron offered to drive me, but I could still steer the
station van, even with my bandaged hand in an arm sling.

"You don't have to talk about it if you don't want to,"

Ron had said when I showed up for work. "I'm just going to say one thing, and then I'll butt out. Do you realize you speak with two voices?"

I shrugged and winced. I had blamed the break on a fall that happened while I walked Wipeout, downplaying the severity of it, but even the slightest movement of my shoulders jarred my hand.

"When Sonny walks in the room your voice changes from chipper and confident to quiet and hesitant. Your tone rises. Every statement sounds like a question."

I didn't know what to say, didn't want to say anything now that even my voice betrayed me. I felt transparent and pathetic, my situation as see-through as an emperor without clothes. Ron had witnessed only the wind blowing on the surface of my life with Sonny. He had no idea how far I'd been pulled underwater since my days in graduate school, before my life had circled back to Puerto Angel, Mexico. Ron meant to help, but his words sliced through the shred of dignity I was fighting to maintain. I cried all the way home from the TV station. Teenage girls speak with rising intonation because they're insecure and immature – not television reporters with master's degrees, not lucky mermaids who are their mothers' princesses.

Alone at last, I looked around the house I was abandoning. My suitcase was spilled open next to the bed where I had started packing the night before. I made room to stuff my passport and some family photos inside and snapped it shut. The face of Jim Morrison sneered down at me from a Doors poster. Giant beach towels with Camel cigarette logos fluttered in front of the screen windows, nailed there as shades from the beating sun. Coke cans punched with holes and rimmed in ashes lined the windowsill. I saw the splintered hole in the fake wood paneling near the door where Sonny had slammed my hand. I would not miss this place. Neither would Wipeout. She jumped into the news van without hesitation while I made my last phone call from the house.

"Hello, Mr. Graber, this is Teresa Bruce," I said. Scott Graber was the lawyer I'd met with early that morning, the one who had told me the bad news.

"Teresa, getting a divorce in South Carolina is far more difficult than calling yourself married under common law," he had said. He carefully replaced the cap on his elegant pen and set it down on the pad where he had been taking notes. "Unless there's abuse involved."

Scott was a soft-spoken, courteous man, given to sipping Merlot and writing graceful opinion columns for the local paper when he wasn't in court. I could have told him why my hand was in a sling except that I was scared the truth would get Sonny deported. And if he got deported, my name would be in the newspapers – local TV anchor in scam marriage to illegal immigrant, faces up to five years in prison for green card fraud. I kept quiet, and Scott continued.

"We do live in a conservative state, I'm afraid. You have to be legally separated for at least 12 months."

"Twelve months! You mean an entire year?" Sonny and I had no property to split up. There was nothing to argue over. We weren't even properly married. "Couldn't I just sign some paper and be done with this?"

"I'm afraid not," he said. "First you move out. I draw up the papers. You sign. We serve him. He signs. A year later, assuming you don't move back in together, you have a hearing and a judge grants you the divorce. It's just a formality, Teresa, try not to panic."

Hours after the discussion, I was still trying. I gripped the phone between my cheek and my collarbone. This was me, keeping my head above water, trying not to fight against the current. Ron, Suzanne and all my friends at the TV station were waiting on the shore with outreached hands. All I had to do was breathe deep and let the tide carry me to safety.

"I've got all my stuff out now and Sonny should be home sometime this afternoon," I told my newly retained lawyer on the other end of the line. "Let's get this over with."

"Good for you," Scott replied. "This is a big step. Deputies will be by with the papers, and I'll call you at the TV station when we've got his signature. Twelve months from today you will be a free woman."

My plan was to rent a room from military friends who lived in a double-wide trailer near Beaufort's Marine Corps Air Station. Sonny didn't know where they lived. They liked dogs, and said Wipeout and I could stay as long as we needed. In the meantime, I would have to tell Suzanne what Ron had already guessed. Sonny would come straight to the station once he was served divorce papers.

"Oh, Teresa, I'm so sorry," Suzanne said. If she was shocked that we were actually married she didn't show it. "I've been through a divorce myself. I know how scary it is. You're going to be fine."

It felt as if she was talking about someone else. I still didn't think of myself as really married, let alone someone who would be divorced in a year.

"We won't let him inside," Suzanne said, as though reading my mind. "If your hand isn't too painful, why don't you take my place on set tonight and let me wait for Sonny in the parking lot. I'll talk to him, gently, and make sure he leaves."

I fought back tears, trying desperately to maintain some sort of professionalism. But Suzanne was the understanding boss who had introduced me to Byrne. When my stories irritated a business owner, or I forgot to mention the names of every lady on an event committee, Suzanne was the one who took the angry phone calls and talked viewers out of writing letters to the state legislature. And now she was offering me her anchor spot so that I wouldn't have to deal with Sonny's reaction. She was willing to take the brunt of whatever emotions would erupt from an abandoned man on the day he was served separation papers. It was a generous gesture and I let the tears flow. I'd never done anything so brave for anyone.

In the days that followed, I hid in plain sight, delivering the evening news as if nothing had happened and then sneaking into my friends' trailer park at night. Billy was assigned to shoot every meeting with me, so I would never be alone. It was overkill. Sonny didn't need to follow me on assignments. He just waited in the parking lot of WJWJ day after day. My co-workers took turns talking him into leaving before the cops made their nightly rounds. I knew it was a matter of time before he found a way to get back at me. The kind of rage that leaves dogs limping and bones broken doesn't self-correct, especially not after public humiliation.

I was the one who had humiliated Sonny, and the specter of retaliation lurked in every corner of my mind. Every rock that flew up from a gravel driveway sounded like a bullet just missing my window. Each time headlights flashed behind me, I was certain my car was about to be rammed. I jumped at the sound of a light switch. The station receptionist intercepted my calls and wrote down the phone numbers to call back and make sure it wasn't Sonny. I quit my second job at the radio station – there were too many places for Sonny to wait along the dawn-darkened islands I had to cross to get there.

Nights were the hardest. I knew nothing of base politics, deployment schedules and movies like *Full Metal Jacket* and *Platoon*. But these were the conversations around my new dining room table, and I was grateful for the distraction. Wipeout thrived in the constant attention, and when it was time for bed, she buried herself under my covers. She slept so soundly that I had to wake each night to poke her and make sure she was still breathing.

The trailer park was an island of sand and dirt, the shade of its live oak canopy too impenetrable for any grass to grow. When Wipeout left the double-wide to do her business, she tracked grit and pee-splattered mud back inside. My new roommates were forgiving, but I didn't want to push the limits of their hospitality. So when my hand was healed, I bought a dog grooming kit and informed Wipeout that she was getting a Marine Corps crew cut on the back deck. I picked a Saturday morning, when all my roommates were out at the beach.

I expected vigorous protest, considering that bathing Wipeout was always a leash-straining struggle. But she had transformed in the six weeks since leaving Sonny. She no longer jumped up and scraped her claws down my stomach when I came home. She had stopped chewing on her tail and nervously biting her own paws. The Marines wrestled with Wipeout on the living room floor and instead of cowering and flinching at the sound of men's voices, she licked their faces until they surrendered. She was once again the puppy on the beach in southern Mexico, reveling in attention, unsuspecting.

I showed her the buzzing razor and let her sniff the oil that lubricated the blades. Then I ran it down her side, tentatively at first. The vibrating noise seemed to put Wipeout into a trance. She rolled onto her back and let her hind legs flop apart. The coarse under-layer of fur came off like strips of shag carpeting while the downy top coat puffed around my head in dandelion wishes. It was worth the mess, I told myself. A close shave would make her quicker to brush off after walks in the woods, easier to bathe when she rolled in fish guts at the public boat landing.

I rolled her over onto one side when suddenly her flank tensed and I nicked her skin – she heard something. I put the blade down, dabbing at the wound and listening. Then I heard it too: the unmistakable sound of Sonny's truck, engine still running as he slammed the door. My mind raced through useless questions like how he found us, or how he knew we were alone. I pulled Wipeout inside, through the sliding glass door and shut her in our room. But before I could lock the front door Sonny barged in.

"Where is she?" he yelled, pushing me over the back of the sofa. His hands closed around my throat, and I kicked against his shins and thighs. "You think you can take everything away from me, even my dog?!"

His fingers pressed against my windpipe, pushing my head into the crack between cushions. The truck, the house, the green card were forgotten offerings – Sonny wanted me to suffer. If Wipeout were my favorite doll, he'd have stomped on her head just so I couldn't play with her, then ripped out her hair to watch me cry. Wipeout began to howl and bark at the commotion. Sonny got off me, slid open the pocket door to my rented bedroom and saw Wipeout cowering on a futon on the floor.

There wasn't time to call the police. He dragged Wipeout by her collar down the front steps. She yelped and braced herself against the yanking, but when she sat down in the dirt, Sonny scooped her up by the haunches and manhandled her into the truck. He shoved her past the steering wheel and climbed in.

I made it to the passenger side door just as he threw the truck into reverse to back up. I reached in through the window to let Wipeout out. Sonny accelerated and I lost my footing. The tops of my sandals scraped along the road and peeled away from my feet. My shoulders felt ripped from their sockets. Dust blinded me. I kicked, trying to get my feet back under me. My weak hand let go first and then I felt my chin slam against my knee and I rolled into the ditch. The truck disappeared into a cloud of dust and gravel and all that was left was the receding sound of Wipeout howling.

I hobbled back toward the trailer, tongue bleeding from where I bit it. I thought of calling 911, but Sonny could have taken her anywhere. I knew he had moved out of our rental house. The phone was disconnected, and the landlord had kept my deposit to pay for damage to the walls. I'd heard Sonny was living on a tiny sailboat he borrowed from another bartender. He had his green card. Maybe he had been waiting until my guard was down to steal Wipeout and then escape – to start a new life someplace where the waves were steady.

I was still curled up on the floor of the deck where I had tried to shave Wipeout when the first of my roommates arrived. I was racked with sobs that interrupted normal breathing, sobs that joined a flood of snot and spit and blood flowing down my face, sobs that couldn't be spoken through. Five minutes later, sheriff's deputies were knocking on the door.

"We can't do anything about the dog unless you press charges," one of them told me. His tone was somewhere between sneering and frustrated. He might as well have said, "You women are all alike, can't make up your mind."

For the next 10 months and two weeks, I would be legally tied to Sonny. I couldn't report anything that might get him deported. While we were still married, any shit-storm would just rain down on me and wash Wipeout away. I stared at a man in a uniform who knew nothing of the fronts that I was battling. He just saw a girl in a trailer park, too dumb to let go of a pickup dragging her through the dirt.

"You sure you don't want to get checked out at the hospital?" the deputy's partner asked, before they left. I shook my head no. It was the first of many suggestions I rejected in the coming days.

"I could get some base MPs to plant drugs in his truck," one of my Marine friends offered. "That'd get him deported for sure."

"I could sic the Hilton Head Island rugby team on him," a normally mild-mannered colleague at the TV station suggested. I wouldn't have believed him except that he once stuffed tampons in each nostril of his broken nose to stop the bleeding and kept playing. "I'm not saying we have to break any bones, unless you think that would be effective."

It would have been comforting, this sense of troops rallying around me. But none of them knew the truth. They were defending a fraud who should have ditched Sonny the very first time he stuck his hand down Wipeout's throat to teach her a lesson.

After nine days, Sonny returned Wipeout to me at the TV station. I had finished my stories early and was curling my hair next to the window in the editing suite so I could keep a lookout over the parking lot. He came 20 minutes before airtime, tires squealing to a stop in a cloud of dust. Wipeout was tied up in the back of the truck.

Suzanne patted my shoulder. "You just keep getting ready. I'll deal with him."

I watched from my hiding place as Suzanne walked beside Sonny along the bank that sloped down to the Beaufort River, putting her arm over his shoulders. Live oaks obscured my view and blocked any chance to guess what they were saying. But I could see when Sonny suddenly squatted to the ground, hands covering his eyes. It was far from the stance of the confident surfer I once knew, able to crouch for hours waiting for the perfect wave. It was the position of a man who thought the moon was sucking the swells away forever, draining the ocean and leaving him stranded.

Suzanne held out a hand and eventually he took it, standing to sob into her shoulder. She tucked a note into his hand, probably the phone number of a counseling service, and walked him to the pickup truck. He untied Wipeout's leash from the roll bar of the truck bed and handed her over to Suzanne.

I was still blinking back tears when Billy started the countdown in the studio. The tiny red light on top of the camera seemed to blink *keep it together, keep it together.* "Good evening, I'm Teresa Bruce. Topping the news tonight ... " *a man's life washed away.*

After the newscast, Ron walked me out to my car. I kept my eyes on the rearview mirror as I drove away from the station, just in case Sonny followed Wipeout and me. I should have gone straight to my new home but I drove, instead, to Byrne Miller's house.

26

The Truthfulness of Friendship

WHEN I PULLED UP to Byrne's house, ready to open a
bottle of wine to celebrate Wipeout's return, there was an
unfamiliar car in the driveway. One of Byrne's collected
daughters I'd met at the Martha Graham master class,
Lisa, was locking up the front door.

"It's Duncan," she told me in her clipped, Swiss-German
accent. "He's at Beaufort Memorial Hospital. Byrne's been
there with him all day, so I'm picking her up and bringing
her home. Would you mind tidying things up and maybe
putting some tea on? She'll need to eat something."

The details were a blur. Something about how Duncan
had tried to swallow but choked instead. EMT's came to
the house. Resuscitation. Then an ambulance ride to the
emergency room. Drifting in and out. Didn't look good. A
living will. Best to be prepared.

Lisa's words flew at me in machine gun bursts, and it hit
me that she had been part of Duncan's life long before I'd
ever met him. She knew what his voice had sounded like,
before it was a struggle for him to even whisper. She knew
what his body looked like, when he could stand and lift

dancers in the air. She knew how his mind once worked, and she knew that Duncan would want Byrne to get some sleep, in her own bed. So Lisa pushed aside any melodrama and assumed the role of dutiful, responsible, reliable daughter. There were things to be done and she was gone.

A phone started to ring and it took me a few seconds to realize I would have to answer it. The cordless phone wasn't in Byrne's office, where it should have been, and I darted from room to room following the sound. *Please Byrne, hang on, I'm coming.* I didn't want her to imagine an empty house, like it would be without Duncan, where she might be alone for the rest of her life. *Where is the goddamn phone?* I found it on its last ring – face down on the porch where Byrne probably dropped it when the ambulance arrived.

She must have stood in the very spot I stood, watching Duncan's eyes turn to hers in utter panic. When he choked, she must have tried to squeeze him from behind. The wheelchair would have kept him from her. In my mind she lurched through the house to answer the doorbell, all the grace and elegance stripped from her legs and arms. I imagined her collapsing into the rattan chair on the porch as the EMTs transferred Duncan to a stretcher, unable to maintain her picture perfect dancer's posture.

I sat in that same chair, and Wipeout backed herself between my feet. The tide was so low that the creek beyond the screen looked like a muddy ditch, and a foul stench of marsh sulfur climbed the bank. This was supposed to be the porch that helped Duncan find his words, a sweet-smelling refuge where he could flirt with girls who arrived by kayak. It wasn't fair, Duncan not sitting here, peacefully sleeping in his wheelchair. I was still staring down at the cordless phone on the porch floor when it rang again. It was Lillian, calling from the hospital.

"She's doing as well as can be expected," she said. "Mostly she's just really angry at the doctors. They keep insisting on a feeding tube."

I tried, but I couldn't picture Duncan connected to a feeding tube. All I could see was Byrne, pushing the glasses up on her nose, pursing her lips to keep from arguing. *Was she crying?* I'd never seen her cry and never wanted to.

"They both signed a living will, but apparently this damn hospital doesn't feel compelled to follow their wishes. If Lisa doesn't come and get Byrne out of here soon, there's going to be a fist fight."

When Lisa returned with Byrne and brought her to the door, I raced into Byrne's arms. The softness of her was a revelation. I expected a *port-de-bras*, muscular dancer's arms defining the space between us. We'd never hugged before and her weary bones seemed to melt around me. I breathed deep for a hint of her perfume, a dab of confidence behind her ears. What clung to her was the smell of syringes and tubes and fear. Her hair was sour and I struggled not to sob.

I would follow the lead of her collected daughters. Lisa was already placing teacups on their china saucers. Just two, her way of telling me she couldn't stay. She had kids and a husband at home to feed. It was my turn to take over.

"I'll be back in the morning," Lisa said as she braced Byrne's shoulders between her sturdy hands and kissed both cheeks. Hers were no dainty air kisses, like someone handing roses to a ballerina. They were the loud, deliberate kisses a mother gives a frightened child, for encouragement and confidence.

"Teresa, only one cup of tea and then make sure she gets to sleep. We're all going to need our strength."

I was reaching for the sugar dish when I heard the screen door close. Byrne stood in the entrance, still holding the heavy oak door open as Lisa walked down the uneven brick path to her car. She kept waving through the twilight as if Lisa could still see her from a block away. At first Byrne's hand pivoted at the wrist and then, like a little girl, her fingers drooped into bye-bye flutters. When she finally closed the door, she gripped the doorknob to keep her balance. A lesser woman would have leaned into the door and sobbed, pounded it with her fists. But Byrne held onto that doorknob and, vertebra by vertebra, straightened her spine and pulled her chin up before she turned to me.

"I could use that cup of tea now, darling," she said. "And a warm fuzzy white dog to rest my feet on."

So this was how it would be. No tears, no rehashing of the medical details. Her face was drained and her glasses rested near the tip of her nose. I wondered what to talk about, what subjects to avoid. I'd never walked in on a charmed life in the process of unraveling. I didn't know how much of the obvious to acknowledge or ignore. I searched Byrne's face for any hint of what she wanted and realized only what I wanted – to see her eyes light up like they did whenever she spoke of Duncan.

I pulled a chair into the bedroom, between the adjustable metal gurney where Duncan slept, and the skinny, long twin bed next to it that was Byrne's. The tea needed to cool, so I helped Byrne undress while we waited. I unbuttoned her blouse and jerked my hand away from a back laced with alarming scars.

"My war wounds," she said. "That's what having five surgeries does to a dancer's spine."

I traced my finger along the longest of five ridges, still purple and puckered. "After the first surgery, weren't you terrified of all the others?"

"Physical pain is something I have learned to accept," she said. In what she didn't say, I heard the dread of losing Duncan. "All dancers do. Fear of pain is for the *hoi polloi*."

The words were ones I would have to look up at the library before I could chew and swallow them. Later, I learned the Greek phrase: Byrne was separating herself from commoners, the masses. But on the night of Duncan's taking, I found my own meaning in her narrow hips and weary spine. Byrne could survive anything. She didn't need sympathy.

"Tell me what it was like when you were first married," I asked.

Byrne closed her eyes and began to describe her first home with Duncan, the tiny yet elegant flat in Greenwich Village where they rented the back two rooms and bathroom of a parlor floor.

"We didn't have a table or chairs, but we had a piano," she said, smiling. "You can always sit on the floor to eat. But like I told mother, if you haven't a piano, you can't make music."

It was working. It might have been the reflection of her nightstand reading light, but I detected a sparkle in Byrne's eyes. She was reciting her personal fairy tale, a land far, far away that gave her comfort. This was the Byrne Miller way of ordering the world and putting pleasure before pain.

It was getting late. Wipeout was fidgeting at the foot of Byrne's bed, ears twitching at every noise outside. I reached out to stroke her silky ears, hoping she felt safe. *I'll never let you out of my sight again. It's all going to be okay.* I almost didn't notice when Byrne's voice picked up again.

"We've been married almost 60 years and Duncan still loves to watch me undress. Not a day passes that he doesn't tell me he loves me."

I'd heard this story before but it wasn't me that she was addressing. She was convincing herself, and when I took the empty teacup from the table next to her bed, I saw that she had wadded up the sheets in both her fists.

"If he can't say the words, then he mouths them to me: *you are marvelous.*"

The fairy tale could end tomorrow. Duncan's eyes might not light up when she walked into his hospital room.

"Nothing will take that away, Byrne," I said. "You will always know he loves you."

"We did have one big argument in the early years of marriage," Byrne said. "I knew he slept with other women on occasion. He tried to cover this one up."

It was as if she were showing me backstage, behind their perfect, public love. I didn't want to see what happened in the wings. I was overflowing with secrets of my own, covering up the aches and bruises of relationships with stage makeup to stay in character, however duplicitous. Duncan was lying in a hospital bed, possibly spending his last night on earth alone, and Byrne was dredging up a 60-year-old infidelity. *Why?*

"It was a lie between two people who were partners, equal partners, in truth."

I exhaled in misery for Duncan. Byrne was angry at him for giving up, for being in the hospital with a feeding tube down his throat, for the fact that he might leave her forever. She was angry because she was scared.

"How did you work it out?" I asked. I wanted to hear the happily ever after part. I wanted to tuck Byrne in and believe in her perfect love story again. I needed it to be true as much as she did.

"After that he never lied to me again," she said. "And isn't it the truthfulness of friendship that re-ignites the passion?"

Her eyes caught mine and I looked away before she could see through me. At the end of what had to have been one of the worst days of her life, Byrne Miller was taking me into her confidence. This was more than the light-hearted womenisms she shared with all of her collected daughters.

When she was at her most vulnerable, she trusted me with a long-ago humiliation. I hadn't shared any of the truth of Sonny with Byrne, or anyone. All the anger, fear and shame of it was still secret. *And isn't keeping secrets from a friend the same as lying?*

27

If you're going to be a snob, be unrepentant.
Mediocrity is distasteful.

~Byrne

St. Thomas

St. Thomas, U.S. Virgin Islands – 1964

Byrne leaned over the apartment's kitchen table and sliced an Exacto blade through smudgy newsprint. The article announcing Duncan's promotion was so far down the page that she had to write in the date and masthead information by hand: *The Virgin Island Daily News, September 28, 1964.* Duncan had probably written the press release himself, she thought. His name was buried at the bottom of two paragraphs announcing that Design Print, a company specializing in promotional materials for Virgin Islands businesses, had expanded its offices.

"The new manager of the St. Thomas office is Duncan Miller, formerly of the Television Bureau of Advertising in New York. Miller has been handling copy and contracts at Design Print for the last three months."

She reread the paragraph, wincing at the way it reduced the last three months to simply "handling copy." She lifted her eyes through the kitchen window and took in a placid, clear blue bay bobbing with yachts and catamarans. To the wealthy and transient boating class, St. Thomas was picturesque and tranquil. For Byrne, three months on the island felt like three years, trapped in idyllically calm waters while her inner world was a churning whirlpool.

"This is only a temporary posting," Duncan had said when he took the job. "A salary to tide us over while I finish the novel. Think of the silence that an island thousands of miles from Manhattan will afford me."

Byrne knew then that this was the truth Duncan would come to believe, just as he had convinced himself that Cream Hill would breathe life into his writing. She looked down at the clipping in her hand. Byrne suspected there would be no future employers. Unexplained detours and self-imposed exiles do not read well on a resume. A 50-year-old man at the top of his career, Director of Sales and Promotions at the Television Bureau of Advertising in Manhattan, does not voluntarily give it all up to "handle copy" hawking landscaping services and charter-boat fishing expeditions.

She considered pasting the clipping into the scrapbook alongside other mementos of a tumultuous year. Perhaps a member of some future Miller generation would be curious how Alison, Byrne and Duncan ended up living high on Mandahl Hill, mixing with the moneyed set as though they belonged. But Byrne wadded up the clipping in her fist. She would save no reminders of Duncan's slide from grace. A 31-square-mile island in the Caribbean was not large enough to cloak her in anonymity or let her forget what she had given up to follow Duncan here.

Her dance career had been the least painful sacrifice. No 53-year-olds danced in the touring companies of Elizabeth Rockwell and Lucas Hoving when she left the mainland, and Byrne would have declined positions even had they been offered. A sojourn from daily dancing would rejuvenate her aching back, some weight might even settle on her bony hips.

Breaking the news of another uprooting to her daughters had been much more traumatic. Alison, at first, seemed delighted. The idea of a tropical island was infinitely more appealing than being 26 years old and living in the basement of her parent's house in Bedford Village, New York. College had been a short-lived, unsuccessful experiment, and Alison spent the subsequent years at home teaching dogs to sit and stay. It was when Alison learned that her younger sister wouldn't be coming with the family to St. Thomas that the unraveling began. Jane's announcement that she was getting married and that her husband-to-be wanted to ranch in western Colorado shifted the very ground under Alison's feet.

"But you can't leave me," Alison had wailed, as if Jane were her mother, abandoning her.

Byrne had closed her eyes against tears that threatened to make a lie of her optimistic façade. What she wanted to remember were her two little girls in their Cream Hill tree house snuggled close as chicks in a bird's nest.

Instead, Jane brushed strands of stringy black hair away from her older sister's frantic, beseeching eyes and smoothed Alison's red-splotched skin with open, patient palms.

"When you get to St. Thomas, you can still rescue dogs," she said. "But it's too mountainous for my horses. I shouldn't leave them here all alone, should I?"

Alison could understand this parceling of the predicament. But not a man who promised her tomboy kid-sister big skies and never to fence her in. Not a wedding where Jane wore a scratchy yellow wool suit and mumbled things like "forsaking all others" and "until death do us part." And not a reception where her father danced every song with her, instead of Jane, because no other man would have asked.

When Duncan left New York to begin the job on St. Thomas, Byrne sent Alison with him.

"I'll come and join you as soon as Grandmama and Grandpapa are settled," she told her leery daughter. "You can help Daddy find an apartment and look after him for me. He'll be too busy to remember to eat without a woman there watching out for him."

In the *bon voyage* photograph Byrne took of the two of them standing on the runway next to a prop plane, the plan looked plausible enough. Alison, in a glamorous green traveling dress and black straw hat, presented no clues to her emotional fragility. She was wearing red lipstick and smiling, and eyes that might have given away her apprehension were hidden by sunglasses and the hat's deep shadow. Duncan clutched a valise in one hand and a silver Zero Halliburton briefcase in the other – a dashing novelist on the cusp of an island adventure. His head was tilted, waiting for the moment to be captured on film so he could be on his way.

Byrne stayed behind to find a renter for their house in Bedford Village, to decide what to leave behind or ship to their new life in St. Thomas and to find a solution for her parents. Fanny and Michael were in their eighties and forgetting to return phone calls, forgetting to check whether the milk was spoiled before drinking it, forgetting to jiggle the flush handle to prevent the toilet from running all night. At first Byrne refused to believe the young man who had taken over Doctor Fein's practice when he told her that Fanny was showing signs of dementia.

"Nonsense. Everyone forgets things when they get old," Byrne had insisted, wishing Duncan were there to agree with her, to defend the woman who had always defended him. She was glad, though, that the girls didn't have to witness the change that was becoming impossible to ignore. It was as if her forever-wise, forgiving mother suddenly forgot how to couch her irritations and disappointments in polite or gentle words.

"Make yourself useful," Fanny had barked when Byrne first returned from taking Duncan and Alison to the airport. "His toenails scrape my legs every time he turns over in bed. It's ugly. I hate him."

"Shhh ... Daddy can hear you," Byrne said, stroking her mother's hand.

Fanny jerked her hand away. "I don't care. You don't care. You're just lazy."

"Don't cry, Mother," Byrne said as Fanny's lip began to quiver. The strap of her mother's cotton housedress slipped off a thin shoulder that was puttied with brown age spots. "Let me get the nail clippers, okay?"

Byrne rubbed her father's limp, scaly calves with lotion while she soaked his feet in a bucket of warm water. When she cradled his heel to lift his right foot from the suds, she saw in an instant why Fanny was striking out at the world. Her frightened mother was flailing against a new reality, one where she was no longer able to take care of even the most basic of her husband's needs. Michael's nails were so overgrown they curled back on themselves and cut into the soft flesh of his toes. But instead of wincing from the pain, Michael Miller hummed Liszt's *Un Sospiro* and smiled.

"My little *tzigane*, I wish you could live with us always," he whispered, and the words were tiny scalpels carving at Byrne's conscience. It didn't matter that she'd done her homework and inspected every rest home in the region. It didn't matter that she found one where moussaka was on the menu and the toilets smelled clean and no residents were parked in wheelchairs in front of blaring televisions. She still felt as though she were abandoning two people who would never have done the same to her.

"Promise me, Duncan," she sobbed into the phone that evening, "promise me this will never happen to us. I would rather die than go through this again."

She needed her husband to tell her she was doing the right thing, that already the peaceful quiet of island life had reignited his writing and taken the edge off Alison's unhappiness. But instead he told her he was sending their daughter back to New York.

"She had an awful spell," he said. "Thrusting herself on a gay business associate I invited for cocktails. It must be some sort of sexual, mental breakdown. I can't handle her, Byrne. She needs to be hospitalized."

The receiver burned against Byrne's temples. The crackling of the long-distance line triggered cruel memories of Alison's shaven head, pressed between electrodes. Duncan's pause was longer than necessary, evidence that perhaps Alison was in the room. Byrne closed her eyes and thought of what Fanny would have said, in the days when her mother was still as unflinching as a lioness but as delicate as a butterfly.

"What she needs is her mother," Fanny would have said, settling it without leaving room for argument.

So Byrne put the phone to her other ear, lifted her chin and for the first time in her life gave Duncan an order. "Take her to a doctor on the island immediately, cut any medication he prescribes in half, and I'll be there in less than a week to take care of her."

It was bad enough that her parents had to be put in a home. She could not bear her daughter's banishment as well. Byrne still believed she could organize Alison's brain, if not cure it. Perhaps it was a good thing, her distant daughter's sudden interest in sex. She just needed to be taught how and when it was appropriate, to be trained in the art of seduction.

Besides, if Duncan were ever to finish his novel, he would need the combination of distraction and reassurance only Byrne could provide. She would take over their social schedule and establish Duncan not as the new manager of an inconsequential printing office but as an undiscovered novelist on an artistic sabbatical. There would be beach excursions and dinner parties, and Byrne would entertain guests by playing the piano while Duncan filled glasses with wine and ears with Shakespeare. St. Thomas would be a triumph. It had to be.

Byrne alighted on the island determined to celebrate her daughter's attributes instead of drawing attention to her deficiencies. The island doctor had told Duncan that Alison only needed time, though in truth he had not known what else to do for her. Byrne arrived to an apartment echoing with silent recrimination. It was clear to her that Alison's lingering shame and embarrassment should be replaced with confidence. St. Thomas would become both performance and stage, and Byrne determined it would be a long and sold-out run. To start with, she declared a moratorium on her husband's heavy silences and her daughter's exasperated sighs. "Methinks thou both protest too much," she intoned with deliberate affectation.

Duncan was the first to break into a grin. "The robbed that smiles, steals something from the thief." He reached for Alison's hand and raised it to his lips for a kiss of forgiveness.

After that, Byrne allowed no discussion of what had happened while she was away. While Duncan put in perfunctory hours in his office and noodled on his novel, Byrne sunbathed along the bay where all the snowbirds moored. With Alison as bait, she set about reeling in visiting socialites and businessmen.

"This is my daughter. She's taking a break from modeling to keep me company while my husband finishes his novel. Do drop by for a glass of wine at sunset? Duncan loves meeting new characters."

Alison held back as her mother flitted over the sandy beach, collecting acquaintances like other women picked up pretty shells. She listened to records alone in her room during the cocktail hours when her mother-the-dancer and father-the-novelist entertained their new, delighted friends. Better to stay away from probing questions than say the wrong thing, stand too close or stare too long. But Byrne insisted on dragging her hesitant daughter along when Duncan accepted an invitation for an afternoon of sailing.

"Alison, wear your pretty, black straw hat," she suggested, "the one that makes your eyes so mysterious."

"Not that string bikini though," Duncan couldn't stop from adding. "I own ties with more substance."

Alison reluctantly obeyed, wearing a modest two-piece bathing suit on the yachting trip that sunny weekend afternoon.

"We quite appreciate the tropical reciprocity," Duncan said, proffering a bottle of champagne to the hosts. "It's a welcome relief from all those annoying agents and publishers back on the mainland."

The other guests splayed themselves on the gleaming wood deck, but Alison scrunched herself under the boom, wrapping long, thin arms around knobby knees. Duncan snatched the black straw hat from her head to snap a color photograph – his pale, wispy daughter in front of the bright, crisp sail. She twisted her neck around to pout at him, uneasy eyes hidden behind dark sunglasses, like she could be blown away and no one would notice.

Duncan turned his camera once again to Byrne, reclined against the bow's railing in a gold and black halter-top bathing suit made even more glamorous by a white chiffon scarf smoothing back her hair. She wore dark, pointed sunglasses too, just like Alison's, but on Byrne they were movie-star playful. As her shimmering backdrop, the ocean seemed a saltier blue. The cut and drape of sails mirrored the statuesque lines of her long, tanned legs and the jaunty upsweep of her breasts. Where Alison looked awkward and frail, Byrne projected poise and power. Yet no amount of bravado or élan made her capable of harnessing the winds that still thrashed about her husband.

Nine months into their stay on St. Thomas, Duncan presented Byrne with what he called his latest re-write. She started to type the manuscript for him, eager to make legible the hand-scrawled pages that had consumed almost sixteen years of Duncan's life. She rolled a fresh sheet of paper halfway down the page and typed *The Silenced Island. By Duncan Miller. Copyright 1964.*

"Shall I put the New York address or St. Thomas at the bottom?" she called out to Duncan, who was smoking a pipe on the veranda.

"Would Hemingway slight Cuba?" he answered.

Byrne smiled and started typing. By the fifth page, the words seemed vaguely familiar, as if she'd seen them before. She had already met the protagonist: a boy who hated noise and invented a machine to kill its perpetrators. Even before she typed the description of his physical appearance she knew what the boy looked like. She knew what he sounded like too, the patterns of his dialog were so similar to Duncan's speech. It was more than premonition; each chapter was an echo chamber hollow with repetition. Byrne leaned back in the wicker chair until she could barely reach the keys, and the chair's canes pressed painful lines into her skin. There would be deep, criss-crossed marks on her back and thighs the next morning, but she didn't stop or change position. The indentations would confess her failings — years of drifting apart, paying more attention to her daughters and her dancing than to Duncan. She typed until her hands cramped and she could no longer lift her neck, but still it wasn't penance enough.

Duncan went to bed a man who believed what his wife told everyone they met – that his was a brilliant mind, his talent as unparalleled as it was unrecognized. While Duncan slept, Byrne typed long into the humid, punishing night. Her fingers pounded the exact same keys they had in the crisp, cool air of Cream Hill. In the 10 years since Duncan had abandoned the first version of the novel, he had changed only its title, from *Shhh ...* to *The Silenced Island.*

28

The Journal

BEAUFORT – 1993

I NEVER REALIZED how many sisters I had inherited by way of Byrne until she took Duncan home from Beaufort Memorial Hospital. She didn't "bring" him home; Byrne's decision was against the will of doctors wanting to extend Duncan's life by artificial means. It was a taking, in every sense of the word. The decision took all of her conviction and strength and brought her no comfort. That was where we all came in: a family of collected daughters rallying around them both. Lillian even slept on the couch in the Millers' living room to spare them the expense of an around-the-clock nurse.

Our schedules seemed to fall naturally into shifts, without anyone planning it that way. Lisa, who checked in with Byrne after teaching middle school all day, was usually about to leave by the time I arrived at the Wilson Drive house. While nurses huddled around Duncan and visitors consoled Byrne, Lisa whisked through the house, taking care of behind-the-scene essentials. Streams of sympathetic friends told Byrne to "let them know" if there was "ever anything" they could do to help. But Lisa simply rolled up her sleeves, tied her ponytail into a knot at the nape of her neck and went to work. She emptied trash cans, folded laundry, changed coffee filters and remembered to water Byrne's roses.

"Okay Byrne, I've got to leave soon," she said, flicking off the light under the stove hood. "I'll say this only once. Should I call Alison or are you up to it?"

There was something unfamiliar in Lisa's voice, like a veiled ultimatum.

"I've already written her, but I think it best you bring me the telephone," Byrne answered. She inched her chair away from the table, as if giving herself space after finishing a heavy meal. "If she hears your voice, she'll probably think something's happened."

"Something has happened," Lisa said. Instead of her usual two-cheek plucks, she kissed Byrne on the top of her head, gently placed the cordless phone in her lap and left. I was opening my mouth, about to ask Byrne who Alison was, when Lillian fluttered out from the living room and handed me an empty wine jug.

"Let's see if we can scrub this label off," she said. Her eyes whispered *not now.* "Our supply of vases can't keep up with all of Duncan's flowers."

Byrne began to dial as we made our way into the kitchen. Her fingers moved slowly, but it was obvious she knew the number by heart.

"Alison is Byrne's oldest daughter," Lillian said when we reached the sink. "You haven't met her because they're not close. She lives out in Colorado."

Not close, what the hell does that mean? The only biological daughter Byrne had ever mentioned to me was Jane, the marine who was killed by a drunk driver the year we met.

"Do you mean oldest daughter like one of us, but from a long time ago, or a real daughter she's pissed off at?" I asked.

266

Lillian smiled. "It's more complicated than that, but Alison is a real daughter."

I pinched my lips, uncomfortable with the answer. The Byrne I'd come to know was a wild azalea garden, outlandish and overflowing with love. A woman "not close" to her only surviving daughter was more stubborn rose, lousy with thorns.

"It's a long way from Colorado, but do you think she'll make the trip to see Duncan?" I asked Lillian. Alison's father was dying, after all. Surely whatever tension existed between mother and daughter could be put aside for his sake.

"With Alison you never know," Lillian answered.

Maybe I have it all wrong. Maybe the daughter is the prickly one. I hoped so. It would be infinitely easier to dislike someone I'd never met. Lillian kept her voice low, and it occurred to me that if Alison did come to visit Duncan, there wouldn't be room in the house for Lillian to maintain her nightly vigil.

"How long are you going to keep sleeping on the couch?" I asked.

"Until it's over," she said and then burst into tears. We walked outside to the azalea garden, two sisters-by-Byrne if not by birth. The vibrant, witty leading man Lillian had known for years was wheezing, caking and cracking before her eyes. "I can't imagine this house without him."

AT FIRST, DUNCAN'S DRIFT into darkness wasn't so different than his life had been before Byrne's decision to take him home. He drank so little water that he had already lost the ability to swallow easily. That was why he'd choked and ended up attached to life support in the emergency room. It'd been months since he'd eaten a full meal. His metabolism was already at a core-preserving crawl. Even before Duncan's hospitalization, visitors were accustomed to the smell of too-strong urine and too-weak bowels.

If anything, there was less his body could release as the days went on. There were occasional, startling muscle spasms and convulsions, but his eyes were the hardest to take. I couldn't pretend that they lit up at the sight of Byrne entering the room. They were hollowed out, sunken pools of despair. Each rasping breath pulsed purple blood through the veins behind his eyelids as he tried to sleep, but that was infinitely easier to witness than the dullness when he tried to stay awake.

That he was dying was not danced around. Byrne often told him someone he loved was "here to say goodbye." She left the room as friends read passages of Shakespeare to him, or whispered to him of their children's accomplishments. Each morning, Lillian tidied up the sofa she slept on so guests could sit down for a cup of tea. She filled in the details no one wanted to bring up: how doctors thought it wouldn't be long now, how Byrne was holding up, how if they wanted to help they could make a donation to the Byrne Miller Dance Theatre.

She always circled the conversations back to the dance theater because, almost unbelievably, there was a movement underfoot to fold Byrne's life's work into the local university's performing arts series, reducing her ownership stake in it. It was as though Byrne was the one about to die, instead of Duncan. It was an indignity that distracted us all.

I helped Lillian and Lisa organize Byrne Miller Dance Theatre grant applications. We prioritized the upcoming deadlines for funding and made sure Byrne knew when each company needed to be paid, in advance. We were determined to keep the hounds at bay because the dance theater was what kept Byrne alive.

But the effortlessness of dance is a calculated illusion.

On stage a dancer's body stretches, soars and spins. Out of audience sight, in the wings, it is stripped of grace and glory. Costumes drop to the floor, breasts bared mid-stride. Paper bags are proffered for hyperventilating lungs, heating pads for torn muscles. Bleeding toes are plunged into makeshift whirlpools of flushing toilet bowls. Shanks of toe shoes are beaten over handrails to soften, the tips pounded into piles of ground glass resin so they will not slip. Torn tutus are stapled closed, ripped hems safety-pinned into place. The air smells of sweat, Ben-Gay and hairspray.

Walking into Byrne's office each night after the newscast felt like sneaking backstage. To her public, Byrne was uncannily poised and polished – describing upcoming performances or raising funds. In the second bedroom of her home, which functioned as the headquarters of the dance theater, she was stripped down, a performer between acts. Stacks of bankers boxes, piled 10 high and tipsy, lined the hallway. They bulged with contracts, grants and programs dating back to the 1970s, more than 80 performances in all. A television and VCR cart overflowed with rejected VHS audition tapes. Performance posters and vinyl banners covered the once-white walls, and cobwebs hung from the low ceiling. Just down the hallway from the smell of bandaged bedsores and ammonia, the scent of Byrne's office was white-out fluid and forgotten mugs of coffee. The hum of an electric typewriter and an oscillating three-speed fan in the corner drowned out Duncan's occasional moans.

Byrne seemed oblivious to the mounting stress. During the day, board members and volunteers marched through the house, tallying season ticket sales or designing ads for programs. At night she was alone, huddled in a cavern carved out of files and overstuffed boxes by the illuminating arm of an assisted reading device. It looked like a microfiche machine holding up the roof of a collapsing library.

"I call this machine my good eye," Byrne told me. On top of losing Duncan, she was slowly losing her sight. The prognosis from her ophthalmologist wasn't good, but that was all Byrne would admit. "I've just got too much work to do to consider going blind. My good eye will just have to work harder."

As if to compensate for it all, her collected daughters worked harder by her side. Judean, a soft-spoken yoga instructor from Savannah, stepped in to teach Byrne's Saturday classes. Mary, one of Byrne's board members who ran a chamber music series at the university, drove Byrne on excursions and errands in her red convertible Alpha Romeo. "You need the fresh air," Mary pronounced, handing Byrne a scarf to wrap around her head.

What she needed was to remember to breathe. When we were alone, I tried to tease Byrne about her entourage. "You're like Tom Sawyer, getting a bunch of people to whitewash the fence."

Byrne's eyes smiled as a short puff of air escaped through her nose. "The trouble is I don't know where the paintbrush is at the end of the day."

That was where I could help, re-filing misplaced papers and putting the most urgent "to do" stacks nearest to her phone. In a shallow drawer under the end table, she kept a log of every call she made and every call she planned to make the next day. Personal conversations were recorded separately from those on behalf of the dance theater, and the length of each was noted to reconcile the phone bill at the end of the month. Volunteers inevitably messed up her system, and Byrne carefully corrected the columns after they went home.

I was putting the phone log away when I saw another notebook in the drawer. It was labeled "Record of Duncan's Illness" and dated back to 1968.

"I dug that up today," she told me. "I think it's time to share it with you. Before he's gone."

Why would Byrne want to bring this up? Months had passed since my last story on Duncan. We both knew the next one would probably be an obituary. He was still breathing, barely, just one room away. *This isn't the time to examine his medical records, like a transcribed autopsy.*

It felt disrespectful when I opened the book and flipped through its musty pages. I recognized the names of dance theater volunteers and friends who dropped by to give Byrne loaves of banana bread or fresh basil from their gardens. But according to the dates in this journal, they were also donors who provided the blood for Duncan's experimental Alzheimer's treatments. Receipts and check stubs served as evidence. It cost $300 for each batch of donated blood to be processed in the hospital's lab. Byrne listed all the different drugs prescribed by doctors – ranging from Pamelon to Prozac. Duncan had been treated, it seemed, for everything from Parkinson's to depression. I kept turning the pages, finding notations in handwriting I did not recognize.

> *Mr. Miller awake and alert when I arrived. Patient was cheerful today.*

"Those inscriptions are from home nursing aides over the years," Byrne explained. "Eventually I got sick of strangers describing Duncan like a lab rat, so I started keeping notes myself." Hers were more personal, emotionally observant recordings. She noticed tiny changes in behavior, and my heart lurched with every hopeful sign she cataloged.

> *Bed time – brushed teeth without reminders from me. Generally aware and sweet.*

By the time I met Duncan, apparently even rising from a wheelchair had become a humiliation.

On fourth try, with much pushing from me, he made it.
But angry at me, rather than himself.

I could feel Byrne watching me read. These were brutally honest stories she'd never shared before. The journal was a how-*not*-to guide: how not to give up or give in. I held the notebook against my chest and closed my eyes, wishing I knew what she needed to hear.

"Have I ever told you the story of when I let Duncan handle our finances?" she asked.

I rubbed her shoulders. *Please let this story be a happy one.*

"He was two hours late coming home, and I was beginning to get worried," she began. The Byrne in the story could barely see Duncan's head for the stack of boxes he was carrying, all from Saks 5th Avenue. The Byrne who was telling the story swept her arms through the air as though she were unwrapping those same gifts a lifetime later. I closed my eyes and imagined the white silk Hermes dress and matching gloves, how perfectly they fit, how proud Duncan was of his selections.

Byrne started laughing. "There was nothing left to pay the rent!" When she took the clothes back the next day, she met the voluptuous salesgirl who had modeled them for Duncan first.

"When your husband believes money, all money, should be used to decorate his wife – all you can do is hug him and realize you had better be in charge."

She was in charge again, dancing on a stage of love and hope and promise. I was in the wings, holding a journal of a different Duncan, reading the less glamorous truth.

Went to dinner for Madison at Land's End. Wonderful house, amazing petit point on chairs and pillows. Home to Duncan who greeted me with a B.M. Felt like Cinderella after the ball.

I flipped through the pages of a woman desperately salvaging a hopeless situation. Each entry was darker than the one before.

I cannot be important enough to God — if there is one who is conscious of individuals — for him to play good cop, bad cop to me, but the extreme alternatives of high and low, very high and very low, continually mark my days.

On one brutal, autumn Monday she went straight from teaching classes to making photocopies at the university faculty building, fell over a telephone wire and wound up with a bleeding forehead, bruised knees and hands, and shattered eyeglasses.

Nothing broken. Finished Xeroxing, had lens put back, GOOD meeting at 4PM. Found my car had a flat tire.

Tuesday — very tired, probably reaction from the fall. Wish I hadn't promised to go with Lillian to City Council meeting but she had said she might need some backup about hanging a banner at Bellamy Curve.

I was confused. I covered city council for the TV station and never heard complaints about where Byrne hung banners to advertise performances. *Her organization was non-profit — why would she have needed backup?* I kept reading and smiled.

Suddenly, Mayor Taub was saying "Where is Byrne
Miller?" After a long list of whereas'es, he proclaimed
Sunday, November 3rd, Byrne Miller Appreciation
Day ... gold seal and standing ovation.

Lillian had never needed backup; my sister-by-Byrne
had created a brilliant ruse. Byrne wrote of being embarrassed, probably of the bruises on her hands and cuts on
her forehead, but surprised and pleased.

I double-checked the dates on her entries. All this
was happening during the same period I began to cover
Duncan's treatments at the hospital in Charleston. I had
been oblivious to the struggle that went into getting him
out to the porch, ready to be interviewed. All I'd seen was
reciprocated devotion so tender it dissolved my pretense of
journalistic objectivity, so powerful that I had thought it
possible to love Sonny enough to save him.

The next entry in the journal catalogued five more bowel
movements, each requiring a bath between.

Ha ha again, 9:20 p.m., another bath. Hard to roll
Duncan over and hold him while I clean. Just too much
for my strength. Cannot face more of this – cannot put
him in Bay View. There seems to be no solution I can
live with.

My eyes tripped over the words Bay View: it was the state-
run nursing home in Beaufort. Duncan belonged in a world
of tall tales told on a porch with a magnificent view. He was
a brilliant novelist who quoted Shakespeare, smoked a pipe
and lifted dancers in rehearsal, not a man reduced to diapers
and sponge baths. I couldn't read any further.

"It must have been so awful for you. Why didn't you ever
say anything?"

"There's no going back," she said. "He's been borderline schizophrenic since the sixties, long before the Alzheimer's kicked in. The truth is he was already gone by the time you met him. The man sleeping in our bedroom isn't the Duncan I want you to remember. He isn't the one I want to remember."

Borderline schizophrenic. The words felt naked, cold and clammy, and I knew by the hesitant tremble in Byrne's voice how much it hurt her to say them out loud. They sounded too vague to be a clinical diagnosis, but it all made sense. She never mentioned Duncan having a job since his days as a glamorous ad man in the 1940s.

"When he was in the hospital, he patted the bed beside his hips. I saw the tube attached to his penis and I pulled away. I still feel guilty about that," Byrne said.

It must have been a catheter, and Duncan was so resigned to suffering that he either didn't notice it or didn't care. Still I cringed to hear the story told out loud when Duncan was only one room away. I had always assumed that, if Duncan were even aware of our conversations, he found comfort in them. In reality how could he? He was a ghost trapped in his own body, talked about as though already gone. The woman he loved could no longer endure the sight of his once powerful masculinity.

"Years ago, Duncan signed a living will, no artificial measures to prolong life. I wish it was already over – I feel like a hostage to this disease."

She was telling me she wished that Duncan would hurry up and die. Byrne took my hand and held it to her heart, as if to prove that it still was capable of beating. I had to let her know that I would never judge her. It was time for the truthfulness of friendship.

"If lightning strikes you down for wishing this was all over," I said, "then it will surely sizzle me as well. In fact,

I'll fry in hell."

"What could you possibly have done to feel as guilty as I do?" she asked.

"I dragged an illegal alien to this country and now I'm divorcing him," I said.

She squinted in confusion, as if I had suddenly dropped out of focus. I looked down at the floor and continued my confession. "I never told you, but Sonny isn't just my boyfriend. He's my husband. And it gets worse. That day I paddled over to your house? Well, that same day, I wished that Sonny's plane would crash – with him in it."

I forced myself to look up at Byrne and confront whatever reaction she might have. But instead of disgust or shock, she seemed amused. I couldn't swear to it, but the sound coming from deep in her throat might have been a chuckle.

"No," I said. "You don't understand. I looked to the sky and visualized him falling from it. I am too much of a coward to kill him with my own hands, so I wanted God to do it for me. The daughter of an atheist no less."

Byrne's shoulders, normally so low and square beneath her long neck, began to jiggle up and down. I hadn't meant to make her laugh. This wasn't a contest of awful thoughts and the women who think them. I was not proud of the person I had become, but if we were competing I would have won. Surely it is a far greater sin to wish a young, healthy man dead than for a disease-ravaged life to simply come to an end.

"Well, now that we've established that we are both utterly reprehensible creatures," Byrne said, her laughter lingering in a smile, "I suppose the sensible thing to do is to stop beating ourselves up over it."

Here was the Byrne I recognized, back from the unfamiliar cusp of self-doubt and blame. I put away the notebook and looked around for something to use as a gavel. An empty coffee mug sufficed. "I hereby declare a moratorium on feeling guilty," I pronounced.

"I will second that motion," she said, raising her hand. I banged the coffee mug again.

"You are out of order, Mrs. Miller. This is not a committee vote. I am the judge and dictator and this is my decree. You must simply obey my command and go about your business guilt-free."

"As you wish," she said. "And I am sure that the real Duncan, the one who lives forever in my heart, agrees."

29

The family you're born with is not the one you're stuck with.

~Byrne

The Miller Pair

Santa Fe, New Mexico – 1965

Weeks after Byrne sat up all night to type his manuscript, Duncan was still picking at the scab that was *The Silenced Island*. He changed the first four pages, setting the action in a place he pejoratively called "Pigtown," and began to write in melancholy, detached second person. "You walk your disenchanted road, high about a blue sea that creams around each of the islands beneath you." By page 26, the tone was one of almost hostile self-examination. "What's the truth about you? Why do you make people turn away from you by your unresponsiveness, your silence?" Before the scab could become a permanent scar, Byrne declared their island sojourn over.

"But there is no closure," he had protested, "the plot is still adrift."

"The book is clearly about you," Byrne soothed him, "so it will follow you anywhere, just as a shadow remains attached to him who blocks it from the sun."

If Duncan's writing was his shadow, then Alison was his night, absorbing heat but giving off no light of her own. Any stars that flickered in her lonely sky burned out in short, downward streaks – a pet iguana that at first brought her attention but later derision, jobs filled before her application was considered. When she aimed suggestive glances at men, they were not returned and her outright propositions were humiliatingly rejected. For Alison the only escape was anonymity. She was eager to leave the claustrophobic island, yearned to go where horses and dogs outnumbered people. And so, after barely a year in the Virgin Islands, the Millers returned to the mainland.

"We left St. Thomas because of all the racial unrest," Byrne would later tell a newspaper reporter about the decision to leave a disastrous year behind. It was a whitewash more plausible than provable and one that invited no probing questions. Returning to upstate New York or Connecticut, the scene of abandoned novels and love affairs, would have been an admission of defeat. So Byrne mapped out a journey west – a grand adventure. Alison would join her independent, pioneering sister and brother-in-law on their Colorado ranch while Byrne and Duncan would join the well-established colonies of writers and artists who had found both inspiration and recognition in New Mexico – from Willa Cather to D.H. Lawrence and Robert Henri to Georgia O'Keefe. A part of her hoped that Duncan would mingle and draw inspiration from the literary colleagues he might find there. But she hesitated to say it out loud. She could still hear his defiant, gilded voice on the day they met at the writers' group in Central Park: "Real writers don't need groups."

He dozed through the long drive West in the Volvo station wagon – curled up on the back seat through loamy Arkansas, desolate Oklahoma and spare west Texas. Alison rode in silence too – sitting in the front passenger seat with her window rolled down, letting her outstretched arm and hand rudder through steady, warm winds. When they reached Colorado, she was to be deposited or reunited with

Jane. Her assessment of the plan depended on her mood. Of the three westward-bound Millers, only Byrne allowed the stark freedom of the landscape to lift and thrill her. She drove with the front seat pushed all the way back to accommodate legs meant more for the stage than a station wagon. With her chin up-thrust and wrists draped over the top of the steering wheel, she could just as easily have been racing a horse-drawn chariot around a Roman coliseum.

She entered Santa Fe like it was a victory lap – using her New England teaching credentials and innate showmanship to win a place on the faculty of St. John's College and to teach movement and improvisation at the fledgling Institute for American Indian Arts. In short order, she found a traditional adobe house on Canyon Road with enough spare rooms for visiting daughters and to house her own dance studio.

The headline in the Sunday, October 17, 1965, edition of *The Santa Fe New Mexican* announced, "Modern Dance School Opened in Santa Fe by N.Y. Dancer." Byrne overwhelmed the local reporter with her far-away and long-ago credentials, and the article mixed and matched the names and companies of Lucas Hoving, Elizabeth Rockwell and a dozen other famous dancers who had studied under or performed with them. She offered classes in basic techniques for all ages, but Byrne lured in non-traditional students with more exotic promises. Younger students would explore the five senses as sources for dance inspiration.

"They learn to paint a dance – and to dance a painting," the article expressed. "A collection of percussion instruments, from a huge Congo drum to castanets, and including instruments from Haiti, Mexico and Japan, inspires the students."

Santa Fe proved a welcoming and open-minded laboratory for reinvention, and not just for Byrne. It took her less than a year to position Duncan as the man she still believed he could be. The headline of a July 31, 1966, article in *The Sante Fe New Mexican* declared, "Miller Pair to direct Fiesta Melodrama."

"It's a marvelous opportunity to showcase your talent," she told Duncan. This time, Byrne was the one who wrote the press release to advertise his new position, and there was no mention of petty copy jobs. Forty years after the artist Will Shuster made the fiesta famous for the annual burning of a giant "Old Man Gloom" marionette, the emerging novelist Duncan Miller would leave his mark on the venerable Santa Fe tradition.

"The husband and wife team of Duncan and Byrne Miller are directing the Fiesta Melodrama which will be performed Aug. 31 at the Santa Fe community theater," the un-bylined article began. "Duncan Miller wrote and directed television scripts for the Television Bureau in NY before coming to Santa Fe. As a professional writer and newspaperman, he has been on the staff of both the Daily Mirror and World Telegram of NYC and Time Magazine. Though busy writing a fictional novel based on his recent experiences in the Virgin Islands, Miller has volunteered to make this year's Fiesta Melodrama the very best of all."

In Santa Fe, Byrne resolved to be more than a too-late typist caught off guard by the spiraling emotions that she knew could trap her husband's talent. She would create a new identity for him and then stitch herself into that costume, making sure of forward progress. For the Fiesta Melodrama, she and Duncan worked together, batting ideas about until one stuck – a satire about the controversy surrounding the round, "territorial" design of the new state capitol building. Byrne volunteered to manage the casting and staging of whatever Duncan created. The fiesta itself would be a deadline, a trigger to bring alive the confident Duncan who had once been able to command an impressive salary in Manhattan.

For months, he paced the portal that ran along the length of their adobe house at 203 Canyon Road, his pipe in one hand and a writing notebook in the other. When ideas came to him, he shoved the pipe between his lips and exhaled through the corner of his mouth, keeping his hands free to scribble down dialog or exposition. He eased into a curved leather Equipal chair to sharpen his pencils or refill his pipe, catching the loose crumbs of tobacco in a soft Mexican blanket folded on his lap. Byrne kept a pot of soup simmering in the kitchen that formed one end of a tiled interior patio, ready to replenish her husband's body whenever his mind reached a good stopping place.

When Duncan finally handed Byrne his completed, handwritten play to type for the actors, she swallowed at the title: *The Sinister Secret of the Sawdust Sepulcher, or, A Capital Conspiracy*. She considered all the gentle ways she could suggest another, less convoluted and arrogant-sounding title. It would take up the entire playbill, for one thing, and could easily be interpreted as newcomers imposing New York aesthetics on a culture they knew nothing about. But in 32 years of marriage to a man she considered her intellectual superior, Byrne had never critiqued his work and she convinced herself the wordiness of the title was a sign that Duncan's curse was broken. However strange and disjointed, he was putting new words to paper and putting *The Silenced Island* behind him.

She was tempted to place all the early versions of that tormented manuscript at the feet of the giant effigy whose annual burning kicked off the Santa Fe Fiesta. Old Man Gloom's bonfire was the night before their play debuted, and Duncan gripped her hand in his and pressed through the crowd to take their place with all the other artists, performers and organizers in the front row. Red- and white-costumed "fire spirit" dancers hopped and pranced around the small fires that dotted the stage, their wild chants and grunts building anticipation and whipping the crowd into a spirit of transformation. Bursts of fireworks sparkled against the black backdrop of the Santa Fe night.

"Burn it! Burn it!" the crowd of onlookers chanted as fiesta volunteers raised the figure of Zozobra, Old Man Gloom, high above the stage.

"I should, I should," Byrne thought to herself. The flames that licked a destructive path up to Zozobra's blood red mouth, vacant green eyes and plastered white ears burned everything in their path, symbolizing the collective hardship and disappointment of the preceding year. It would have been so easy to toss her hidden doubts and heartache on the stage. As Zozobra's muslin robes and light wooden frame caught fire, the draw of oxygen would inhale the redundant pages of *The Silenced Island* as kindling. Out of the ashes, a new novel might rise.

"Burn it! Burn it!" continued the hypnotic chants, causing Byrne to jump when Duncan slid his arm around her waist and rose up on his tiptoes to speak into her ear.

"Paganism at its artistic finest. How fitting to celebrate the fulcrum of our future."

His face was pink with heated purpose and his fire-brightened eyes burned to the core of Byrne's guilty fantasy. Duncan had never, in their entire marriage, judged the worth of any effort she undertook, even when it was to support the dreams of another man. Knowing that her belief in him had faltered, even for a moment, shamed her. She would never destroy his manuscripts; she would champion them instead. She would take charge of sending *The Silenced Island* to editors in New York and re-dedicate herself to finding a publisher who would validate Duncan's efforts. So what if his writing seemed self-indulgent and the language, at times, coarse? It couldn't be anything more shocking than what editors found when they accepted journals and manuscripts from the likes of Anaïs Nin, William S. Burroughs, Jack Kerouac or Allen Ginsberg. She would re-type page after page of whatever Duncan was compelled to write if doing so fueled the flame that first drew her to him. Duncan's fire was what kept her warm and on that August Santa Fe night it was enough that they were there together, just the two of them, starting over.

As the embers of Old Man Gloom swirled around the feet of the fire spirit dancers, Byrne wondered if Alison's absence was the reason she felt lighter. She looked to the sky and instead of a foreboding blackness, she saw only a lack of color. When she shuffled into the inner patio of her adobe house the next morning with a cup of tea, the sky that greeted her upturned eyes was not the heavy blue of expectation and disappointment but the brilliant blue of peace and purpose.

That Duncan had found peace and purpose too revealed itself to Byrne when she read the first handwritten page of his new novel, *The Air Drawn Dagger*.

Perhaps it is strange that I do not remember her name or see her face, yet see the opal in her hands clearly. But that may be the way of memory which, like a river rolling on to its mouth, picks up debris along the way.

She wondered, for a second, who Duncan was trying to remember, then kept reading.

The first of the things which I touch for the last time is the fire opal I gave to the little girl who used to play in the tree house with me …

She held the single, fluttering page to her heart and inhaled the remembered fragrance of the white oak tree in Cream Hill.

30

We are capable of bearing so much more than we pretend.

~Byrne

Duncan's Dance

BEAUFORT – 1993

A SMALL GROUP OF friends gathered in front of wild
azaleas on the banks of the Beaufort River after Duncan
Miller died. There were no speeches, no recitations of
accomplishments or readings from his novels. Instead,
his favorite lines from Shakespeare lifted up and over the
banks. The famous monologue from *As You Like It* ferried
Duncan's spirit to the outgoing tide. "All the world's a
stage, and all the men and women merely players. They
have their exits and their entrances and one man in his
time plays many parts."

Duncan hadn't wanted a funeral and directed that his
body be donated to the Medical University of South Carolina for research. Alison sent a telegram from Colorado,
but when the time came, Byrne couldn't read it aloud.

"All this time I thought I was ready," she apologized to
the hands-clasped group before her. Her voice wavered but
her eyes released no tears. "I told myself I was ready but,
Duncan, my darling, I am not."

Inside the house, it was as if a hurricane had blown
through and sucked out all of the humidity. Hospice

volunteers retrieved Duncan's hospital bed and wheelchair. The details of his death hung in the stillness, bone dry, but it was in a dance created by one of Byrne's collected daughters that his loss was clear.

Judean was Byrne's most dedicated and advanced student. She made the 50-mile drive from Savannah to Beaufort each Saturday to take Byrne's two-hour class in a tiny YMCA activity room. But one Saturday after Duncan died, Judean rented a studio in Savannah so that there would be space enough for a crowd of dancers. She lured Byrne out of Beaufort with a request to teach a master class and surprised her with a dance tribute to Duncan.

It began with two women in unitards, Judean and another dancer, gliding across the floor of the sun-streaked studio. They danced for an audience consisting only of other students stretched out on mats and draped on a ballet *barre*.

Byrne stood in a ballet position, wide fourth, supported by Duncan's cane. Her chin was tilted, neck elongated and her upper body weaved slightly, as if a breeze was lifting and swaying her. She beamed with the sum total of all her life experiences, beautiful and tragic.

Judean's delicate face, always softened in smile outside of class, was deep in concentration. She danced not for an audience but for a memory. In an intimate, internal way, her chin and eyes followed the movements she created. She looked at the hand, the arm, the leg, but saw something far away.

The music pulled and swept both women across the studio, upstage and downstage, leaping above the floor and sinking level with it. They danced the same steps, each leading and following like a spiral, never looking at each other for timing or reassurance. It was a duet of equals, both bodies interpreting the movements in unison, individual and not identical.

There was strength in the separateness, tenderness in the connection. It was impossible to tell which dancer represented Byrne and which Duncan. The connection of a steady partnership was the whole Judean honored – more than *grand jeté* and *pirouettes* of passion and devotion.

The dancers moved apart, one following a few beats behind the other. The music slowed and faltered as Judean's movements reduced and contracted. She reached a point on the sidelines of the dance floor and stopped, arms slowly lowering to her sides. She was Shakespeare in the azalea garden then, spirit freed from muscle and bone. At her feet, her partner lowered to the floor, back curved over gathered legs. She hugged herself as she rolled and recovered, rolled and recovered, in a smaller and smaller circle until the music stopped and all was still.

That was when Byrne allowed herself to cry.

31

If the family you're given cannot make you happy,

or vice versa,

collect another.

~Byrne

The Walls Between

SANTA FE – 1967

BYRNE AND DUNCAN did not set out to replace Alison, but the terracotta and rose backdrop of the desert Southwest all but erased their pale, drifting daughter. When the dust settled out of the thin, dry air of Santa Fe, it was a young Navajo man who stood at the center of their new world. Ben became the first of Byrne's collected children. She discovered him among the curious students who signed up to take her modern dance class at the newly opened St. John's College. Years later, Duncan would proudly write of him as their Navajo son and would name characters after him in future novels.

It was Duncan who suggested inviting the St. John's students, including Ben, to dinner at the house on Canyon Road. "They're probably all homesick and could use a break from campus," he said. "And you can give a master class in our studio to whet their appetites."

Ben helped Byrne peel carrots and scavenge through drawers for spices and dried fruits that might complement the ham hock simmering in a giant cauldron.

"This clunky apparatus is meant for canning fruits and vegetables," Byrne said, adding water to her concoction, "but it's the only vessel big enough for the task at hand, so I'm teaching it a new role tonight: Hungarian soup kettle."

Ben leaned over the speckled blue metal pot, closed his ember-black eyes and inhaled the soup's aroma.

"It is good. This way you never have to end the making of the soup," he said. Byrne turned the heat down to let the soup simmer and steered Ben by his broad shoulders to the room she had converted into a dance studio.

"This is where the real magic happens," she said. She pulled a tall stool behind an even taller drum and perched so she could grip the base with her knees. "Dancers, let's begin."

Ben sat cross-legged on the floor in front of Byrne as other students, mostly women, paired up to stretch each other's legs and arms. Even Duncan joined in, trading his customary cabled sweater and corduroy pants for black long john leggings and a white t-shirt.

"Reporting for duty," he announced, winking at Ben. "Young Ben here cannot be expected to lift all these ladies by himself."

The three became regular companions. On weekends, Byrne and Duncan picked up Ben from campus in their aging Volvo station wagon and went on long drives in the surrounding desert. The Millers told Ben of how they met in the Central Park writers' group that Duncan promptly disavowed and later how they married twice – once in secret. Ben sat in the back seat, brown arms stretched out on either side of him as wide as the skies, absorbing it all without comment.

"Jump in anytime," Byrne teased him, winking into the rearview mirror. "If not with questions, then with your own stories of conquered love."

"But I don't wish to interrupt," Ben said, leaning forward, folding his arms between the head rests of the two front seats, resting his chin on his wrists and listening so intently to their stories that they became part of his memory.

He took them to meet his family near Lukachukai, Arizona, where he had lived until he was sent off the reservation as a teen to learn English at a federal boarding school. From a distance, the two domed structures Duncan drove toward looked like termite mounds rising from the earth itself. But Ben explained they were traditional, eight-sided *hooghans* with doors facing east, dirt floors and roofs made of logs. "The stone one is where I stay, and the other *hooghan* is where my father stays."

His parents were the same age as Byrne and Duncan but they, too, refrained from asking questions of the imposing pair who seemed so interested in their son.

"When you come to Santa Fe to visit Ben, it would be our honor if you would stay with us, at our house," Duncan offered before leaving.

"Will they accept?" Byrne asked Ben on the long drive back.

He considered her question for several minutes before answering. "My mother has not left the lands, but Father, yes. He is Catholic and speaks English."

With Ben as their companion, Byrne and Duncan had access to more Navajo culture than other wandering artists and academics passing through Santa Fe in the 1960s. Byrne, in particular, was fascinated with the native dances.

"Can you arrange for us to attend a powwow, or some other kind of ceremony where they perform your dances?" she asked.

Ben considered the question and then pointed to a spot on Duncan's tattered map. "We will have to go here," he said.

"But why so far from Lukachukai?" Duncan asked.

Ben explained that his clan family did not have a ceremonial healer who used dancing.

"But now they have you," Byrne exclaimed. "You're a wonderful dancer."

Ben pointed to the map. "It has to be arranged. Your parents have to commit you to that healing path when you are born."

He didn't tell Byrne how his mother had reacted when he had told her of his growing interest in dance and how Byrne had offered to prepare him to audition for professional companies when he finished college, or to show him the art of teaching dance if that's what he preferred.

"Our people are not allowed to dance," Ben's mother responded. "You know this is not our way."

Ben did not interrupt or question her, but his face must have betrayed his disappointment.

"Even clans that use dance to heal do not dance for entertainment," she said. Ben only realized that his mother was pausing the discussion, not ending it, when she caught him practicing one weekend. He was using the top rail of an out-of-sight wooden sheep corral as a ballet *barre*. His mother watched him rehearse his *pliés, battements* and *développés* without saying anything. She watched him when he stepped away from his makeshift *barre* and practiced the isolations and spiraling twists of modern dance. She had not said anything to the elders.

Ben was still thinking of his mother's silence when Byrne patted his hand and playfully snatched the map from him. "Let's go to this other community you recommend, but trust me, parents have nothing to do with picking this particular path. You find dance on your own."

Byrne found the colorful Navajo ribbon dance to be her favorite – with the dancers weaving fabric streaks of white, turquoise, yellow, black and red into complicated patterns through a central space. Ben explained how the ribbons represented the seasons of life and the six directions, but

Byrne saw more than symbolism in the choreography.

"It's rhythmic, almost hypnotic," she said, patting the tops of her thighs in time to the drums.

The unsmiling, moccasin-footed dancers moved with the softness of rabbits and the spring of desert deer.

"Wonderful use of the *plié*," she continued. "It's as if they're afraid to trample or offend the soil." She was searching for words to express the constrained solemnity she saw, the separateness of men and women portraying their traditional roles. "It's so … representational."

To Duncan, later, she would confide how beautiful yet repressed the native dances seemed to her. "In a way it is both elevating dance to spiritual importance and reducing it at the same time – to formula and repetition."

Duncan merely grunted agreement. He was too busy jotting down thoughts and observations in the spiral notebook at the side of his rustic Mexican chair. Byrne went inside to prepare for bed. She removed the desert dust from her hair with the soft bristles of her grandmother's ivory-handled brush. She unclasped the coral and turquoise bracelet she bought on Ben's reservation and placed it on the middle shelf of the simple glass vitrine that had belonged to her mother. And when she was naked in front of the long mirror with a nightdress ready to pull over her head, she saw Duncan's reflection, watching her.

"You are marvelous," he whispered, and she let the fabric drop to the tiled floor instead. This was perhaps her favorite dance of all, the one that changed every time she was inspired to perform it. The music that accompanied her in her mind varied with the light, with the hour, with Duncan's urgency. This night it was a resonant, rumbling drumbeat that drew her to the bed. Instead of soaring over their thrusting bodies the drumbeat kept her grounded, a part of him. The steady rhythm of it sustained her connection to

Duncan through the night and into the next day, when the first of his rejection letters arrived in Santa Fe.

"Darling, would you mind opening this envelope and reading its contents to me?" Duncan asked. "Listening to whatever they have to say through your voice will temper it at least."

The letter he handed to Byrne would be followed by 20 other rejections. They came from all the biggest publishers of the day: Curtis Brown, Doubleday, Harcourt Brace, Alfred Knopf and Houghton Mifflin – most just standard rejection slips or notes with courteous platitudes. But Burroughs Mitchell of Scribner's at least turned Duncan down with flair.

Byrne's eyes scanned over the lengthy response, stopping on phrases that Duncan might find comforting. "Your ability is so strongly evident in *The Silenced Island,* and the core of it is an intensely imagined story," she began.

Duncan's chin lifted, just a little, and Byrne continued in her cheeriest voice. "It seemed to all of us who read it ..." She paused, looking down at Duncan sitting in his favorite chair. "It's made the rounds, darling. That's something, isn't it?"

He pulled his chin into his neck and tilted his head, seeing through her veil of encouragement. Byrne found where she left off and continued.

"...to all of us who read it that you had realized your hero and heroine and their intricate relationship in a remarkably interesting way."

Duncan interrupted. "Let me play editor now. Skip to the unfortunately, comma, won't you, darling?"

Byrne cleared her throat. "It is an unpleasant duty to have to decline the work of so able a writer."

"Far more unpleasant for me, I'm afraid," Duncan said, standing to pat Byrne's hand. "Would you mind filing it for future reference? I've got to get back to work."

Duncan's new novel, it seemed to Byrne, was both a startling and promising departure from his earlier work. Duncan was using the typewriter himself, transferring pleasing passages from hand-scribbled notes to neat paragraphs he could cut and paste like stanzas of a poem. He described *The Air Drawn Dagger* as dealing with injustice, a familiar theme, but this time injustice centered on a Southwestern battle between the "Anglo" and Spanish descendants. It abandoned the pretense of second person and started, more naturally, with a first-person narrator as protagonist.

To Byrne, the writing opened like a deep sigh, as if responding to a gentle reader rather than declaring or demanding reaction.

> *Yes, I tell myself, I am loved! Look at the glass case on the table at the foot of the bed. It is filled with mementos of those who loved me! Home is where the heart is. I have no other home than that glass vitrine, which contains all the furniture of my life, there on those three glass shelves within the foot-square walls and ceilings of glass.*

Byrne smiled to herself. Duncan was describing Fanny's delicate, steel-hinged glass box – the see-through treasure chest where Byrne kept her Navajo bracelet, silver rings and other artifacts of their nomadic life. Duncan watched her open it every morning when she dressed and close it at night when she undressed. But the very next line in the manuscript suggested he felt something different about the ritual.

> *I wish I could be free. I wish I could shatter my glass home and cast into the canyons and deserts all the memories embodied in the objects lying rampant, ready to spring out at me from those glass shelves.*

Instinctively, Byrne reached out to touch the glass case, as if to protect it. She ran her fingers along its delicate, welded steel edges and rubbed a fleck of dirt from its clear surface. She counted the glass shelves. There were three, just as he had described, layered within walls and ceilings of glass. But what was precious and comforting to her was somehow constricting to Duncan. After 34 years of marriage, there were still mysteries between them – like why he never spoke of his family or his life before she saved him from it.

Until he asked her to, she vowed to read no further. The walls between them were not ones Duncan wanted to discuss. But how could she help him, then? How could she free him to fly through the canyons and deserts without the memories that clearly haunted him?

She sat at the foot of the bed and stared into the vitrine until the answer came to her. She could still see through the walls. Duncan's heart was transparent to her even if his past was not. If he so desperately wanted to be free of walls that he was willing to put his pain into words, then she would make it the focus of her work, too. They would move side-by-side along the same path, always making forward progress.

"Duncan, darling, you've inspired me," she told him at dinner that night. She brought the glass vitrine from the bedroom and placed it on the center of their heavy, hand-carved Mexican dining room table. "All this time I've been teaching students the choreography of others. I've deciphered and notated the choreography of a giant in the field of modern dance. But I have never created a full length performance piece myself."

Duncan reached for her hand. "Every time you walk into a room, it is a dance," he said. "But I admit it is rather criminal of me to hoard such talent."

Byrne placed a tea candle at every corner of the glass vitrine and handed Duncan a box of matches to begin lighting their tiny wicks.

"I have a title for the piece already," she said as four delicate flames struggled for oxygen to leap to life. "If you'll permit me some slight plagiarism I'll call it *The Walls Between*. It will explore all the ways we divide ourselves from each other."

Emotions flickered over Duncan's face like an ancient cave drawing illuminated by the torchlight of a hesitant audience. His eyes were glint and shadow both. His breath quickly caught then returned to stillness in exhale.

"There is more to this than one performance," he said at last. "*The Walls Between* should be the debut of your own company: The Byrne Miller Dance Theatre."

They were the Miller Pair again, each the other's biggest champion, and the adobe house on Canyon Road was their chrysalis. Instead of holding auditions that would divide and intimidate her students, Byrne found roles in the cast for them all – including Ben.

"I don't see you partnering with another man, or a woman," she explained to Ben. "I haven't worked it all out but I want you to convey a sense of apartness."

She gave him a prop to partner instead: a rattan chair with sturdy wooden legs and graceful, gently curving arms.

"I will choreograph the steps but you will give them meaning," she told him. "The chair can be anyone you want, anyone you miss. I don't want you to tell me who it is. I want to know who it is and what she means to you when I watch you dance."

Ben sat cross-legged in the Canyon Road studio and took it all in without asking questions. He closed his eyes and listened when Duncan played the music composed for the dance by noted jazz trumpeter Jack Loeffler. The rhythms were unfamiliar but inviting.

"Don't try to count the beats," Byrne said, resting her hands on his shoulders. Ben stiffened, but didn't interrupt.

"Do you feel the pauses? Those are the holes we will fill with magnificent leaps through the air."

Without asking questions, he stood when Byrne asked him to stand. He marked out the steps when she asked him to move. He followed her instructions when she wanted the men to cluster in a knot, fists gripped and chins thrust forward as they moved across the floor together.

"You're a pack. Hunters. Your survival depends on being in unison."

Their movements were too tentative and Byrne swept in front of them to demonstrate. "Feet flexed," she ordered, "We're not ballerinas. Now use your *pliés*. Pound the floor. Tear down walls. Show me!"

In class, Byrne simply instructed and Ben knew where to stand and when to take his turn. In rehearsals, he was more instrument than student, tool more than chosen son. Byrne experimented with the bodies of her dancers, spacing and posing them in constantly changing combinations, tempos and direction.

This was like no dance he had ever seen at a Navajo healing or Blessingway celebration. There, the steps were learned comforts: stars explained and stories re-lived. Byrne was not passing down rituals, she was creating her own. Instruction got in the way of inspiration. She didn't take the time to explain her frustrations or parse the difference between abandoning a fleeting idea and finding fault with the skills of those who attempted to articulate it.

Even so, Ben came to the Canyon Road adobe house night after night for rehearsals, along with students from St. John's and older dancers Byrne had recruited from the community. He did not miss rehearsals even when his grandmother died and everyone else in his family went to the funeral on the reservation. He couldn't interrupt the passion of Byrne's vision, let alone ask for permission to grieve. But when Byrne wanted him to leap through a curtained backdrop, into the waiting hands of four other male dancers, he could not do her bidding.

"I do not trust that they will catch me," he said.

"It is not your job to trust them," Byrne replied, gripping a wad of her long, silk dance skirt in irritation. "It is mine."

She did not apologize when, after he did find the courage to leap through the curtain, the four male dancers crouching on the other side could not stop Ben's momentum and he landed on his knees.

The dancers helped him up, morose with apologies, but Byrne cut in.

"Good instincts, men. At least your hands broke the fall," she excused them. "And you, Ben, magnificent! You held a perfect stag forward leg position even in the landing. I had no idea you could do that leap. I'll put it in the opening act."

It was only when the rehearsals moved to the St. John's College stage that the power of the current Ben had been swept into became clear. He saw a hundred empty seats in the auditorium, seats that would be filled with strangers watching him.

"It's not Lincoln Center but it's a start," Byrne whispered in his ear as he stared out into the black sea of space below the stage. "Congratulations. You are a principal dancer in the Byrne Miller Dance Theatre."

A cold weight settled in the small of his back and he was suddenly, uncomfortably thirsty. He worked his lips and tongue inside a mouth that couldn't open to form a protest. What had until then been an intense, exciting workshop in choreography and modern music would culminate in a public performance: dance for entertainment's sake. It was forbidden. He couldn't go through with it.

A wardrobe mistress came up behind him and tapped the back of his elbows with a measuring stick.

"Arms out, second position wide," she ordered, and ran her hands underneath his outstretched arms and across his chest.

"The costume needs to be loose enough to move but tight enough to cling to those muscles," she said.

Ben jumped back when she pressed the top of the tape measure against his hip bones and squatted to the ground, eye-level with his pelvis.

"Relax. I don't bite," she laughed. "I'll just put you down for medium in tights, okay?"

He wanted to leap down from the stage and bolt through the darkened doors, but Byrne clapped her hands to begin the rehearsal, and dancers took their positions all around him as the music began. He had to tell Byrne to find a replacement for him, but not then. He would dance one last time, for himself. The movement settled into his muscle memory and stuck to his skin. The music lifted him, over the empty seats and into a space without fences or boundaries. He was free when he leaped above the stage, a stag released from gravity. He was home in the pack of hunters pounding the floor with flexed feet. He was fluent in his body, not dragged under the weight of a foreign language forced on him in a federal boarding school. He didn't need mirrors; the steps danced him.

And when it came time for his solo with the chair, he danced with his dead grandmother. All that he hadn't asked his elder, he told the chair. All that he hadn't dared, he danced instead. The steps Byrne gave him were the stars from which he drew a constellation. It was his grandmother's form that would float above him in the night sky, watching over his creation story. But it was Byrne who would take credit for it.

She listed his name and hometown in the April 21, 1968, edition of *The Sante Fe New Mexican*. She thought he would be proud, that he'd want to send the article to his parents and invite them to the upcoming performance. But the hands that she clutched with excitement had turned cold in her grasp.

"You don't understand," Ben said. "This belongs in the white world. Wearing makeup, performing, letting people look at your physical body and not your speech or your thoughts is your world, not mine."

Byrne hid the flash of panic that momentarily made her pale face even paler. Ben was one of her stars. She had no understudies to take his place if he refused to perform. She saw the desperation in his watery eyes as evidence of something almost like abuse. The ties to his past were strangling his future.

"I can explain it to your father for you," Byrne offered.

She still wanted to believe that her unwavering certainty and devoted dedication could repair anything – Alison's mind, Duncan's despondency. Ben was just being stubborn. Surely, his parents would listen to reason. Dance could be Ben's path to success and independence. He was beautiful, she would tell his parents. Their son was a trusting soul with a gift she had never been able to develop in her own children.

"It is my mother who decides all things Navajo. She must not know," Ben told her. Byrne was asking him to tear down a wall she couldn't see. "I will do this dance for you but I am very uneasy. To my people, dance is only for healing."

Byrne agreed to keep Ben's family unaware of the performance, not because she understood his reasons but because she understood secrets. She reminded herself that when she was Ben's age, she had kept her marriage to Duncan hidden from her family. She didn't think of the secret as a lie but as a wall between a passionate truth and her father's pride.

What Byrne hid from Ben, the wall that only she could see, was that she needed him. He was more than just her star pupil. When he danced she saw something she created, something joyous and wonderful, a reflection of herself. That light did not shine in Alison. Ben was proof it wasn't her fault.

He danced with his grandmother chair in front of people who had no idea of the risk he was taking. He displayed his body in a white man's world, wearing a costume that had nothing to do with the six directions or the seasons of life. He danced without realizing that *The Walls Between* was a healing ceremony – not for Ben, not for anyone in the audience of the Great Hall of St. John's College, but for Byrne Miller.

32

Happy Hop

Alongside neatly typed shopping lists, phone trees and schedules for upcoming Byrne Miller Dance Theatre concerts, it was easy to overlook the faded newspaper cartoon Byrne taped to the side of her refrigerator. It was a single cell of Snoopy, laughing and waving his arms, saying "If you can't dance, you should at least be able to do a happy hop."

In the first few months of widowhood, Byrne managed to keep dancing, but it seemed to me she had lost some of her happy hop. Without Duncan's cause to keep her in fighting form, I saw moments of fragility. When I drove away after visiting her each night, she still stood on the brick stoop to see me off. But the arm that waved goodbye looked worn out by the effort. It bent only at the wrist instead of an enthusiastic elbow.

Without Duncan watching her dress each morning, Byrne sometimes wore the same outfit two days in a row or forgot to put on earrings – even to meetings of her board of directors. She resisted pressure to slow down and present fewer performances each year. It was a slippery slope, she said, and the university would pounce on any signs of weakness.

The state arts commission, responsible for most of her grants, began to question the Byrne Miller Dance Theatre's plan of succession, and I suspected she was grooming me, along with the other daughters she had collected. The expectation was as heavy as the humid air. I didn't want to think of the day when Byrne could no longer defend challenges to her artistic supremacy. I was still a chick in the nest of Byrne's conviction, able to fly away each day but content to return and feed on our screen porch conversations.

She never asked about the stories I reported on each day or commented on such trivial aspects of my job as a new shade of lipstick or a different part in my anchor helmet hair. Instead, she would wait until I poured us each a glass of wine and then ask how the documentary was coming. In between city council meetings and court cases, I was filming the story of an effort to preserve the Gullah culture through its music.

She was as excited as I was when I got permission to film a river baptism and record the spirituals sung by the audience on the banks. When I arrived at a title – *God's Gonna Trouble the Water* – she raised a toast in delight.

"How perfectly foreboding," she exclaimed. "*Wade in the Water* would have been too predictable."

Without being able to devote myself to the documentary full time, I knew it would be years before I finished it. By then I doubted Byrne would be able to watch it. The sight in her eyes continued to fade. She saw the fringes of whatever passed in front of them – the lovely border on a piece of stationary but not the words themselves, the arch of a dancer's pointed foot but not the extended leg, the children riding tricycles on the sidewalk but not the traffic on the road ahead. She abandoned the leafy shade of the magnolia tree, where she had always parked her car, in favor of the baking hot but open expanse of the front lawn. Instead of using the rearview mirror, the back bumper informed her when she parked too close to another car on her daily errands in town. Eventually there was a fender bender, no one hurt, and she asked me to come with her to stand in front of Judge Ned Tupper.

"I could use some moral support, reprobate that I am," she said. "It wouldn't hurt if you wore that darling yellow dress with the low-cut back."

I knew the judge from covering his courtroom for the news. He managed to swagger with masculinity even under the shapeless folds of a black robe. A deep tan set off sparkling blue eyes, and he was known throughout Beaufort for his flirtatious, mischievous sense of humor. I hesitated for a minute, wondering what kind of mother figure would parade her collected daughter in front of the court as she was suggesting. But Byrne saw it simply as an opportunity to advance her own cause. She knew full well that the judge was a bigger fan of television news than modern dance.

"Teresa, I need to talk to you," Judge Tupper said before the proceedings began. He was holding the docket, so he already knew that it was Byrne facing a moving violation and not me. There was a theatrical crinkle in his brow, and I knew he was up to something when he motioned me over to the corner of the courtroom, where no one else could hear. "Your dress is on backward," he whispered, pretending to be concerned.

"That's so low, you owe me one," I laughed.

Then his smile faded. "If I go easy on her, you must promise to convince her to give up driving."

"I promise," I told him.

"I'm going to hold you to that. The next person she whacks into better not be me."

Byrne got the lowest fine allowed under the law, Judge Tupper didn't take away her license, and her courtroom victory put a spring in her step that I hadn't seen since before Duncan died. The Byrne who had performed nearly naked in vaudeville shows, handed out communist leaflets during the Vietnam War, and who told her collected daughters to have affairs was back. Nothing so plebian as haranguing would convince her to give up her independence and stop driving. She would simply arch her eyebrows in defiance and tie any moral argument in knots. No, I would have to employ techniques of persuasion that she herself perfected: subtle innuendo, personal anecdote or creative alternative presented with great spontaneity and enthusiasm.

"Byrne, it occurs to me that since neither one of us finds grocery shopping or doctor's visits particularly interesting, we could combine our errands on the weekends," I suggested on the Saturday after her court appearance. "I can do the driving and your role will be to keep me awake and entertained."

If she knew what I was doing, she was graceful enough to pretend otherwise. Not that I was being altogether duplicitous. Even picking out the ripest grapefruit from the Piggly Wiggly was entertaining when accompanied by Byrne. She held them at arm's length, squeezing and circling her wrists in my direction and giving an exaggerated wink with her good eye.

"Let it not be said that sweet and luscious melons are the most sensual of fruit," she declared. "A little tart goes a long way too."

It felt good to be her conspirator, a relief to make her laugh. We made grand, goofy entrances together, me bowing as I presented a shopping cart for her to lean against. Most of all, I looked forward to long drives with Byrne. We combined doctor visits in Charleston with dance performances; lab tests in Savannah with art exhibits. Both cities took at least an hour to reach from Beaufort on two-lane roads through arched canopies of live oaks and swamps of cypress and saw-tooth palm. We paralleled the island-dotted coastline 30 miles inland. The scent of the breezes that followed the tannic, black-water rivers on their way to the sea was earthier than those that drifted over our screened porch conversations. When the sun was a gauzy white net cast over vast salt marshes, something like a trance fell over me. I was drawn, eyes forward, into the beauty of the place that bound me to the woman at my side.

It was on these drives that I slowly offered up the past that I had kept from Byrne. How I met Sonny. How long ago I had known it was over but kept making excuses for him. Why I had never told. I could slip these secrets into the silences, between bridges, across savannahs, and know that I would not be pressed for more than I was willing. I kept my eyes on the road so I was freed from looking at Byrne's reaction, safe from any judgment. I learned to trust that none would come, only gentle questions and soft segues into mistakes she too had made. And when we invited other daughters along, these drives became a chance for me to learn what bound me to her collected daughters.

It seemed ages earlier that I had met Lisa and Lillian in the Martha Graham master class. Duncan's decline had kept us in constant overlapping circles, more like members of the same team than friends. I knew what worried these women and how they handled stress but not what delighted them. That changed when Byrne announced that she had free tickets for dance performances at Spoleto, the 17-day fine arts festival in Charleston.

"It's one of the perquisites of being a presenter," she said, grinning. "No company turns down a Byrne Miller request to see a performance. It's like getting a free audition."

Byrne had remembered to put in earrings, and they were dancing a happy hop. "One of my children, Marlena, has an apartment in Charleston," Byrne began to explain. I'd heard stories of a brilliant German architect working in Charleston who spent the weekends at home in Beaufort. She had been a Saturday student of Byrne's for years. "Since Marlena will be in Beaufort, she says we're welcome to stay at her apartment. Our only expense will be meals and I insist on treating."

I hadn't been to Charleston since the immigration interview. I was avoiding anything that reminded me of my impending divorce, and Charleston was where the lie of my marriage had been consummated. Still, I longed for Byrne to dress up in her long black skirt and jeweled collar once again. For Spoleto, she would paint her lips with color, even without Duncan watching. So I volunteered to play chauffer, mostly for an excuse to eavesdrop.

Lisa served on Byrne's board of directors, seconding motions with a Swiss-German accent as proper as her posture. But all I knew of her softer side was that she baked breads, cakes and ginger cookies to take to the dancers, backstage, after each Byrne Miller Dance Theatre performance. I'd seen ballerinas beg for more of her nut cake or another slice of buttery yeast bread. They told themselves it couldn't be fattening – not when the smiling woman who made it was so tall and muscular. Lisa started dance too late in life to twirl and leap and bend like a dancer, but she studied with Byrne long enough to sit like one, walk like one, stand like one.

Mary was the physical opposite of Lisa, compact and curvy, with masses of fading blond curls that bounced with every giggle. She taught art and ran a chamber music series at the university, but I knew her mostly as the lady with the wine glasses. For university concerts and fundraisers, as well as for Byrne's, Mary stuffed her Alpha Romeo with padded boxes of stemware – hundreds of sparkling, clean glasses delivered on demand. She fluttered over catering tables like a butterfly, smoothing flat the linen tablecloths and adjusting bottles in the ice bucket to their most inviting angles.

"Mary's here," Byrne declared as we put our overnight bags into the trunk. "Now the festivities can begin!"

"Let's play the usual game," Lisa said, once we left the city limits of Beaufort. "Since we three are now four, I want to know how Teresa would arrange the world."

I drove over the Whale Branch River, open windows drawing in the breeze of brackish water. The banks on either side were black with pluff mud, still slick, like they'd just slipped out of the current.

"Marvelous idea," Byrne said. "Oh driver, darling, can you concentrate both on the road ahead and what you would change if you were God? It makes Highway 17 ever so much more interesting."

"For the time being," I said, "I'll exercise first right of refusal. The world looks just about perfect to me."

Groans greeted me from the backseat and Byrne swiveled to shush them.

"She's young and naive," she said. "We have the whole weekend to cure that. Mary, you go first."

"Small things first," Mary began. "If I were God, I'd make Spoleto come to Beaufort, just for our convenience."

Lisa interrupted, laughing. "Don't you dare. I like to get away from time to time."

"That's it!" Mary exclaimed. "What we really need is time travel and a concierge who could get us front row tickets to any performance we've ever dreamed of."

By the time we reached the fresh water swamps and swaths of abandoned rice fields along Highway 17, weighty solutions to the world's troubles swirled through the open windows. Fanciful laws were decreed. Imaginary funds were bestowed. I drove a party of dictators, lavishly generous to those deemed deserving.

Miles passed in uninterrupted conversation, and I was almost disappointed to reach the congested snarl of traffic lights that marked the outskirts of Charleston. I still hadn't figured out how I would change the world until I drove past the building where I had talked an immigration officer into granting Sonny a green card. Suddenly I knew how a world with me as God would operate.

"Divorces would be completely private," I declared. "If the man runs back to Mexico, the woman would never have to advertise it for three weeks in the newspaper for everyone to see."

There. I'd said it, even if no one in the back seat of the car knew what I was talking about. Sonny had not responded to any court documents delivered since our separation had begun. As the person petitioning for divorce, I had to prove that I'd done everything I could to find him. According to the same byzantine South Carolina laws that recognized co-habitation as marriage, I was required to advertise our upcoming divorce so that anyone who might know where Sonny was could inform him of the shocking news.

"I didn't know you were married," Lisa said. "I thought that person was just your boyfriend."

"I never told anyone except Byrne and a man inside that building," I said, pointing to the immigration office. "It's like it was a different lifetime, and I can't bear the thought of dredging it all back up again and trying to explain what isn't explainable."

I told myself not to look in the rearview mirror for Lisa and Mary's reactions. I stared straight ahead, as if the highway was my teleprompter. After all, I sat at the WJWJ anchor desk each night, with perfect hair and perfect diction, and reported on arrests and convictions as if they happened in a different world than mine.

"On the bright side, no one other than you and the immigration officer knows this Sonny-person by his real name, right?" Byrne said. She meant it as a consolation. His name, listed in fine print under the word "defendant," would not set off any light bulbs. But it wasn't Sonny's identity I was trying to keep private.

"Try not to worry," Lisa said, squeezing my shoulders from the back seat. "The only people who read *The Beaufort Gazette* legals are people who snoop into foreclosures and dock permits. No one in his circle will ever see it."

The good part, in other words, was that no one was likely to track down Sonny and tell him when to show up in Beaufort Family Court. But every busybody in Beaufort would have the chance to read about their local news anchor getting a divorce. My name in the paper would transform me from news reporter to newsmaker.

But for two fragrant days of the Spoleto festival, I could put all that behind me. I was drawn in to a circle of confidence, each of Byrne's collected daughters unrestrained in her opinions and certain of her acceptance. When Byrne reached for a check, we got there first and split it evenly. We traded silk shoulder wraps, earrings and bracelets that matched another's outfit better. We took turns hailing bicycle rickshaws to fetch us from Marlena's sleek apartment and deliver us to dazzling performances.

"I am still capable of walking," Byrne protested on the first night. We were headed to the Dock Street Theatre, where Lillian had arranged to join the four of us. "But I will acquiesce to your collective judgment only because these rickshaw drivers have sublime physiques. Not quite the elongated lines of a dancer but thicker, more thrust."

She was adjusting to life after 60 years of marriage.

But instead of leaning back with the posture of a grieving widow, Byrne reclined with regal grace. She braced herself for the backward tilt of the tiny carriage. Her long legs jutted out precariously close to the bicyclist's behind, and she drew her face into mischievous contemplation.

"Couldn't I just blame the cobblestones?" she whispered, a sudden bump away from illicit contact.

We pedaled past stone walls dripping with purple wisteria blossoms and peered into the long, hidden gardens that slid between the antebellum mansions.

"I'll take that one," Lisa said as we passed a mansion with an in-ground lap pool lined with variegated hostas.

I looked at Byrne and saw her surveying all of Charleston's wealthy excess without a hint of envy. This was the woman who had cheerfully returned a fairy-tale gown to Saks 5th Avenue because Duncan's intent meant more to her than the gift itself.

"I can picture you floating in the water like a lily on a pad," she told Lisa. "Gloriously unclothed, of course. It makes a beautiful canvas in my mind."

When we arrived at the theater, Lillian greeted Byrne with a fanciful curtsy, like a maiden of a long-ago court. She was an altogether different woman from the one whose eyes had teared up on the steps of the Silver Slipper. Her relaxed shoulders floated far below her triumphant chin, and she stood in defiantly tall boots, towering over all the other patrons on the sidewalk. Her divorce had released the woman Byrne had always known Lillian was. The look that passed between them sparkled brighter than the rhinestones in Byrne's jeweled collar.

"I bet she took Byrne's advice after all," I whispered to Lisa. "She looks like a woman having an outrageous affair."

Byrne took Lillian's hand and stepped down from the rickshaw. "Now all I need is a carpet of roses at my feet and for the crowds to part. I must say I could get used to having my darlings all around me."

Five of us huddled over a program between acts, saved places for each other in the lines for powder rooms, and dissected the acoustics and lighting of every venue.

"I expect brilliance. Nothing less," Byrne said. "If you're going to be a snob, be unrepentant. Mediocrity is distasteful."

Byrne reveled in the company of women who understood her snobbery. And she relied on them to hold her back when that snobbery overcame civility. At one performance, hip-hop dancers in drab camouflage-patterned street clothes moving to a blasting beatbox prompted Byrne to lean forward and whisper, "Not terribly imaginative."

She removed her hearing aids. "That's better," she muttered, "muted to a dull roar."

Lisa and Lillian looked at each other and rolled their eyes. Mary gave us all an index finger shush, but her eyes locked onto Byrne's. There was a smattering of applause between movements and then a costume change into prison garb. Dancers swaggered across the stage, grabbing crotches and flashing gang symbols.

"When will they begin to dance?" Byrne grumbled. "This is half-hearted mime."

Suddenly patterns of projected light pummeled the stage, and graffiti appeared on the backdrop and side curtains in blood-red streaks.

"Is the choreographer trying to distract us from the lack of discernible movement?" Byrne complained in a voice muscling beyond a stage whisper. Her irritation was audible for rows around us.

Lisa drew her chin into her neck. Her feet were following the rhythm of the pounding music, and her fingers tapped the beat. She was making an attempt, at least, to feel the message.

"I've seen enough," Byrne declared, swinging her feet into the aisle. "I will never invite this company to perform for the Byrne Miller Dance Theatre, so let's go."

She was feeling around for the other end of her shoulder wrap when Lisa leaned over me and put a hand on Byrne's arm.

"I am not leaving until the first act is over," she said. The measured staccato of her accent gave the declaration gravity.

"Don't you recognize the superficiality?" Byrne said. Her tone was somewhere between exasperation and incredulity.

"I agree it's dreadful," Lisa said. Byrne let out a sigh, relieved. "But there are people in the audience enjoying this performance, and it shows disrespect for them to interrupt it."

It was the longest sentence I had ever heard Lisa say, and Byrne slouched back in her seat in resignation. At intermission, she attempted to redeem herself.

"Shall we stay for the next half?" she asked innocently. Lisa, Mary, Lillian and I burst out laughing.

"I'd love to but there's a bottle of Cabernet back at the apartment that must be close to room temperature by now," Lisa said.

She slid an arm through Byrne's and we marched out five-strong into the warm Charleston evening.

"I can't believe anyone would sit through more of that than we were able," Byrne said as we prepared dinner at Marlena's apartment.

I looked at Lisa, skinning cloves of garlic by crushing them between the heels of her palms, then mincing the flesh with lightning-fast blade work. She threw her head back and laughed.

Mary stepped in. "Not everyone knows as much about dance as you do, Byrne," she said, smothering the rebuke in praise.

So this is how you reason with Byrne, I said to myself. I thought of Judge Tupper and the promise I had made to keep Byrne off the road. I would need every trick I could learn from these women.

"I say if dance of any kind moves someone in the gut," Lisa said, "then it has some intrinsic value."

"Well said and point taken," Byrne said, raising her glass of wine with one hand while draping the other over the counter. With her feet planted in fourth position and her chin tilted up like Degas' sculpture of the 14-year-old dancer, her face was radiant with pride. I realized she was taking credit for Lisa. She took maternal, even boastful pride in a woman with the courage to contradict and challenge her.

"How did you manage to collect so many brilliant daughters?" I asked.

"My innate intelligence is surpassed only by my impeccable instincts," she answered. "Blood relatives are simply people you were born with, not necessarily people you are stuck with."

I recognized the womenism in her colorful quip and knew not to draw a literal line to Alison.

"If the one you're given cannot make you happy, or vice versa, then I say choose a family. It works magnificently for me. Just look around."

I did, and smiled at the women hand-selected for their strength, their dedication, their devotion. It was just as Byrne always said, one person could not possibly expect to be everything another needs. This was how she had survived the loss that would have broken an ordinary heart. She didn't ask any one of us to be everything she needed, or to even try. But taken together, she found in the women at her side what Duncan had found in her: a substitute family.

33

There is not a contract on earth,
let alone between a man and woman,
that cannot be rewritten.

~Byrne

Into Another Room

SANTA FE– 1969

IN THE SUSPENDED SECONDS before the impact, Byrne saw the paved road ahead of her as a center aisle. It stretched between rows of seats in front of a desert stage, floodlit in sunset red. She twisted her neck to the side, looking past the steering wheel that Duncan gripped, and wondered why there was suddenly a pickup truck in the wings. Her glasses lifted from her nose and cartwheeled in slow motion, the lenses catching and reflecting prisms of light before the stage went dark.

The drunk driver of the pickup truck that careened into the driver's side of the Millers' station wagon put Duncan in the intensive care wing of a Santa Fe hospital but left Byrne with only minor physical injuries. She could still walk like a dancer, sit like a dancer, bow like a dancer. But after nearly 40 years of partnering, she was forced into a solo. Duncan's absence was so disorienting it was as if she were still pinned in the car rolling over on the highway. At times, bandaged and plaster-casted into immobility, Duncan was so heavily sedated he did not even recognize Byrne's face or respond to her voice at his ear whispering "come back to me."

It was weeks before Duncan returned to their adobe house. With him home again, Byrne felt as though she could finally reattach the muscles of her heart to the empty cavity that was her aching chest. His physical recovery was something she was certain she could speed, knowing as she did how bodies stretch and strengthen over time.

She sat behind him in their bed and, with the gentle pressure of her thighs, taught him to align his hips and relieve the pressure on his spine. She massaged his atrophying muscles and loosened the tendons that still twisted and torqued under his skin. She showed him how to use his lungs like a beggar's accordion, drawing air slowly inward so as not to irritate his broken ribs. In the mornings, when he settled into his chair on the portal to have his coffee, she wrapped his legs in the Mexican blanket and cupped his heels in her palms, coaxing flexibility from his cramped hamstrings. When she kissed him she squeezed his face between her outstretched hands to gently lift the pressure from his upper vertebrae. When she at last drew her lips away and released the traction, he draped around her like a heavy cloak.

"Will you type the rest of the manuscript for me?" he whispered. "I cannot summon the resolve."

She willed her body not to stiffen, giving the tender and vulnerable man in her arms any cause for alarm. The last time he had asked her to type a novel it had been like a sea had parted and dropped her to its dry, desert bed. That Duncan had been swimming in circles at the surface was as unforeseen to Byrne as the car that careened into the driver's side of their car.

"Of course I will," she made herself tell Duncan.

She began to whisper calming thoughts to the instincts that threatened to topple her resolve. This time it would be different; Santa Fe was not St. Thomas. What she had seen

so far of *The Air Drawn Dagger* inspired her first choreo-
graphic work and the creation of the Byrne Miller Dance
Theatre. Besides, readying a new book for submission
would distract Duncan from the stream of rejections that
had resulted from *The Silenced Island*. If he needed closure,
she would gladly be the instrument.

Her faith in Duncan's talent, in the worth of the stories
inside him, had sustained her from the day they met in
Central Park. From that day forward, she had told anyone
who asked that she was the luckiest woman in the world to
be the unique combination of attributes a man like Duncan
could not live without. She told herself her husband's
brilliance would someday be as evident to everyone as his
elegance, sophistication and kindness. As much for her
sake as for Duncan's, her dazzle demanded a worthy mirror.
Still, she was nervous. She waited until he went to sleep
before she sat down under a reading lamp with a generous
glass of Gallo at her side. On her left, she put the stack
of pages Duncan had managed to type out himself before
the accident. On her right, she balanced a collection of
tablets, notebooks and scraps of paper filled with Duncan's
imperial, almost hieroglyphic handwriting.

"All right, my beautiful glass vitrine," she said as she
picked up the first chapter, "when last I read of you, there
were simply three shelves with walls between. Let's see
what he has made of you."

She reminded herself that Duncan's book was a work
of fiction, not a confession, that the voice speaking in
first person from the typewritten pages before her was a
created character, not her husband. But what this character
described was too personal to dismiss, too close to be
coincidence, too raw not to be real in some way. The glass
vitrine Duncan described with melancholic nostalgia on
the first page of *The Air Drawn Dagger* became a horrifying

trophy case as the novel progressed. Instead of displaying things of beauty, her Navajo bracelet or her silver rings, the glass walls in Duncan's novel enclosed objects the narrator described as "feelers": a piece of satin cut from his mother's evening gown, a piece of lemonwood carved into the shape of his father's head, a stiff wad of women's underwear stained with menstrual blood and semen.

Beyond the description of the vitrine's contents, there was a thread of injustice to Hispanics – mentions of the Treaty of Hidalgo and revolutionary slogans like *"Tierra o Muerte!"* – but the plot felt like a collection of discarded shells for its viscous narrator to crawl inside of and fester. The words were wounds – wounds worse than those she'd seen across the crumpled front seat of the wrecked car. The Duncan revealed in the pages she clutched in her hand was bloodier than the man who had been wrapped in a steering wheel and plunged through the windshield. In the soundless slow motion of the minutes before the ambulance arrived, she had seen that Duncan was still alive, that even unconscious, his pure, true heart was beating. In the silent eternity before she turned off the reading lamp, she wondered if she had ever known that heart.

There had been signs, she saw that now. Duncan had described his first book, *Sit in Dark Places,* as about a boy's sexual love for his mother, and Byrne had been the one to suggest that he refrain from sharing the details of it with Fanny. She had felt wise and protective then, sheltering both her old-world mother and her avant-garde, uninhibited husband. Now she wondered what she had encouraged and whether it had grown into something too dark to publish.

Her heart contracted at the thought of what a psychological professional might diagnose, someone who did not know the sweet consistency of Duncan's nature. He had committed no crime, demonstrated not an inkling of the disturbing fixations laid out in the pages of his manuscript. But if even his wife had trouble separating the man from the narrator, how could the outside world? She had allowed such an intrusion into a private painful place, once, and Alison was still searching for the part stolen from her as a child.

There was a shuffling sound in the hallway and she looked up to see Duncan at the doorway. The legs peeking out from under his nightshirt were so pale and thin she could see veins feathering up his translucent skin like cracks in an adobe wall.

"It's three in the morning. You mustn't strain your eyes, my love," he said. "Come, I've drawn you a bath and there isn't much wick left to the candle."

Byrne decided, then, that she would simply type the words as though they bore no witness to the man who had created them. If a publisher found them worthy enough to print, let a court of law determine where freedom of expression ended and obscenity began.

"Just close the door to this room and walk into another," she told herself when she mailed off the first half of the manuscript to Mary Yost, an agent who had not been unkind in her rejection of *The Silenced Island.* The ability to disengage from the present and step into the future, to put distance between disappointments, had always preserved her optimism. So when a generous settlement from the accident was deposited in their bank account, enough to pay off all of Duncan's medical bills with thousands to spare, she suggested he close the door on Santa Fe and walk into another room as well.

"You've always loved the water," she began. "Perhaps we could buy a cottage somewhere near the ocean, where the air is moist and healing."

Duncan, still frail and wrapped in three Mexican blankets

against the chill of the desert winter, licked his lips enough to slide them into a smile without cracking. "I am utterly transparent to you. Hold me to your ear and you will hear the waves," he said. "I yearn for the undertow of ocean currents, but where?"

It was Jane who provided the answer when she called her parents to announce that she had enlisted in the United States Marine Corps. She and her husband were reporting for duty at a small Marine Corps air station in Beaufort – less than 60 miles from the city where Duncan was born.

No bomb Jane could have dropped – pregnancy, jail, divorce, illness or converting to Hare Krishna – would have shocked Byrne more than her youngest daughter telling her she was volunteering for military service, especially four years into the Vietnam War. But before Byrne could react, let alone compose herself enough to launch a counter argument, Jane told her mother not to worry. Alison had friends and a life of her own and had decided to stay behind in Colorado.

"She'll be better off on her own two feet. And, before you bring it up, I know you protested the war and every-thing," Jane said. Byrne's stunned silence was an opening Jane jumped through. "But I'm not you."

34

The Mosquito

I was about to go on air when the phone on my desk in the WJWJ newsroom rang and I picked up. "Hey listen, don't freak out or anything. I'm not, like, stalking you, but I'm back in town," Sonny said.

He doesn't know where I've moved. He can't possibly get Wipeout. The carpet under my feet felt like it was dissolving.

"Dennis told me to give you a heads-up so you don't just run into me in the street without any warning," he continued. "Don't worry. I'm not moving back. I just think we should talk. Can you meet me for a coffee?"

"I'm not sure," I said. His voice was an undertow, sucking me below the surface. I sat down hard and leaned against the edge of my desk.

"Well, I'll wait for you at the café on Bay Street after the news. I'll wait, even if you don't come. So come," he said and then hung up.

I glanced around the room to see if anyone had seen me talking to him. *Suck it up. It doesn't matter what people think.* One phone call from Sonny should not shrivel me, I told myself. Neither should meeting him in a café. *I am a different person now. Maybe he is too.*

At least he had considered how I might react if he didn't warn me he was back in Beaufort. He wasn't staked out in the parking lot of the TV station, where I couldn't avoid him. He was waiting in a public place with no guarantee that I would show up. *Am I really scared, or is this just pride?*

I still wasn't sure when I parked across Bay street from the café. To my right was the wide open water where the Beaufort River bent due south, where snowbird retirees moored their yachts and paddled their tenders into town. It was low tide and all its hazards were exposed, rivulets too shallow to navigate, oyster rakes too sharp to walk across. I took a deep breath of mud and marsh. Like the smell that comes before a soaking rain, the scent promised the waters would rise again.

At first, I didn't see Sonny. He was a shadow, dark and small, tilting back on a chair turned the wrong way around, like his baseball cap.

"I didn't think you'd want to see me," his voice reached out, tentative.

"I'm not sure that I do."

"Will you always hate me?" he asked. "If anyone deserves to hate me, it's you."

Years earlier, I would have found this enticing: a bad-boy's "forgive-me." His face was still hidden, but I saw right through him. He was swimming forward and sideways at the same time, wanting forgiveness before he offered an apology. He hadn't really changed, and I no longer cared enough to try to change him.

He babbled through my silence. He pointed to a car in the parking lot, a shiny red convertible with a black cloth top folded down into the seat. I didn't ask how he got the money.

"Nice ride, eh?" he said. "I traded in that piece-of-shit truck."

There was a replacement dog, drinking from a Styrofoam bowl on the pavement next to the passenger door. I didn't ask to be introduced. I didn't want to imagine what would happen to another dog when he tired of the responsibility. Back in Mexico there was a replacement woman, too. Her name washed over before I could pull it out of his stream of words. He was saying how she really understood him, how he never knew how amazing sex could be. I let it swirl into the slipstream behind me, with all the other proof that he had moved on. I sat up straight, like a dancer, but inside I curled up like a little girl, trembling in anticipation of a horrible injection.

I knew even as the panic rose up inside me that it was Sonny's stinging presence triggering the memory. I clutched at the wrought iron table between us for balance. I had always been afraid of shots. When I was a girl, sweat would drizzle down the backs of my knees and the palms of my hands, my racing heart and the buzz of panic between my ears making it hard to hear voices. That last part was actually merciful when it became clear that I wouldn't outgrow the reaction. There wasn't a lot of sympathetic conversation in a doctor's office when a fully grown woman behaved like a terrified child.

In my defense, I had a reason for this. Needles were how my parents discovered I had epilepsy as a child. Each time I got a shot I had a seizure. The room began to overheat and pulse. Then the overhead lights spiraled and pressed in against my eyeballs – like a boa constrictor wrapping itself around my head, squeezing and squeezing until I blacked out and my body began to twitch and convulse.

I hadn't gone into seizure in almost 15 years, but just when the surroundings began to go dark, I felt a cool, fresh breeze off the Beaufort River. Slowly, my diaphragm squeezed my fear like a gentle embrace, my lungs started to expand and my body felt lighter. No doctors huddled over me. The noise in the distance was only Sonny buzzing, like a mosquito.

How could I have stood still, for years, baring my naked skin to him? I let this sad, small man convince me that I deserved to be infected, to share his misery. He seemed so inconsequential and powerless, showing off his toys. He'd asked if I would always hate him but the strongest emotion I could summon was regret. I wasted so much of my life enduring him. He used up years that I would never get back.

Byrne said nothing when I told her Sonny was back in Beaufort. She only raised her eyebrows and leaned across the kitchen table to top off my glass of California merlot. I was proofreading her grant applications, carefully brushing white-out over the plethora of exclamation points, dashes and semicolons. I thumbed through another pile of papers: contracts for the companies Byrne had hired for the upcoming season. A thick, stapled-together stack labeled Dayton Contemporary Dance Company sat on top. It was the most expensive company ever hired by the Byrne Miller Dance Theatre, and the grant applications were a sign of the scramble to cover costs.

"Do you think you'll get money from all these sources?"

"I'd better," she said. "Or else I'll have to mortgage the house to pay the dancers."

The exuberant phrasing and punctuation of her grant writing suddenly made sense. Byrne committed to these world-class companies long before she found the money to pay them. For Dayton Contemporary, a leading African-American dance company, she was tapping every organization from the South Carolina Humanities Council to Penn Center, the famous St. Helena Island campus that was the nation's first school for freed slaves.

"But aren't you ever afraid they'll turn you down?"

"It's my job to make sure they do not perceive rejection as an option," she explained. "I have a whim of iron, remember?"

Byrne flipped through the stack of contracts, reading some parts aloud.

"This one wants private hotel rooms for the dancers," she said. She reached for a black felt tip pen in the center of the table, removed the cap and inked out the entire phrase. She took a thinner ink pen and, in block letters, inserted a phrase of her own. The dancers would be housed in donated accommodations.

"If we get a hotel to offer free rooms by show time, marvelous," she said. "If we don't, I'll ask my wealthy board members to house them in their guest rooms and beach houses."

I was watching a ballet mistress correcting flexed feet and hunched shoulders with a swift tap of the cane, always in control. Her black felt tip marker crossed out one company's required stage dimensions, another's dressing room preferences and replaced them with what was available in Beaufort, within her budget.

"That, my dear, is how you handle unacceptable demands," she said.

As Byrne walked me to the screen door, I thought of Sonny and all the unacceptable demands I had allowed him to make. The sun was fading and her hand was on my shoulder, not for balance but to turn me square with her eyes. All of this had been her way of steeling me for my divorce.

"Teresa," she said. "There is not a contract on earth, let alone between a man and a woman, that cannot be rewritten."

SEASONS ARE TOO POLITE to change in the Lowcountry. They refuse to rush each other: *Bless your heart. No, you go right ahead.* Fall is the most patient season, letting summer linger long past its welcome. I did not appreciate this in the autumn of my divorce.

I had been counting the days since my state-mandated, 12-month period of separation began. I held my breath in anticipation of humiliation, but not a soul had mentioned seeing the summons printed in the newspaper. Sonny's 30 days to legally respond had gone equally unnoticed.

Finally there was a court date to circle and triple underline in my calendar, the first day of September, and I waited for an unmistakable sign to herald the next phase of my life. I wanted the new season to bring haze-free blue skies and a nip in the air. The arrival of fall would push the humid, suffocating wait into my past. If it were cool enough to wear pantyhose, I reasoned, it would mean that Sonny wouldn't be waiting for me on the courthouse steps.

I hadn't heard from him since he drove away with his new dog in his new car to his new girlfriend back in Mexico. After months of talk therapy, my hands had stopped shaking when I saw a white truck in my rearview mirror. I no longer woke in the middle of the night tangled in sweaty sheets, grasping in the dark to make sure Wipeout was still at the foot of my futon. I wasn't frightened of Sonny anymore, just dreading that he would show up in court. I had rehearsed all of the possible scenarios: an angry Sonny, demanding alimony, or worse yet a pleading Sonny, worried that his green card would become invalid. I didn't want to have to feel anything for him anymore, good or bad. I wanted it to be over, that part of my life sealed with the passage of time.

But the first of September was oppressive and stagnant. The air smelled of mold and reluctance. Shrimp boats still anchored off shore, waiting for the open-season signal to spread their nets and trawl the waters. The droning hum of air conditioners drowned out birdsong, and hurricanes brooding in the Atlantic clouded what should have been blue skies. It was hot but I wore the pantyhose anyway. Sweat pooled between my reinforced toes and stunk up the new high heels I'd bought to feel tall and powerful.

I was glad I hadn't asked Byrne to come along. She had offered, of course, when I found out that I needed a "corroborating witness" at the hearing.

"I'll sit next to you, all delicate and well-behaved, and if that Sonny person shows up, I can innocently trip him with Duncan's cane," she had said.

A part of me wanted to hide behind her skirts like a child without culpability. But it wouldn't have been honest. She couldn't truthfully corroborate my marriage to Sonny – he existed only as the person I told her had broken my hand and stolen Wipeout. Bringing her as my witness was what a woman who had never learned anything from Byrne would have done.

Her mantra, we are all of us fine sumpter asses and assesses, was now my own. I was finally strong enough to handle the burden. So I asked Ron from the TV station to be my witness. He was the person who first told me that I spoke in two different voices, one confident and one cowering, when I was around Sonny. This would close the circle.

Sonny didn't show. The sheer relief of it made me appreciate the logic of what I had considered the most draconian of divorce laws. Twelve months of separation reduced the procedure to a formality. There was civility in this Southern courtroom instead of accusation and melodrama. There was no victim or abuser, just a plaintiff in sweaty pantyhose and a defendant in abstentia.

The judge's voice was monotone, his question whether there was hope of reconciliation perfunctory. He made no attempt to pronounce Sonny's Spanish surname correctly, or to pause between the sentences he was reading verbatim.

He sounded utterly bored, plodding through "the above-mentioned separation" and "furthermore, that of this common-law marriage no children have been born" without looking at me.

Then he got to section eight under findings of fact where it said that the plaintiff owned and cared for her five-year-old husky dog named "Wipeout" continuously since separation and "is the proper person to continue to do so."

He put down the pen that he used to follow along the lines of the agreement as he read. His black-robed body slumped forward toward the empty rows of seating. Instead of twisting his torso to look at me, he just leaned his head back at an angle so that it rested on rolls of neck skin. His left eye bulged in my general direction and I could hear an unspoken "what is the world coming to?" in his tone.

"I usually deal with the custody of children, not who gets to keep the dog," he said. "Is this language really necessary?"

For a fleeting moment I felt a giggle surfacing. I was in a courtroom defending the one wonderful consequence of my Mexican mistake. The judge was right. Language wasn't necessary. Not anymore. At last, in the very near future, I could picture laughing at myself.

"It was at the time, Your Honor," I said. "All I can say is that it was at the time."

In less than 15 minutes, the judge granted my divorce. Ron asked me if I wanted a drink to celebrate and I didn't. All I wanted to do was go get Wipeout, sit on the porch with Byrne Miller and tell her I would not affect to be so delicate again.

35

When what is painful can't be fixed,
close the door behind you and walk into another room.
 The brain has more chambers than the heart.

~Byrne

The Unanswering Sea

BEAUFORT – 1971

DUNCAN'S ENQUIRY TO Mary Yost began innocuously
enough, asking the Manhattan literary agent whether she
had read the first half of his latest novel about injustices
perpetrated on the American Indian. She had seemed so
considerate of earlier attempts that Duncan saved one of her
rejection letters. "A marvelous ending," the now years-old
response had proclaimed. "A good funny book, which is rare."

So Byrne had supported Duncan's decision to seek out
Yost's opinion once they settled in the Deep South. She
reasoned that if his lurid language or provocative perspective
was a problem, Duncan would listen to warnings from a
credible source, would change course before the tide carried
him too far out to sea. But her fingers tensed when she began
to type the second paragraph of his hand-written query. "As
you might guess, this area is something of an intellectual
vacuum and the possibilities of finding responsive minds on
which to try out works-in-progress are limited."

She thought of the smart and well-traveled friends they'd
made over the course of almost two years in Beaufort:
professors at its tiny two-year college, the manager of the

local public television station, the inspiring Quakers who served on the board of the first school for freed slaves, even the young military wives Duncan cheerfully assisted in lifts during the Saturday morning improvisation classes at Byrne Miller's School of Dance. Yet in the third sentence of his query letter to Mary Yost, Duncan described a self-imposed exile in an intellectual vacuum.

"Frankly, other than my wife's sound perceptions, there is only the unanswering sea."

Even the acknowledgment of her "sound perceptions" felt hollow to Byrne. She knew she was not the sounding board Duncan described to the agent; she never had been. From the day they'd met, she considered herself intellectually inferior. She was Fanny's daughter, a woman who "figures out where everything belongs because that's what women do." It wasn't Byrne's opinion of her husband's work that mattered but her unconditional support.

Duncan's letter to Mary Yost ended with the question Byrne dreaded typing. "May I impose upon you to say yea, or nay, and why?"

She despaired of the answer that would in all likelihood arrive in the mailbox at the end of their sandy driveway. If Yost thought this novel more marketable than Duncan's other attempts she would have responded already, without any prodding. Perhaps life in tranquil but isolated Beaufort was dulling Duncan's edge. Leaving Santa Fe, with its world-renowned artists and writers' colony, might have been a mistake.

Beaufort County was a collection of so many barrier islands that many of them weren't even named. It was, however, possible to buy a two-bedroom cottage with a spectacular waterfront view for less than the settlement payoff of a terrible automobile accident. Duncan had been certain that the tides he could watch from the screened-in porch would refresh his writing and his spirits. Neither of them had fully anticipated the tradeoffs of life behind the picture postcard beauty. The Department of Motor Vehicles closed its doors every tenth of May to honor Confederate Memorial Day, the closest branch of the League of Women Voters was 60 miles away in Charleston, and in the history of Beaufort city and county government, no woman had ever been elected to public office. Byrne folded Duncan's query into a business envelope, admitting that her husband was not alone in yearning for more than an unanswering sea.

"There are not enough electric fans in all creation to stir this suffocating air," she told Duncan as he watched her undress that night. She placed even her wedding rings inside the glass vitrine atop the dresser. It was too hot to sleep with anything against the naked skin. The single-pane, casement windows in their bedroom were cranked all the way open and the drone of nightly fighter jet training competed with the rattle of unseen armies of cicada bugs. "Let's escape to Cream Hill for the summers and return here only in October when it's humanly habitable."

Duncan leaned back onto his elbows on the twin bed closest to the window. They slept in separate beds now, close enough to reach out and hold hands as they fell asleep each night but not so close as to trap any heat between their sweaty bodies.

"But what would become of your dance theater?"

There was no Ben in Beaufort, but Byrne had managed to recruit the 16-year-old stepdaughter of a squadron commander at the air station to play an alienated girl in a restaging of *The Walls Between*. A Marine Corps sergeant stationed in Beaufort for a few years had starred in her Beaufort Elementary School rendering of *The Emperor's New Clothes*.

"The beauty of the Byrne Miller Dance Theatre is that it

travels wherever I do," Byrne said as she reclined long and glistening on the bed parallel to Duncan's. "Besides, so much closer to New York, I'll have access to trained dancers again."

A smile fluttered across Duncan's face like a breeze. "Have I ever mentioned that you are marvelous?"

THE STEEP UPHILL DRIVEWAY made the two-story house at Cream Hill appear off-kilter, jutting out of a cluster of peeling paper birch trees. It wasn't until Duncan rounded the last curve and reversed the car into its overgrown parking spot that distant mountains leveled the horizon. When the engine knocked and rattled to a stop, he sat behind the steering wheel for a moment and closed his eyes.

"Do you hear that, my love?" he asked Byrne.

"Absolutely," she answered, flexing the palms of her hands against the dashboard. "Utter, blissful silence. Welcome back."

Tall, fuzzy stalks of velvet dock and wind-tussled Queen Anne's lace obscured the pebbled path to the front door, but Byrne declared the shaggy carpet of weeds the most fertile welcome mat she'd ever seen. The key stuck in the lock, relinquishing its hold only after persistent sawing motions dislodged bits of rust. Inside, the four stacked rooms were more camp cabin than mountain retreat. Cold air carried the stagnant scent of forgotten paperbacks and empty coffee tins, so Byrne took the bottle of Chianti she found abandoned in the pantry, and they sat outside on Adirondack chairs to enjoy it.

"To the muses," Byrne offered in toast.

"Those present and otherwise," Duncan said, clinking the lip of her glass with his.

Eventually, though, without daughters or pianos or lovers to share the cluster of rooms in Cream Hill, the house felt almost too quiet for Byrne. So while Duncan passed the mornings smoking his pipe under the shade of quaking aspens, she set up her tape player on the kitchen counter and dragged the rustic table and chairs to the sides of the main room. She pushed the play button and Carl Orff's *Carmina Burana* sneaked up on the silence and filled the space between four walls.

At first she stood, feet bare and eyes closed, listening with the intense focus of the trained musician she was. She lifted both arms in front of her to shoulder height and began to conduct an invisible orchestra. But it wasn't enough to flick the wrists and cue each section of imagined musicians with lifts of the chin. What began as subtle tilts and rotations of the neck became sharp twists and pointed poses. The hand released its phantom baton and began to explore the space – reaching and plunging in time to plaintive flutes and tubas. She could not stay rooted in one spot. The haunting call of oboes drew her spine into spiraling contractions. Changing meters forced her feet to follow. The rhythmic pull of the cantata enveloped her, and it wasn't until a smiling Duncan tapped on the window glass that she was even aware she had been dancing for hours.

"I see Connecticut choreography has commenced," he said as she pulled open the heavy door to let him in. "Is it too early to ask what the next addition to the Byrne Miller Dance Theatre's repertory will be?"

Strands of greying hair stuck to the sides of Byrne's long neck and the low scoop neck of her black leotard rose and fell with every heaving breath.

"I'm loath to give it a storyline," she said, turning down the music. "But I suppose there is a reason ballets are so accessible to the masses."

Duncan gave a theatrical shudder. "Not the *hoi polloi*, I beg of you. Adorn whatever you create with only the vaguest of meanings and retain your dignity."

334

Byrne smiled. "If only I had half the talent of your way with words. I am, however, beginning to hear individual parts in the music, like characters. Six so far."

"Well," Duncan said, rubbing his chin. "As I am only one man, it seems we need to find five other willing supplicants to bring this masterpiece to life. Let's drive into the village and telephone your darling Elizabeth. She'll surely donate some dancers to such a worthy cause."

It had been nearly 20 years since Byrne was a guest soloist for Elizabeth Rockwell's "Ballet Etudes," but the former High School of the Performing Arts teacher of Robert Joffrey, Arthur Mitchell and Edward Villella was still a close friend. Their trail of correspondence bore the postmarks of two wandering confidantes. Byrne's letters from St. Thomas had been answered from Elizabeth's tour stops in Israel. Updates out of Santa Fe had been returned from dance residencies in California. Rockwell's latest modern dance company, Rondo Dance, came full circle and settled in the town where she first met Byrne: Bedford, Connecticut.

"We'll invite her for supper," Byrne exclaimed, already imagining the reunion. "I'll build a soup worthy of a soul mate."

Dancerly kisses to both cheeks were nowhere near celebratory enough to consummate the reunion of Byrne and Elizabeth a week later. They gripped each other's shoulders like exultant ballroom partners and spun around the kitchen, alternately knotting into huddled embraces and holding each other at arms' length to take in the measure of time passed.

Duncan ducked behind them to reach a rusty metal garden pail filled with wild geraniums and freshly chipped ice. The loud pop of a flyaway cork spun the women around to look at him. "Can either of you two be trusted to hold still enough for a glass of champagne?"

They were well into a second bottle when more cars began

to pull up in the Cream Hill driveway.

"Ah, the potential dancers have arrived," Duncan said, giving Byrne a kiss as he stood up from his seat in front of the fireplace. "I'll give the soup another stir whilst you greet them and begin the recruitment seduction."

Elizabeth laughed. Instead of dancers, she had invited a young editor from *The Lakeville Journal*, John Parker, and his brother, David. "You'll love the Parker boys. And more importantly, they'll love you and the experimental … no … make that the *avant-garde* summer residency of the Byrne Miller Dance Theatre."

Byrne put down her glass and gaped at her friend and mentor. It was like watching a tornado form from the barest whisper of clouds. Elizabeth's confidence and ideas pirouetted around the room, her eyes touching down on Byrne's after every spin.

She reached out and grasped Byrne's hand. "In all my years of running schools and dance companies, I've learned that dancers come and go, but good press is irreplaceable."

By evening's end, the cauldron of thick Hungarian stew was as empty as the champagne bottles, and Byrne had secured much more than just the endorsement of the well-connected Parker brothers. Elizabeth volunteered three female dancers she knew to be summering in the area, and both John and David agreed to join Duncan as the women's partners.

Byrne clasped her hands together, twisting Duncan's wedding ring around and around in excitement. "It'll be a workshop version of the Byrne Miller Dance Theatre. Strong, handsome men are instrumental in staging choreography for the first time, and mine will be the envy of the eastern seaboard."

In the months that followed, Duncan devoted mornings to his thoughts and the long walks through the woods that seemed to clear them. By afternoon his 58-year-old body was sufficiently warmed up for Byrne to put it through stretching and balance exercises. The rest of the workshop company joined them for rehearsals in the evenings, after the Parker brothers got off work.

Soon, articles in the *The Lakeville Journal* began to document the approaching performance. Newspaper readers learned that Byrne Miller, choreographer and former Elizabeth Rockwell soloist, was debuting her interpretation of a theme from Ecclesiastes, "A Time to Hate and a Time to Love," set to the score of *Carmina Burana*.

Cast members included the novelist Duncan Miller, husband of the choreographer, and Marjorie Stevenson, whose dance experience included summer workshops with Helen Tamiris. Broadway actress Helen Townsend had studied under José Limón, and the third female dancer, Susan Smith, danced with the up-and-coming modern dance star Dan Wagoner.

Photographs of rehearsals began to appear in the papers next, building anticipation for the performance. In one of them, Townsend's long blond hair streamed out behind her in a graceful *grand jeté* – a beautiful dancer captured at her zenith. Byrne clutched each article and flattering photograph to her chest and blew a silent kiss to Elizabeth Rockwell for the publicity money couldn't buy. Even without the backing of an arts-friendly university like St. John's in Santa Fe, the Byrne Miller Dance Theatre was building an audience along with a reputation.

"I'm going to have to kidnap these dancers and take them back with us to Beaufort," Byrne told Duncan. He and the two other men were holding their own, facilitating the lifts and turns with increasing coordination and confidence. But the steps she labanotated each morning took flight and form when women with years of training loaned Byrne their bodies. "It isn't fair that only New Englanders get to witness talent of this level."

Duncan laughed. "I'm not sure Helen would trade Broadway for the Beaufort Little Theatre, but I'm sure you'll think of something."

Byrne's summer workshop company premiered "A Time to Hate and a Time to Love" on Sunday, October 3, 1971, at the Colonial Ballroom in Canaan, Connecticut. John Parker could not dance and take photographs at the same time, so the final photograph that appeared in *The Lakeville Journal* was actually of the last rehearsal before the performance. It showed a side-lunging Duncan, in black tights and form-fitting t-shirt, supporting the waists of Helen and Susan as they arched their backs and necks away from him in *arabesque*. The cutline reported that the audience had responded enthusiastically. Byrne smiled, remembering Duncan's stiff-waisted bow and the way his fingers had twitched and pointed face blushed when the applause continued. When, as the cutline reported, "many joined the dancers in a group improvisation," Duncan had slipped outside to smoke a pipe and reclaim his privacy.

Days later, Byrne's lungs still inhaled with delight in her spontaneous decision to invite the audience on stage. Seeing her artistic vision articulated and expanded by talented, trained modern dancers would have been triumph enough. That Duncan so believed in her that he offered his untrained body as clay for her to mold was testament to a love she treasured. But the eager, unselfconscious response of an educated audience thrilled Byrne.

The people who filled the ballroom that night were teachers and merchants, artists and architects. Because they knew and appreciated the work of pioneers like Elizabeth Rockwell, Martha Graham and Lucas Hoving, they were willing to take a chance on a workshop performance. At 62, Byrne knew she would never be one of the great modern dancers. Her attempts at choreography would not earn her commissions with renowned companies like Rondo Dance or reviews in *The New York Times*. But she saw something even more rewarding in the forward-leaning, eyes-bright audience she could not let slip out into the cold, Connecticut night. When the music faded out, she stood up in the front row and lifted welcoming arms.

"In the beginning there was dance because people just needed to move," she said. She signaled for the music to continue. "Come, join the dancers who have moved you tonight." When they did, she was certain that the sun could never cast another shadow. She had swallowed it whole.

BYRNE CLIPPED THE striking photograph to send it to Alison, her father the life-long novelist in a new role: modern dancer. But the man in the photograph looked absent, detached from the movement and emotion around him. His lean, sallow face had the same faraway look she'd seen in Santa Fe after the accident, when his world was shrinking just as hers was expanding.

It was about to shrink again. In two weeks, they would shutter up the Cream Hill house and ride out the winter in Beaufort. After a blissful summer of writing, rehearsals and fireside discussions with dancers, actors and writers, how could he not dread returning to an unanswering sea?

She grabbed the keys to the car and left Duncan a hastily scribbled note – *need to ask Susan about something, be back by supper*. The curves of Connecticut country roads partnered the twists and bends of the plan formulating as she drove. Susan Smith, the third woman volunteered by Rockwell to join Byrne's workshop company for the summer, was hoping to go on tour with Dan Wagoner's modern dance company. There was already one performance scheduled for 1972 in St. Louis.

"Why there, of all places?" Byrne wanted to know. Susan wasn't sure of the details, except that an organization called Dance St. Louis had raised the funds to sponsor the company's performance.

"But I don't know of any modern dance company in all of Missouri, do you?"

"Exactly," Susan explained. Wagoner's small company wasn't being shipped out to Missouri as guest performers for an existing troupe. The dance aficionados and university academics who founded Dance St. Louis weren't performers themselves. Their mission was to share top-level modern dance with a city that favored traditional ballet and to build audiences by having the likes of Dan Wagoner teach master classes in the local schools.

"It's brilliant," Byrne whispered, more to herself than to the graceful girl whose hands she grasped. "Tell me, do you think this Dan Wagoner of yours could be persuaded to add another leg to his journey?"

There was still enough daylight when she arrived back at Cream Hill to see Duncan at the base of the giant oak tree, staring up at what had once been the girls' tree house. The spare structure looked brittle and unstable, and the ladder that leaned up against the trunk was decomposing, rung-by-rung. Spotted brown leaves blanketed a scattering of acorns at its base.

"Now you've got me pondering Ecclesiastes. How does the verse go again?" Duncan asked as Byrne wrapped her arms around him from behind. "To the place from where the rivers come, all return again?"

"Something like that," she said. "All rivers run to the sea, but the sea is never full." She knew then that it was the same with Duncan. She could never fill his unanswering sea, but she could bring rivers to Beaufort to sustain them both.

36

A whim of iron simply rejects rejection.

~Byrne

Dinosaurs with Hula Hoops

BEAUFORT – 1972

LETTERS FROM ALISON were like fragments of a drift-wood raft that washed up on the banks of the Beaufort River. Each time she opened an envelope postmarked Colorado, Byrne was never sure if she would find signs of survival or disaster inside. Alison was a worry that hung from Byrne's shoulders like the soft grey Spanish moss draped over every oak tree. On the azalea-scented walk from the mailbox to the screened porch, Byrne wrestled with how to paraphrase the content of her daughter's let-ters. Duncan almost never read them. He just looked up from his wicker chair, pipe in one hand and pen in the other, and gave his theatrical wife her cue.

"And what of manifest destiny today?" he'd ask Byrne with a gentle smile, or, "News from our wild Westerner?"

Alison had not protested the wholesale transfer of her family to Beaufort. She said she was proud of Jane and her brother-in-law for their service to their country and of her free-spirited mother immediately introducing modern dance classes to the Deep South. But the letters she mailed to Beaufort were evidence of upheaval – disjointed

341

reflections on a world she alternately described as amusing and annoying, but still always a world she struggled to accept. Some spoke of ordinary complaints and observations – itemized details of the daily rituals involved with feeding, training and bathing her dogs.

"It's a good one this week," Byrne would tell Duncan when those letters arrived. "She seems grounded and focused."

Others told of plans to sell her trailer and hitch rides across the country.

"A flight of fancy, this one. There is no mention of the animals. Unless those doodles in the margins are meant to be dogs."

The only consistency from letter to letter was Alison's child-like handwriting, which clumsily filled the space between ruled blue lines. The block letters were so emphatically penned that they ridged the backs of every page, and Byrne read Alison's emotional unevenness as clearly as if the letters were written in braille.

"Her thoughts don't connect. It's as if she is transcribing whatever she remembers of a strange dream."

Duncan took the pages from Byrne's hand and refolded them to insert into the envelope. "Think of the parallels," he said. "We are here, beside a river that ebbs and flows without any interference, and Alison writes to us in stream of consciousness."

Byrne looked out at the live oaks leaning over the banks of the river as if to shade the harsh reflection of the sun on the water's surface. Across an island of spartina marsh grass, beyond the red and green buoys marking the channel of the Intracoastal Waterway, a red light flashed atop the radar tower at the air station. Jane could look up from her job on base at any time, day or night, and see the same pulsing light her parents did. But Alison drifted along with no such guiding beacons.

A letter arrived one day that was too much for Byrne to decipher alone. There was no opening salutation, no sloppy attempt at a return address in the upper right hand corner. Alison leaped right into words as though she did not claim them as her own, a series of clichéd phrases set off by quotation marks.

"'Let it all hang out'; 'Tell it like it is'; 'If it feels good do it' – wistful anachronisms," the letter abruptly began.

Byrne smiled at Alison's cynicism, savoring the sight of a multisyllabic word before continuing.

> *The Peace Corps; the Woodstock era – paid by Vietnam; the sins of Agent Orange visited on the sons ... and Woodstock only a funny little bird with a war hero Beagle buddy.*

She wondered if the military references meant Alison was struggling with her sister's absence. This letter was written in red ink on yellow notebook paper and looked as though it had been wadded up and then smoothed out with indecisive hands. There were no paragraph indentations. No sentences began with capital letters and none ended with periods. The spelling was erratic and an entire section of the second page was crossed out, smothered with white typewriter correction fluid and re-written with a different pen. It looked like the rantings of a fourth-grader with a precocious vocabulary, and Byrne needed to hear Duncan's comforting interpretation. She handed him the letter without preamble.

Duncan took a deep breath of the sulfur-tinged marsh air and began to read. Byrne paced the length of the porch, flicking at a palmetto bug that clung to the outside of the copper screen. She heard Duncan's foot tapping before she heard his voice, murmuring snippets of Alison's letter as if he were reciting a poem in a smoke-filled coffee shop.

"'And the nitty gritty now a dirty ditty,'" he began and a smile rose in his voice.

Byrne leaned against a wooden post and folded her arms across her chest to listen.

"'They marched away singing but most of them died,'" Duncan continued, picking through the lines like a woodpecker selecting seeds from a bird feeder.

"'The concern was more hellfire than history and the Last Supper replaced the First Crusade as a wall hanging. Then, nobody gave a damn.'" He looked up at Byrne, whose eyes were closed. "Darling, are you listening? This is not merely a letter. It is verse."

"Only if you leave half of it out and ignore the grammar." There was a catch in Byrne's voice, as if the humidity in the air was stifling her. "Or the fact that we sent her to the very best boarding schools. And a year of college."

Duncan sat up a little straighter in his wicker chair and tapped the ashes from his pipe into an ashtray before resuming.

"'Man is the only animal to talk to others after his time by little black marks on light-colored surfaces. These marks may be cast in stone, marked in marble, inscribed on parchment or written on toilet paper.'"

Byrne ran her fingers through her graying hair, lifting it off her sweaty neck to catch the breeze from the porch's wobbly ceiling fan. But she did not interrupt Duncan's reading.

"'What they tell us is that mankind has stayed much the same, that fashion repeats itself and we find no bones of dinosaurs with hula hoops. Signed, Alison Miller.'" Duncan beamed as he handed the letter back. "Byrne, it's brilliant."

Byrne studied Alison's signature as if it might be a forgery. Alison had chosen to end the letter not with "Until next time" or "Yours truly" or "Love, Alison," but with the shyly possessive "Signed, Alison Miller." The cursive letters that formed her name were so fragile and uncertain they looked to Byrne as if they were traced by another's hand.

"'Dinosaurs with hula hoops,'" Byrne whispered. She held the crumpled yellow pages to her chest and exhaled. "Duncan, I finally understand."

He stood up and wrapped his arms around her waist from behind, and the breeze from the wobbling ceiling fan encircled them both.

"Our daughter is 32 years old and her words literally fall over themselves. She still can't control the way her hand grips a pen," she said. "And she can't control her mind. I am certain that the two are connected."

Sixteen hundred miles from a daughter whose mind raced in circles, Byrne stepped into another room. Left behind in its timeless beauty, Beaufort might not offer up another Ben, so Byrne might never have as promising a dancer to shape and champion. But surely there were Alisons, children she could reach and teach before the walls between became permanent divisions.

BYRNE MARCHED THROUGH the entrance portico of Beaufort Elementary at high tide. The morning sunlight sparkling off the brilliant blue Beaufort River competed in intensity with the building's four white neoclassical columns that towered over a landscape of scrubby palmetto trees and a patchy, expansive lawn.

"Euclid himself might think this edifice a tad geometric," she muttered, smiling to herself as she drew the knot of her bright silk neck scarf a little off center.

It was cooler inside, the heat drawn up through transom windows along the top of 12-foot ceilings. The stacked heels of her strappy dress sandals clattered on the wood floor like mahjong tiles, and the principal's loud voice announcing her arrival bounced off the solid plaster walls of the fourth-grade classroom.

Byrne adjusted the glasses on the bridge of her nose to get a better look at a 10-year-old boy repeatedly lifting and slamming the front two legs of his desk onto the tops of his feet.

"Germaine comes from St. Helena Island, and he has difficulty sitting still," the principal of Beaufort Elementary explained. "Not surprising, given the degree of his handicaps."

"All the more reason to teach him how to move his body," Byrne replied. "We'll start with simple skips and happy hops – for improving balance. That's why he fidgets. He doesn't know how to readjust his body to feel secure in the chair."

"Movement therapy?" the principal questioned. "We already have a special ed teacher."

"You need a dance teacher," Byrne interrupted. "I've studied under the greats of modern dance. I've taught everywhere from ballet studios in New England to Indian reservations in New Mexico. Let me have these children, and I will write a grant to pay my salary."

Without waiting for his reply, she dragged a chair in front of Germaine. She reached over and drummed a galloping rhythm on his desk with the palms of her hands. Then she lifted the boy's hands and placed them on her desk. "Your turn," she said, and when he copied the pattern she lifted her arms on either side of her body and danced to it.

"Let's play a guessing game," she said to a girl shyly sneaking up behind Germaine for a closer look. She reached for the girl's hand, spun her around and traced the capital letter "Z" between her protruding shoulder blades. Then she steered the nervously giggling girl to the blackboard and put a piece of chalk between her fingers.

"Show me what you think I'm writing," she said, tracing

the letter on the girl's back again. "Can you feel how it starts on your left side, then moves straight across to the other side, then down a diagonal, like when you go down a slide in the playground?"

The girl rocked from her left foot to the right, following the pressure of Byrne's hand, and began to transfer the movement to the surface in front of her. She couldn't see the tall woman with dangling earrings and a turquoise Navajo bracelet light up with a toothy smile. The shaky, uneven "Z" slowly taking shape on the chalkboard could have been traced from any one of Alison Miller's letters from Colorado.

"I see where you're going with this, Ms. Miller, but we don't have a special room for dancing," the principal said. "All the classrooms are used for learning."

Byrne took a deep breath and let the unintended insult dance off into another room before she responded.

"That's quite all right. The four walls of classrooms sometimes prevent learning," she said. "Let's take this group out into the hallway, and I'll show you what I mean."

A troupe of would-be dancers with wobbly gaits, funny-looking glasses and clunky hearing aids followed Byrne through the doorway into another world.

"We are going to pretend without talking," she told the students, so that her impromptu dance class wouldn't aggravate the teachers in surrounding classrooms. "Pretend this hallway is the Beaufort River at low tide, the walls I'm touching are its muddy banks and all the boys and girls are really alligators."

She quieted the eruption of giggles with a finger to her pursed, crimson lips, and the students dropped to their bellies on the hallway floor.

"I'm not sure what they're learning here," the principal began to interrupt.

"How do alligators move?" Byrne asked the kids at

her feet. As they began to squirm in experimentation she leaned close to the principal's ear. "These children have trouble differentiating between right and left and between the concepts of the same and opposite, am I correct?"

The principal nodded.

"Dance helps the muscles to lead the mind."

She lifted her right leg and right arm at the same time, both of them bent and flexed to the side at 90-degree angles, and the kids mimicked her movements. "Let's see what happens if alligators try to walk with only one side of their bodies, like this."

The kids veered toward the walls like rudderless boats.

"Now let's try using the arm from one side of our alligator bodies and the leg from the other side at the same time," she said. She lowered her torso into an *arabesque* position parallel to the floor and demonstrated the coordinated movement of opposition.

A smile spread across the principal's face as he tiptoed through a hallway river of writhing alligators.

"I WAS ASKED TO CREATE a dance curriculum for handicapped and deaf children at the elementary school," she told Duncan that afternoon.

"Was asked or was not refused?" he said, looking up from his typewriter with a sly smile. "I did not know sign language was among your many gifts."

"Dance is a universal language," she said, twirling on the floor of the porch with outstretched arms. "And these sweet children deserve as many ways as possible to express themselves."

Duncan drew his left hand through the humid air and flipped it over with flourish to an open palm, acknowledging yet another of his wife's accomplishments, and returned to his manuscript.

37

Pretend without Talking

I MIGHT HAVE BEEN the first woman in South Carolina to divorce an illegal alien she never married, but the official legal notice of my double life still had not appeared in the area newspapers. Some part of me hoped it had slipped between the cracks, but I knew eventually my name would show up in print. So every Saturday I went to the Beaufort County Library to scan through all the publications it carried: *The State*, out of Columbia; *The Post and Courier*, Charleston's daily; the local edition of *The Savannah Morning News*; and *The Beaufort Gazette*.

It was in a back issue of the local paper that I came across a feature about Byrne, and my eyes were drawn to a sidebar headlined "Bon Mots from a Maven." It was a collection of quotes that apparently made an impression on the reporter and in the bottom right corner was one that seemed to point its finger at me.

"I forced marriage on my husband. He said no, because there had never been a happy marriage in his family. I said there had never been an unhappy one in mine, so I had enough for both of us."

I sat down less gracefully than a dancer should, reminded of how far from happy, or even real, my marriage to Sonny had been.

"I was the first to marry out of the Jewish faith, but Duncan loved my parents, who accepted him as a changeling."

I submerged myself in the salty waters of dozens of articles about Byrne and her adoring husband, dating back to 1973 when the Byrne Miller Dance Theatre presented its first nationally known modern dancer: Dan Wagoner. The former Paul Taylor and Martha Graham dancer was on a tour funded by the Sears Roebuck Foundation and the National Endowment for the Arts, but somehow Byrne had convinced him to stop in South Carolina and teach a class of special needs students at Beaufort Elementary School.

Dan Wagoner's actual performance, from what I could gather, was promoted as a dance festival and barbeque. The brochure listed the address of a private residence, but sometime in the intervening years the site of the dance festival/barbeque had become Beaufort Tire and Appliance. I could imagine a trim, stylish modern dancer from New York City getting off the plane at Frogmore International, its one paved landing strip eye level with alligators and other swamp creatures. Byrne would have picked him up and driven him through miles of slash pine forest, past trailer parks and hunting clubs. When he saw the long line of pickup trucks parked all along the dirt driveway Byrne pulled into, poor Dan Wagoner could have been forgiven for wondering what he had gotten himself into, whether he was the main draw or the pulled pork.

"I was pleased to perform in a place I'd never heard of," Wagoner graciously told a local reporter.

Every article about Byrne raced through her professional background as though the reporters were handed her eclectic resume and didn't know quite what to make of it. Her early work with modern dance pioneers like Lucas Hoving and Elizabeth Rockwell were just lines of type, uncorroborated footnotes in the history of this charismatic transplanted Yankee. The reporters heaped much more praise on the wonders Byrne created in local schools.

"It was Byrne Miller," one article contended, "who brought dance to Beaufort and self-respect to its handicapped children."

I sat, thumbing through articles, piecing together the connections between the woman I knew and the one she had been when I was still a toddler. When Byrne followed her daughter to Beaufort in 1969, it was a sleepy military town. But somehow she got a grant for a three-year, pilot dance project in the public schools.

"I was wandering down the halls looking for something to do and I walked into a hearing-handicapped class," one article quoted Byrne. "Dance is such a universal language. I can stretch their imaginations and get them to feel capable."

By 1974, Byrne's Beaufort Elementary dancers apparently felt so capable that they went on the road. The education reporter for *The Beaufort Gazette* followed Byrne and her unlikely troop to neighboring Mossy Oaks and Broad River Elementary, covering her latest piece of choreography: *There Was an Old Woman Who Swallowed a Fly.*

A three-year grant turned into 16 years, and a dance program for the handicapped and hearing impaired blossomed into the creation of full-time dance positions at every middle and high school in Beaufort County.

"Byrne Miller is the Johnny Appleseed of modern dance," another article intoned.

She did it all in a state that still flew the Confederate flag over its capitol dome, a state whose legislators supported prayer in public schools, not modern dance. Because of work she had started in the 1970s, 20 years later every student in Beaufort County had the chance to study dance and come to dress rehearsals of companies like Martha Graham's. When Byrne won the Elizabeth O'Neill Verner award in 1989, the state's highest cultural honor, reporters didn't have to look very far for corroborating sources.

"When we went to Beaufort, I thought it was just another play," began the quote of an eight-year old student named Tim who had just seen the annual Byrne Miller Dance Theatre presentation of *The Nutcracker*. "And then POW!!! I loved it."

A boy named Germaine described Byrne's dance therapy class as, "It's a fun place to be. You could learn to use your imagination in ways you never used it before. You learn to pretend without talking."

Some of this I already knew from my own TV stories about Byrne's dance programs in the schools. So the enthusiasm of the reporters didn't surprise me. What struck me was how, in almost every article, there was a segue to the love story of Byrne and Duncan. It didn't matter if it was an editorial encouraging more funding for dance in the schools or a feature about an upcoming performance. Somehow their romance slipped in, as though each reporter were equally enchanted.

"From having a giant-sized inferiority complex, I now have reversed myself entirely. And most of it is due to my husband."

At first, I thought quotes like this were simply Byrne trying to include Duncan in her glory. Maybe she was canny enough to know it made a more interesting story, that it attached a mystique to the Byrne Miller Dance Theatre. Then I saw that even if she didn't bring it up, others did, especially after Duncan became too weak to talk to reporters.

"He just adored her," was how one board member described Duncan. "They were so close. They went everywhere together. To lose that is immeasurable."

The great dancer who loved the great writer – it was an irresistible story.

38

The Naked Emperor

THE AZALEAS THAT THRUST themselves out of every hedge and bush around Byrne's house, flaunting their cerise and magenta petals, seemed indecent as the anniversary of Duncan's death approached. The delicate, tidy camellias that had returned the winter after his passing were more respectful of his absence. *Pardon us*, their nodding buds had seemed to say as they unfolded to the glancing sun, *we know how much he delighted in us every year, so we thought it time to bloom again.* They quivered in the easterly gusts of winds that blew in off the water, unsteady in the reordering of the world that had resulted from Duncan's departure. Modest, really, at most they dared to mix a dusting of white with their kitten's-ear pink blush of color.

Not so the wild azaleas that replaced the camellias when spring arrived in 1994. They crowded the view from the screened porch where Duncan used to watch the river. Their lipstick-red throats, variegated blotches and vulgar stripes were more garish than grieving. *Who cares,* they shouted to the sun. *He's gone but we're back, brighter than ever.* They sprung from the well-drained soil in such

354

quantities as to crowd out his memory.

"It's odd," Byrne told me on an evening leading up to the one-year mark, "the azaleas seemed so loud the day of Duncan's gathering that they blocked out the words everyone read. I'm sure there were wonderful passages but I can't remember any. What a shame."

It might have been the almost full bottle of California merlot we'd shared, but when I blew Byrne a goodbye kiss that evening, I was twitching with a good idea. I would scour the shelves of the Beaufort County Library on Saturday and check out each of Duncan's novels. I'd say it was for research, to get around the three-at-a-time limit for borrowing. There was enough time, a week or so, to read through them all and pick out passages to read aloud. I would practice in my apartment, to do them justice, and bookmark the best pages with azalea clippings. I might ask Lisa and Lillian to join the reading. Byrne would beam with happiness – the words of her life-long love celebrated by her collected daughters.

Beaufort was a literary town, a colorful setting for novels and the authors who wrote them. Whenever Pat Conroy signed copies of a new book, the line at the local independent bookstore stretched the length of Bay Street. No less than five community newspapers printed book reviews and social calendars of book clubs and writers' group meetings. So I thought I'd start by searching the microfiche collection in the library's newspaper reference section. Depending on how far back in time the library kept copies of the actual publications, I could make photocopies of any wonderful reviews and maybe even pull quotes from them to make some sort of card for Byrne.

I adjusted the focus on the flat reading surface of the microfiche machine. I cranked the advance handle and allowed my eyes to adjust to the orange glow of the light source. But roll after roll of microfilm purred through the machine, and I found no references to book signings or literary reviews. If Duncan's novels had ever made a splash, it must have been in a bigger pond than Beaufort.

I told myself Byrne never cared what the unsophisticated public thought of anything. The books themselves were the proof of Duncan's brilliance. I reversed each roll of microfilm through the spools and handed back a stack of boxes higher than my head.

Like any library, the fiction section was arranged alphabetically by author's last name. Duncan Miller's novels would be somewhere in the middle row of shelves, which was opposite the front door, flung wide open to catch the breeze. It was April, and horse-and-buggy tours were at the peak of spring garden season. The timeless clopping of horseshoes down Craven Street was the soundtrack to my search. Surely, a town so steeped in history would preserve the artistic triumphs of its residents.

I scanned the little white stickers at the base of each book's spine and squatted for a closer look at the FIC-MIL labels. But the books on the shelf skipped from James Michener's *Mexico* to Sue Miller's *The Good Mother*. I checked again but Miller, comma, Duncan still wasn't there. I stood up, swatting at a cloud of sand gnats that must have swarmed in through the front door.

I was irritated. I'd obviously given the town too much credit, assuming a small library like Beaufort's would carry books that must have gone out of print. It was the only explanation that relieved the queasy feeling in my stomach. Byrne had said Duncan started writing when they were first married, in the Great Depression. He must have been good. The editor of *The Atlantic Monthly* said Duncan wrote like Thomas Mann. Still, Byrne never said how long his career lasted, and I never thought to ask.

It wasn't until I pulled open the L through N drawer

of the card catalog that I acknowledged my suspicions. It was stuffed full of titles in circulation and out of print available in the Beaufort location or on loan from sister branches. There were books with copyrights much older than the range of dates that would have spanned his career, and still I found not a single reference to Duncan Miller. I returned my slip of recycled notepaper and half-sized, eraser-less loaner pencil to the basket atop the card catalog and pushed the L through N drawer back along its metal rails. It felt like abandoning a tiny wooden coffin; I couldn't give up yet.

I was filling out a multi-state library request for any publication by Duncan Miller when I saw Lisa browsing through a back issue of *The New York Times*. I would have recognized my sister-by-Byrne anywhere. She sat just like Byrne, with perfect posture, even in a sagging, low-slung reading chair. Her silver hair flowed down her back, gathered like a bouquet of flowers with a twist of ribbon. She smiled to herself as she read, as though delighted with how the words were arranged on the page. If the Beaufort County Library was at that moment a stage, Lisa was bathed in a warm spotlight, and I had somehow fallen off into the orchestra pit. I wanted her hand to hoist me back up into the enchanted story we shared, but when I asked her about Duncan's novels she couldn't help me.

"Actually, I haven't read anything he's written," she told me. "Nobody has, except Byrne. His novels have never been published."

If she had said Duncan never walked the earth it would have felt no less a lie. Lisa must have been mistaken. Byrne wouldn't have led me to believe in a success that wasn't real, she and all her talk of the truthfulness of friendship. I suddenly needed to sit down but all that was available was a tiny, molded plastic chair in the kids' reading corner.

I folded myself into it and clasped my hands around knees that seemed awkwardly enormous and shaky. It was as if the Hans Christian Andersen collection my mother gave me back when I believed in mermaids had come to life and Duncan was the naked emperor. In the story, the tricky weavers said his new suit was invisible to the stupid or unfit, guaranteeing complicity from all who valued their reputations.

I couldn't push the story's ending out of my head. Only an innocent child had dared declare the truth, and the proud and embarrassed emperor believed he had to bear up until the end. Was that how Duncan felt, exposed but for his wife's faithful championing, or was Byrne the duplicitous weaver all along?

The woman sitting in the grown-up chair in front of me spoke as though Duncan not being published was entirely the fault of editors in New York, in no way passing judgment on Duncan's gift or Byrne's omission.

"He lived for literature," Lisa said. "A group of his friends used to gather every month in Duncan's living room to read aloud from Shakespeare. He was magnificent, before the Alzheimer's."

Unlike me, Lisa seemed to need no proof of Duncan's talent. It made perfect sense, I told myself. She was one of Byrne's oldest collected daughters and her loyalty extended to Duncan. I had met him at the point when he forgot where his sentences were headed and abandoned them with frustrated snorts and strange, gurgling noises. I was the unfit follower who still needed fairy tales.

"His manuscripts are sitting in boxes underneath the sofa in Byrne's living room," Lisa said. "I think there are six complete works of fiction in all. Byrne typed each and every one."

I reeled with the heartbreaking futility of it. Thousands of pages, the work and dreams of a lifetime were yellowing with age under a homemade sofa in Beaufort, South Carolina. Clearly I had not been the only woman who tried to be everything to a man, only to find out that it didn't work.

39

The mind is meant to operate on a higher plane
than guilt.

~Byrne

Grand Grotesque

BEAUFORT – 1978

THE WIDE, TIDAL RIVER in front of Byrne and Duncan's
house rose and fell in eight-foot increments. From the
porch where Duncan watched and wrote, it was as if the
Beaufort River periodically swallowed the marshy islands
that divided its channels and swelled into a vast lake. Six
hours later, those same clumps of marsh towered over
millions of fiddler crabs scurrying across a muddy ditch.
It was at those extreme low tides that Byrne and Duncan
risked the onslaught of mosquitoes and sand gnats and left
the screened porch. At water's edge, down a path from
the 13-foot bank to a natural landing, it was possible to
submerge from sight.

The sun dropped below a horizon they couldn't see, the
proof of it reflected in a sky streaked with flushed pinks
and marsh grass stalks of solid gold. Sometimes, before
the inky blackness of full night, they could see a strange,
solitary light hovering in the distance. Too steady to be
the landing lights of a fighter jet at the air station, it could
have passed for a star dangling itself low enough for ad-
mirers to touch.

"Well, the snowbirds are returning," Duncan said, reaching for Byrne's hand. "I'd wager it's one of those new C&C thirty footers. One would think a mast light that bright would melt the fiberglass hull, but what do these people care? They'd just buy a new model next season."

Duncan tracked the progress of the passing seasons by the number of luxurious sailboats that plied their way down the Intracoastal Waterway each fall and back up again each spring. Enough for an invading armada, he would joke with friends who stopped by to watch the sunsets and share a glass of wine.

So Byrne wasn't surprised by the title of Duncan's latest novel: *Jane's Fighting Ships*. Or that Duncan said it dealt with hatred, again.

"Of what?" she asked, leaving *this time* unspoken.

"The arrogance of youth," he answered and she pressed a soft kiss to the place on his head still sheltered with threads of silver hair.

But when she began to type the pages of the manuscript, it seemed to Byrne less about hatred of the arrogance of youth than the humiliation of growing old. The epigraph was from Louis Ferdinand Celine's *Journey to the End of the Night*.

"Man is only himself when he is on the toilet or on his deathbed; the rest is histrionics."

The protagonist was, once again, a first-person narrator, this time a malcontent named Jo Jo Cates. Duncan set the novel on a houseboat in Sausalito, California, in the 1960s, where Jo Jo obsesses over base bodily functions, especially his digestive system. In the first four pages alone, Byrne typed the word "piss" six times, "toilet" four, "bladder" twice and "dung," "bowel" and "shit" once each. Then she arrived at a passage when Jo Jo argues with himself over whether to spray perfume to hide the smell but resigns himself to the futility of it.

"No: smell how foully you stink, the sewage that has sprayed out of your bladder and lower bowel is no worse than the garbage that seethes in your brain and spews out of your mouth."

Byrne could hardly recognize the world that spewed from Duncan's imagination, full of coarse characters speaking in an awkward, almost foreign-sounding dialog of washed-up hippies, prostitutes and drug users. She typed mechanically day after day, never leaning into the keys with anticipation or suspense. She stopped only at the sound of the margin return bell, and each completed page she pulled from the carriage seemed to weigh a pound.

When it was done, she took the 212-page manuscript out to the porch for Duncan to check over and box up for shipping. He fingered the fluttering pages, tapping them on the wide arm of his rattan porch chair to keep the edges in line. "Marvelous," he muttered, "simply marvelous."

Byrne looked out at the river on the other side of the screened porch as an old wooden sailboat motored its way up the Intracoastal. Duncan's dreams too would travel north for dispensation, and Byrne knew a rejection of *Jane's Fighting Ships* was as likely as the snowbirds returning the following winter.

It was that summer, before any of the dozens of agents and editors had responded to the unsolicited manuscript, when Duncan had his second accident. He was driving Byrne to Hilton Head Island for a procedure to remove a calcium growth from her spine. They were running late and Duncan was in the passing lane. The sky was a hazy white, heavy with humidity. Even with rolled-down windows, the air couldn't cool his skin.

Perhaps it was a bead of salty sweat in his eye that made him blink when he should have checked the mirrors. His hands might have slipped on the steering wheel when he tried to make a right hand turn and bashed into a car on the inside lane. Byrne could make any number of excuses for the collision, but not for the next accident a few weeks later.

That time, they were returning from another of her spinal procedures and it had just begun to rain. Byrne noticed that Duncan was drifting to the right, off the pavement, and thought he was dozing at the wheel. She blurted out a warning but Duncan overcompensated. The car spun a full circle across the two-lane highway, the watery marsh vistas on either side blurring into elliptical streaks of blue and gold in Byrne's peripheral vision. The ditch they landed in was deep and muddy. Although neither one of them were seriously injured, the car was wrecked and the accident forced highway patrolmen to close the road in both directions while they investigated.

A week later, Duncan was nodding off for a nap on the porch when Byrne heard the phone ring in the room that served as the dance theater office. She got to it just before the tape in the answering machine began recording.

"Yes, Duncan Miller is out of the hospital, but he is unavailable at the moment," she said. "This is his wife. May I be of assistance?"

She did not recognize the voice of the woman on the phone because she had never met Duncan's sister. The nearness of the voice with its soft and polite Charleston accent made Byrne forget to ask how Duncan's sister had heard about the car accident. Or why she'd waited until 1979, ten years after they'd moved to Beaufort, to make contact with her blood brother. A thousand questions could have been answered, but all Byrne could register was that the voice on the other end of the line didn't sound evil. Duncan's family had always been a chilling absence, and yet, in the pauses of an awkward telephone call, she heard remorse.

She waited until Duncan woke from his nap before handing him the Byrne Miller Dance Theatre flyer she had grabbed at the end of the call to take down a 10-digit telephone number.

"It's a Charleston prefix," she said when she saw Duncan's eyes squint. "One of your sisters called while you were sleeping. She must have read of the accident in the newspaper."

She expected Duncan to be surprised or even irritated by the sudden gesture of concern. So the silence that initially greeted her announcement didn't seem out of place, until she felt the weight of it. Duncan, normally so quick with witty responses, seemed to be inhaling words from the air. His silence created a physical vacuum, and Byrne felt it suction the breath from her own lungs. The vein at his temple throbbed a blue warning to the white-hot rage that followed. He stood without releasing his grip on the armrests of the rattan chair, lifting it off the floor like a weapon clenched behind his back. When he spun in Byrne's direction, the chair flew the other way, through the delicate screening and onto the variegated hostas and English ivy below the porch.

"I told you never to speak to my family!"

"Duncan, darling, this is irrational. I merely answered the phone."

He shredded the brochure implicated by the hand-written phone number.

"I forbade any contact with those people!"

She stared at the spot where she had just seen her 65-year-old husband stomp the porch floor like a child in a temper tantrum. His cheeks were as flush as freshly slapped skin and his eyes pooled with tears before Byrne realized she was watching a man dissolving in shame. She had to convince him he was safe, that the walls he'd built around himself had not been breached.

"I did not initiate the conversation. I did not promise her you would return the call. I didn't tell her anything about you, or me, or us."

Byrne stretched out her hands to steady her husband's trembling, but Duncan slapped them away.

"You betrayed me."

She looked down at her stinging hands. It was the first time Duncan had ever touched her in anger. But his voice was more wounded animal than attacker and Byrne heard in it a panicked danger. She could not disarm him with logic. She had to console him first.

"I'm sorry, Duncan. I should have let the machine answer. I will never forgive your family for whatever they've done to you. I don't need to know what happened."

She held out her arms again and this time Duncan pulled her to his chest. She made herself limp and leaned into him, letting him hold her until she felt his breathing return to normal. She didn't stiffen even when she heard mosquitoes buzzing at the hole in the screen the chair made. She didn't pull away when she felt them feeding through the tender skin behind her ears. They would fly away filled with her blood and leave nothing more than a red welt, but she knew if she left Duncan's side, it would drain him completely.

They never spoke of the call again, or Duncan's violent reaction to it, but Byrne couldn't get his sister's voice out of her head. It whispered to her, soft and complicit, when she reread a passage in *Jane's Fighting Ships*: "How could I have been so stupid as to believe that any man could be my friend and so trusting as to believe he would keep my secret?"

That line, on page 25, was both Byrne's proof and torment. Some part of this created character was Duncan's truth. There was a secret shame in his hidden childhood, a shame his sister knew or shared. It explained his desperation to keep the life he had created for himself separate and safe from the one he was born into. Even a phone call threatened to expose him, betray him. The book's protagonist, like Duncan, took solace in the music of Vivaldi.

"With Vivaldi might come, unpredictably, a recall of that moment when I had been lost as only a child can be, in infinity, a drop of water joining an ocean, mystically becoming one. No longer old Jo Jo Cates, who pretends to be of an age with the kids he befriends and seduces, no longer harnessed into his corset, copped by wig, toothed by dentures, becoming no one, staring at the sky, becoming the sky. The loss of identity had never occurred with the same transcendent joy remembered from childhood, but muted echoes of it could sometimes still submerge the clamor of the moment."

Byrne read in the words of Jo Jo Cates that Duncan wanted his past to be lost, sucked out in a sea of anonymity. If writing these twisted stories about wretched, depraved lives so different than their own somehow set him free, then it was worth the pain of every rejection letter that arrived in their mailbox.

Duncan actually seemed pleased when he showed Byrne the one that came from Bob Cornfield of Dial Press when the snowbirds began to sail south again.

"*Jane's Fighting Ships* is a kind of grand grotesque that shows tremendous energy and boldness, but which overwhelms me," the editor wrote.

Byrne could not let the truth of it overwhelm her. She smiled at Duncan and presented the rejection letter back to him as though it were a bronze medal to hang around his fragile, brave neck.

40

Her Only Regret

BYRNE AND I SAT PARALLEL to each other in scratchy wicker porch chairs, listening to a chorus of squirting oysters in the creek below. In the South Carolina Lowcountry, oysters clump together vertically, adapting to the extreme tides by stretched necks and elongated shells. They are not the pearly, teardrop-shaped delicacies of gourmet raw bars and chilled champagne. They are mud-coated, jagged survivors who would wash away without each other. When Lowcountry oysters have taken from the nutrient rich rivers as much as they need, they spit out the brackish waste cleaner than it was before. It sounded like a squirting symphony, hiding an awkward silence.

I had planned a very different observation, one where voices reading lines from Duncan's books would have drowned out the sounds of oysters. But it was just me and Byrne sharing a bottle of wine at sunset, on the porch where she had first introduced me to her husband, the writer. It was all I could do not to spit out my discovery that Duncan had never been published and watch how Byrne would dance around the truth.

"Duncan was a marvelous writer," she said when her glass was almost empty. "He submitted his first novel to *Atlantic Monthly* when we were first married, and we had such hopes. It didn't win the prize of publication but an editor there wrote to an agent on his behalf. He said Duncan was the only one this side of the Atlantic writing like Thomas Mann."

I refilled my glass. This excuse was clearly going to be a redundant, convoluted one, filled with name dropping.

"Did the agent like the novel?" I asked.

"No one since has recognized his brilliance," she answered, slipping into present tense as imperceptibly as a sand gnat landing on her skin.

She spoke of a span of 60 years as if it were a ship lost at sea, she still waiting for its return.

"He has written six novels in all, and I type every one of them, revision after revision. I also type his responses when his novels are rejected, over and over." She caught herself and adjusted her glasses back to the bridge of her nose. "I mean were rejected. Come, I want to show you something."

We walked back into the living room, and Byrne opened the door to a square glass vitrine that balanced on a bookshelf. She handed me an envelope, postmarked 1982, and I pulled out two pages that looked like a carbon copy of a query letter.

"I would match the number and quality of letters of rejection I have received in the last 10 years with anybody else's in the country. They include such as these:"

The body of Duncan's letter was a series of quotes from editors, famous and not, who had turned down every one of his books.

"From Eugene F. Saxton of Harper's: 'We have read your manuscript, *Sit in Dark Places*, with great interest and I am sorry to say that the verdict is in the negative. Of course, the central theme is a difficult one under any circumstance.' From Fredda Isaacson of Warner's: '*The Air Drawn Dagger* was turned back to us by the agent as requiring too much editorial work.' From Bob Cornfield of the Dial Press: '*Jane's Fighting Ship* is a kind of grand grotesque...'"

The rejections went on for 10 paragraphs before Duncan finally wrapped up his plea.

"The yes-but's go on *ad nauseam* from some of the country's leading naysayers. But the possibility of adding to my collection from another source – the world of the university press – never occurred to me till I saw Mitgang's piece in the *Times Book Review*. May I send simultaneously two of the novels that have received the most inspired no's? Sincerely, Duncan Miller."

The sheets in my hand amounted to a dare. *Go ahead reject me*, Duncan all but taunted, *everyone else has*. If I had been the recipient of so petulant a query letter, I might not have bothered to read the submission. I glanced at the sofa pushed up against the back wall of the living room. Underneath the homemade wooden frame were six bankers boxes yellowing with age. I wondered why Byrne kept them, what good she thought was served by these reminders of failure?

"Those boxes contain his life's work," Byrne said. She brought her hands up to her face, removed the dangling, garish earrings from her ears and rolled them in clenched fists. Her neck seemed even longer then, naked of adornment. "My only regret is that I could not get the words of my brilliant husband published."

The part about a life's work, the brilliant husband, flowed past me like the familiar waters of a racing tide. Three words anchored me in place – a stubborn sandbar in the river of my understanding, forcing it to slow down and pass on either side. She couldn't get Duncan published. She did not call it her biggest regret, as if there had been many. She called it her *only* regret. I thought of the devastating setbacks in her life – Alison's schizophrenia, Duncan's Alzheimer's, Jane's death and her own spinal surgeries – but it was as if Byrne knew she had done everything within the limits of her power and because she fought so valiantly, failure wasn't her fault. Not getting Duncan published was her only regret because she must have thought she missed something, that she could have done more.

She couldn't talk about how cavernous her bedroom looked without Duncan's hospital bed wheeled up against the window. She didn't bristle at the marks along the wall where a gurney had scraped on its way to a different patient. In the year since his death, she hadn't let herself break down, wondering who would watch her dress each day and tell her she was marvelous. Instead, she allowed six boxes of manuscripts stuffed under a sofa to torment her.

"A very wise person once told me that one woman cannot possibly expect to be everything to a man. Trying will just pull her down," I said.

Byrne smiled, slowly. "Well, my dear, is there a moral to this ridiculous story?"

It was my stage and Byrne was the one who needed someone to dance for her.

"You are the unique combination that was all Duncan truly needed," I told her. "He couldn't have loved you more if you ruled the world of New York publishing. Yours was the only opinion that mattered."

So much had flowed between us since the day on this very porch when I first saw the love that bound and lifted Byrne and Duncan Miller. Years later, their love slipped into the thoughts I whispered to myself in private moments. *Marvelous,* I told the mirror just before I went on air to deliver the nightly news. Or, when I ate breakfast alone on the futon in my Spartan apartment, *who needs tables and chairs?* I had my own piano: freedom.

"We're always," Byrne started to say before she shifted back to past tense. "We were always joined at the hip and people used to tease me, asking if Duncan always held my hand or if it was just for show."

I was surprised Byrne cared what others thought.

"I knew that we were equals, true partners in life's journey. But I got all the attention, and he got lost in my shuffle."

It was a sad truth, the kind that hangs in the air with inevitability. The lyrics of Byrne's history drifted through the heavy air like the sounds that signaled the passing seasons. From the porch, we listened as the snip of pruning shears after the spring azaleas wilted gave way to the clank of shrimp nets on the public piers. The snap of canvas sails when the snowbirds headed south left the diving ducks to grunt and croak over winter. Byrne had never lied to me. She just let the truth find the right time to arrive.

"The Gullah have a saying," I said to Byrne. I could sense she wanted to be alone with the regret that kept Duncan close. It was time for me to kiss her cheeks and say goodnight. "It goes something like this. All shut-eye ain't sleep. And all goodbye ain't gone."

41

Love is more disarming than logic.

~Byrne

Fate's Whirling Wheel

BYRNE WAITED UNTIL turning right onto Highway 17
to Charleston before she pushed the cassette into the car's
tape player. The grove of centuries-old live oaks at the
crossroads known as Garden's Corner was her cue to begin playing her favorite recording of Carl Orff's *Carmina
Burana*. She was driving Duncan to the Medical University in Charleston for an injection of dialyzable leukocyte
extract, a blood-derived substance called transfer factor
that a Charleston researcher claimed could diminish the
effects of Alzheimer's disease and autism.

She heard the first D minor chord of timpani drums and
thought of Dr. Hugh Fudenberg, who had been treating
Duncan, along with about 80 other patients, for several
years. Duncan seemed to be losing words at a slower rate
than before, but his continued access to the treatment and
Dr. Fudenberg seemed less certain now, as both their fates
hung in the balance.

"*Oh Fortuna velut luna*," the chorus began. Byrne knew
the Latin words by heart as well as what they meant in
English. "O Fortune like the moon, you are changeable,

ever waxing and waning." The lyrics enveloped her, filling the space between the doors of the station wagon with comforting, rhythmic force.

Dr. Fudenberg's methodology involved drawing blood from patients and their "normal" household contacts, such as spouses or caretakers, and then extracting and combining white blood cells in a centrifuge and re-injecting healthy "transfer factor" back to the patients. His theory, that this would stimulate and transfer immunity, had shown inconclusive results in bone cancer patients, so he'd moved on to patients with Alzheimer's and autism. Each treatment cost $300 and five of Byrne and Duncan's closest friends had donated blood to Duncan's cause, some more than once.

Byrne turned up the volume, letting the cantata's building momentum match the frustration raging inside her. "*Vita detestabilir, nunc objurate et tunc curat,*" the voices sang out. Byrne's fists gripped the steering wheel as she mentally translated. "Hateful life, first oppresses and then soothes as fancy takes it."

The first signs of fate's fancy came when a doctor in Illinois filed a $1 million suit against Dr. Fundenberg on the grounds that transfer factor treatments made his patient worse. Then, in September of 1989, the Medical University of South Carolina had suspended Dr. Fudenberg because his methodology had not been approved by its institutional review board. A local judge intervened and Duncan's treatments had resumed, but the tug-of-war had unnerved Byrne. She needed another ally in the fight to save Duncan. But who?

Duncan stirred beside her, awakened by the music blasting out of the car speakers. He seemed agitated. She was relieved. He walked better and remembered more words when he was angry. In truth, she didn't know whether Duncan's incremental improvements had more to do with the traditional medication he was on or Dr. Fudenberg's unconventional transfer factor treatments. But until the doctor was proven wrong, she would sing his cause with operatic passion.

Her foot pressed harder against the accelerator pedal and her hands gripped tighter on the steering wheel. "*Sois immanis, et inanis, rot a tu volubilis.* Fate – monstrous and empty, you whirling wheel."

She pictured a full staging of the cantata with Dr. Fudenberg on the conductor's stand. Instead of a tuxedo, he wore his white lab coat and directed the musicians by waving his Sherlock-Holmes-style calabash pipe through the air. Stage light bounced off his bald crown and backlit the tufts of unruly grey hair still attached to his throbbing temples. The choir sang on in thunderous unison.

"You are malevolent, all well-being is vain and always fades to nothing. Shadowed and veiled, you plague me, too."

At the hospital, Dr. Fudenberg seemed almost gruff with Duncan, impatient with how long it took to secure the IV in his flaccid arm. It worried Byrne as much as it irritated her. If Dr. Fudenberg so clearly lacked bedside manner, how could he win the public relations battle to remain in practice? Duncan seemed oblivious to his harsh surroundings: the flickering fluorescent light, the mechanical hum of a straining air-conditioning system and the long, echoing halls smelling vaguely of disinfectant. His eyes were closed and his head seemed to float atop his neck, bobbing slightly as if he were still listening to *O Fortuna*. He winced when the needle found an insertion point, then smiled when Byrne took his hand and squeezed it. He couldn't see the tears welling in her eyes.

"*Hac in hora, sine mora,*" the last measure began. "So at this hour, without delay, pluck the vibrating strings. Since Fate strikes down the strong man, everyone weep with me."

IT HAD BEEN 10 YEARS since fate struck down her husband's health. Duncan's moody withdrawals, increasing forgetfulness and frustration, and then two accidents on the same South Carolina highway had been warning signs, more obvious to Byrne than him. When Dr. Herbert Keyserling, their family physician, gently closed the privacy door of his office on Bay Street in 1981, Byrne elected to stand behind Duncan's chair so her husband couldn't see her reaction. The memory of Alison's diagnosis, nearly 40 years earlier, was still vivid. When doctors gave a name to her four-year-old daughter's condition, schizophrenia, the sound of it had sliced through the deep muscle tissue of her dancer's balance, leaving her to stagger through the steps of motherhood. For Duncan's diagnosis, she braced her body for bad news, keeping her knees in slight *plié* and her stomach muscles clenched for impact.

Please let it be cancer, she thought. With cancer, there would be chemotherapy, or perhaps radiation treatments. At worst, there would be a timetable she could turn into a grand finale, partners until the very end. Instead, the stage of her life went suddenly dark when Dr. Keyserling said two words: Alzheimer's and Parkinson's. They hung in the air like cymbal crashes. She drew her hands away from Duncan's shoulders and covered her ears – not to block out the ringing but to trap it forever. When the vibrating sound waves settled into silence, she knew she would lose the one thing she treasured most: the company of Duncan's mind.

It seemed like weeks before she could hear again, and weeks after that before she was willing to listen to any well-meaning advice. "The important thing is to keep his mind active," board members and friends encouraged her. "The brain cannot be allowed to atrophy."

She had never considered Duncan's brilliant mind a muscle, strengthened or atrophied depending on degree of effort. But when she visualized his physical brain, withering and weakening inside his hard skull, she made a connection that seemed natural. Dancers kept their muscles limber by stretching, so she just needed to apply the same technique to Duncan. Her plan began by inviting talented, literary friends to the house to join Duncan in reading aloud the plays of Shakespeare. The aroma from a pot of Hungarian stew on the stove encouraged the guests to stay for hours.

"I'm fully aware that oft expectation fails," she told the gathered group. "But I'll happily play Helena to heal my king."

Duncan extended one spindly leg in front of his armchair, bent at the waist in an abbreviated bow and summoned his own line from *All's Well That Ends Well*: "Where hope is coldest and despair most fits."

As much as Duncan seemed to enjoy the readings, Byrne worried they were not enough to keep his mind supple and challenged. She determined he needed something more.

"It's time for a change of scenery," she announced after dropping off the New York dance mime duo of Steve Colluci and Robert Ruggieri at the airport. "There are four months until the Marcia Plevin residency, which is plenty of time to drive out West to be with family."

Jane and Alison were close again, both living in the town of Loveland, Colorado, but it was her youngest daughter on whom Byrne pinned unspoken hopes. Forty-year-old Jane was back to the nature-centered life she had led before the Marine Corps and the marriage that had resulted in a child but ended in divorce. Jane could take Duncan horseback riding and introduce him to his grandson John. Maybe *he* might grow up to be a dancer or a writer – an apple closer to the tree than Jane or Alison. Regardless, a million questions from an affectionate preschooler would surely keep Duncan's brain active.

Reconnecting with Alison was more difficult. It was all Byrne could do to save her disappointment for the pages of a journal she would begin when she and Duncan returned to Beaufort.

"Al's house was a rat's nest – horror of yapping dogs, piles of paper, boxes all covered with a thick layer of brown dust," she wrote. "Al, herself, about the same: immature, defensive, apprehensive. Careful to be non-judgmental, I calmed her, we cleaned, put the place in order as she is eager to invite men over for dinner. Jane is doing well through the difficulty of living with Al and John. Though she, also, is aggressively vocal about it."

THE PROGRESSION OF DUNCAN's disease accelerated in the years between the trip out West and the beginning of his transfer factor therapy. He couldn't fully share in Byrne's relief when Jane met Scott, the man who somehow harnessed her aggression and convinced her to love again. In Jane's telephone calls and visits to Beaufort, she seemed happy and fulfilled. It was as if the whirling wheel of fate had allowed one daughter, at least, to find her own Duncan.

Jane and Scott hadn't been married long enough to produce a child of their own when the big Western sky of their future collapsed. Byrne was never sure how much of it Duncan comprehended, for which she was grateful. She documented it after the funeral in the journal she knew Duncan would never read.

"Jane was killed in an automobile accident on July 25th, at 8:30 in the morning. She and Scott were riding in the back seat of a friend's car, after Scott and his friend had been bungee jumping off a bridge, tied to elastic rope!

"The driver who ran into them is held for manslaughter. Scott has a spinal compression, but will be all right, in time.

His mother and I feared he would kill himself, with the pain of Janey's death. He clung to me, and I to him. It saved us both."

It was the 20th anniversary of the Byrne Miller Dance Theatre, and Lisa, Lillian and Mary had helped secure a performance in Beaufort by the First International Glasnost Ballet. What should have been a celebratory bottle of wine the four friends shared on the porch, became instead a way to comfort Byrne when she returned from Colorado after the funeral. She couldn't shake her son-in-law's anguish in surviving what Jane did not.

"I am finally old enough not to accept guilt," she told them. "It is a waste of the mind and I have set mine on a higher plane."

In truth there wasn't enough room in her mind for guilt. It was too full of desperate strategies to keep Duncan on transfer factor. The Fourth Circuit Court of Appeals in Richmond, Virginia, had ruled that Dr. Fudenberg could not use his experimental immune therapy to treat patients with Alzheimer's or autism until it was approved by the U.S. Food and Drug Administration. In the meantime, the Medical University was debating what to do with its controversial healer. Losing Dr. Fudenberg altogether was a finality Byrne could not accept.

"I'm thinking of calling Suzanne at WJWJ-TV," she told Duncan as she tucked a dish towel under his chin and scooted his chair closer to the dinner table. "Maybe she will assign that new reporter, Teresa something-or-other, to come film us when we go up to Charleston next week. She's new and probably looking for a juicy story to build her resume. A fresh dose of publicity couldn't hurt our cause."

"Marvelous," he croaked.

THE DAY OF THE INTERVIEW was muggy, and the living room felt clammy and too stifling for TV lights. So Byrne spent the morning feeding Duncan and then transferring him to his wheelchair on the screened-in porch. She turned up the ceiling fan so he would stay cool while she changed to greet the reporter.

"Ah yes, the linen," she muttered to herself as she picked out an outfit. The TV station's cameraman had told her to stay away from all white, that it caused some sort of zebra pattern in the lens. But she knew that the white linen pantsuit she bought when they moved to St. Thomas, paired with a bright scarf, drew attention away from the folds in her neck and made her complexion seem rosier. She pulled it from the closet and held its hanger under her chin. The fabric draped down her long dancer's legs and swayed with her as she posed in front of the mirror. "The hell with Billy. What does he know of fashion?"

On the hallway wall, she straightened the photograph of Duncan in the striped sweater, smoking a pipe, then pulled a *Carmina Burana* album from its sleeve for appropriate background music. She watched through the kitchen window as the WJWJ news van slowed in front of the mailbox and then pulled into the driveway. It was just the girl at the wheel. Billy wasn't with her. That Suzanne hadn't sent the cameraman along must have meant the new reporter was competent enough to shoot her own stories.

Still, when the doorbell rang, Byrne decided it wouldn't hurt to offer to carry the lights or the tripod.

"I am not as feeble as my advanced age suggests," she said when the young reporter hesitated to let her help. She didn't look much more than 20 years old, but then again all the reporters that cycled through the tiny Beaufort station seemed absurdly young, on their way to bigger and better markets. She almost reached out to tug the poor thing's skirt down. The heavy equipment she hoisted over her shoulder had not only popped a button on her blouse but somehow velcro'ed itself to her panty hose on the way up a muscular thigh. Interesting, Byrne thought to herself as she held open the door. With thighs like that, this one might have been a dancer.

She let the possibility settle in the back of her mind, food for later thought. What was important here and now was to bring the new reporter into her fold and create a supporter. The sooner she got the girl and her clunky gear past the scuff-marked walls of the house and out onto the porch to meet Duncan, the better. But Teresa seemed to be taking her time, filming everything along the way, even the collection of Shakespeare lining the bookshelf. Maybe there was more to her than the blond, cookie-cutter TV reporter hairstyle and too-bright lipstick suggested.

Her thighs were Byrne's first clue, but watching the way she moved with and around the camera confirmed it. Teresa *was* a dancer and the camera was her partner. When she stepped away from its viewfinder and reached out to adjust the light stand, her arms and legs moved with the natural opposition of a dancer. She didn't just bend over at the waist to check the sound meter on the video recorder; she lowered herself in fourth position *grand plié*.

Duncan was drooped over the side of his wheelchair, sound asleep by the time they reached the porch. While Teresa noisily locked the camera into its plate on the tripod, Byrne discretely wiped a strand of drool from his chin. "Duncan, darling," she said, hoping he'd wake without an awkward jerk or startled shout. "This is Teresa, the new reporter from the television station. She's going to interview us and then film your next visit with the doctor."

Suddenly the sounds of equipment clanging behind her stopped and she sensed irritation in the reporter's silence.

Byrne knew better than to seem pushy, but there wasn't much choice if she was to set in motion more than just a one-time feature story. She could bear almost anything. She would change Duncan's soiled bed sheets twice a night if necessary, stand behind him in the shower to keep him from falling as he bathed. But her husband was a writer being abandoned by more and more words every passing day, and Byrne would hijack the TV camera herself if that was what it took to get Dr. Fudenberg good publicity. Duncan's blinking eyes searched for hers, and she waited for his gentle smile of recognition before she pivoted the wheelchair around. He was trying to say something. "If – there *is* another visit," he muttered.

Byrne reached for Duncan's hand and watched as Teresa leaned in to catch Duncan's voice.

"A pleasure ... to make ... your ..."

Byrne held her breath, hoping this man who once had charmed every woman he met would be able to finish the sentence. But when she saw what happened next, she knew it didn't matter. Teresa leaned over the eyepiece, loosened a black plastic knob at the side of the tripod head and slowly pushed the zoom button as she tilted the camera down. Byrne followed the trajectory of the lens. It was capturing a close-up shot of their clasped hands.

Byrne settled into a wicker chair next to Duncan and watched the scene she had choreographed play out in front of her. It was more than just the gentle way the reporter attached a lavaliere microphone to the fabric next to Duncan's diaphanous, tender skin. Or the way, when she noticed a dark shadow on his face, that she moved the entire camera setup instead of asking Byrne to adjust the position of his wheelchair. It was when Duncan insisted that Teresa call him by his first name that Byrne knew he had collected another admirer.

"Okay then, Duncan it is," Teresa said, as though it was nothing. The young woman distractedly brushed a strand of hair away from her face, and there it was, the hint of a blush. Byrne allowed herself a deep exhale as the curtain rose on her screened porch.

42

The Bastard

BEAUFORT – 1995

RECYCLED, THREE-QUARTER-INCH beta tapes lined the entire back wall of the WJWJ newsroom in a floor-to-ceiling shelving system that housed the television station's file footage. When reporters were assigned to cover a murder trial, they went to the wall for the original crime scene footage to combine it with fresh video from the courtroom. It was also where, after the managers went home, reporters turned for footage to update their resume tapes. But it fell to an assortment of unpaid, questionably motivated interns each year to alphabetize the corresponding index card database. Even after six years of working at the station, I couldn't intuit the way the mind of a Beaufort High School senior worked. Footage of accidents might be listed under "Ax" instead of "Acc." Coverage of airshows at the Beaufort Marine Corps Air Station could be filed under "P" for planes, "F" for Fightertown, or "J" for jarheads.

I groaned at the thought of deciphering the intern code when it came time to put together a resume tape of my own. But my journalism professors in graduate school had warned against staying at one station too long; the TV news business was about market jumping. Since anyone with a press credential can cover accidents and trials, I decided what would land me job offers were visually compelling features instead. I wanted to find a series of stories I'd shot back in 1991 when Byrne's city arts funding had been threatened over a performance by Mark Dendy. I should have known looking under "D" for Dendy was too obvious and rational, but I started there anyway.

It was before Duncan died. The years-ago spark that had turned a modern dance concert into a controversy was a review in another city that had described Dendy's touring show as "mildly homoerotic" and mentioned that the female performers often danced without tops.

The word "homoerotic" was enough to draw the moral ire of a born-again, evangelical Beaufort city councilman whose last name happened to be Queener. I had never seen the squatty, middle-aged, ultra-conservative politician at any Byrne Miller Dance Theatre performance, but Jack Queener was no stranger to WJWJ audiences. He was constantly on the news, objecting to everything from sex education in public schools to the sale of beer at Beaufort's annual water festival.

Byrne reluctantly agreed to let me interview her about Dendy's upcoming performance when Queener introduced a resolution to withdraw city funding.

"I hate to give that bastard the honor of a reply," she said over the phone, "but I suppose I can clear my schedule this afternoon. When you come though, do me a favor and come directly round to the porch. That equipment makes so much noise."

I assumed she meant Duncan had gone through a rough night and was napping inside. But it was actually Mark Dendy asleep on the sofa in the living room.

"Didn't he like the hotel?" I asked.

"It's more that the hotel didn't like him. Even his dancers have had enough of his drinking and cocaine habits. They threatened to walk out on the performance."

The deal Byrne had negotiated in a Beaufort hotel room at two in the morning was that if she sobered Dendy up, his dancers would honor their contract. Which was why, when I peered through the window into Byrne's living room before our interview began, I saw a tangled lump of blankets and a bare arm dangling off the side, still clutching a bottle of Sherry.

"I let him keep it," Byrne shrugged. "He just hasn't figured that out it's empty yet."

I couldn't imagine the added ammunition the pious councilman would have if *this* got out. But Byrne made light of Queener's moral objections, like he was something unpleasant smelling on the bottom of her shoe.

"What's wrong with a little homoeroticism?" she said, shrugging her shoulders at a slight angle to the camera. I knew what her body language meant. Dance presenters of her caliber didn't let such trivial people interfere with their artistic vision. Byrne had shown me Dendy's audition tape, and it was easy to see why his satirical and athletic choreography was in demand by modern and ballet companies around the world. But I also knew that every year, the Byrne Miller Dance Theatre struggled to keep in the black financially. I pushed the pause button and looked up from behind the viewfinder.

"We're not rolling," I told her. "Aren't you worried Queener will follow through with it and kill the grant?"

"I'm sure it's much ado about nothing," she answered. "What *would* be distressing is if this provincial thinking somehow infiltrates my work in the schools."

Freedom of speech, topless dancers, religious intolerance,

cocaine addiction – yes, even four years later, I knew this story could still liven up my resume tape. I gave up on "D" in the footage index and skipped up to "Q" for Queener, but there was nothing there either. Eventually I found the story under "B" – even high school interns surmised that Byrne Miller's legacy would outlast any elected official's. I laughed out loud. The "B" category was perfect for another reason: ever since that story aired, Byrne and I had referred to the interfering councilman as "The Bastard."

I JUMPED WHEN THE phone on my desk rang and debated answering it. I didn't want Suzanne knowing I was staying late, working on my reel. She was such an encouraging, patient boss, it felt disloyal to think of leaving the station. But then again, this call might be the one that would generate a story worthy of a top-tier TV news market.

"You've reached WJWJ," I answered. "This is Teresa Bruce."

"Miss Bruce?" came a tinny voice trying to sound cheerful. "We've got Byrne Miller here at Beaufort Memorial, and she wants to talk to you before we move her. Hang on … ."

My hands felt rubbery and numb. Did Byrne crash the car? Where were they taking her?

"This is a touch melodramatic, even for me," Byrne said when the nurse handed her the phone. "I've managed to wind up in the emergency room for a fat leg."

Somewhere deep in the veins of Byrne's left thigh, a blood clot had formed, and in the course of a single day, her leg swelled to triple its normal size. I sat on the edge of my desk while Byrne spoke, willing myself not to picture IV tubes slithering over her thin arms and machines monitoring her heart rate. I could tell she was lying down, probably on a stretcher. Her words carried none of their customary grand resonance.

"Can you come, darling?" she croaked. I hung up the phone, held my shoes in my hands and ran barefoot along the bluff of the Beaufort River between the TV station and the hospital. It was quicker than driving.

"Are you family?" a doctor asked me, flipping through a chart when I arrived.

"Yes," I answered, without hesitation, and in that moment I knew that I had made a choice. Somewhere in the years of knowing Byrne, she had become my other mother, fearless and larger than life. I couldn't have explained to the doctor or anyone when or how it happened any more than I could pinpoint the first time I became aware of my own name. But the doctor's question was just a formality.

"Then you need to make sure she doesn't move this leg," he said. "I've ordered complete bed rest until the clot dissolves."

He told me about blood thinners and other medications she was on, how if she scratched herself, the cut wouldn't seal or heal. It sounded messy, but not that serious.

"The danger is that if she makes a sudden movement a piece of the blood clot might break off," he said.

"Isn't that what we want, the blood clot to disappear?" I asked.

"We want it to dissolve. If a piece breaks off and travels up the veins toward her heart it could block an artery in her lungs," he answered. "That's what we call a pulmonary embolism. If the clot is large and blocks blood flow to the lung, it is usually fatal."

I stood with my feet in fifth position, trying to keep my legs from shaking, sure that he meant to say something else. "Usually fatal" was a phrase I was accustomed to reading on the teleprompter. Like the Rotary Club raising money for a man with a rare type of cancer – usually fatal. Or engineers, advocating wider highways to prevent head-on collisions between Beaufort and Charleston – the kind that are usually fatal. The context of the phrase was all wrong. "Usually fatal" belonged with footage of yellow police tape and flashing ambulance lights. I would look under "C" for crime scenes or "P" for poisonings. "Usually fatal" didn't match the visual in front of me: a woman wearing dangling parrot earrings, pursing her lips and shaking her head no.

The look Byrne shot me from the stretcher said *Nonsense. Surely none of this applies to dancers. Our bodies are our instruments. They obey and express our wishes.* But she was not wearing her jeweled collar, and she wasn't standing on a stage. Under garish, florescent hospital light, her skin was tissue-thin, stretched too tight over a frightened face. The flimsy gown thrown over her body split open at her thighs. Her leg looked like a tree trunk stripped of bark, pink and fleshy.

Make sure she doesn't move the leg, the doctor had said. How could anyone, let alone an 86-year-old woman, lift that swollen mass that used to be a lean, long leg? But as soon as the question formed in my head, I knew that Byrne would try. Being unable to move is a form of death to a dancer. Byrne didn't just walk into a room. She slid her foot through the folds of the curtain, allowing the audience a glimpse of the ankle before the rest arrived. She walked the way she thought, big and full of purpose. Now I had to.

"Looks like you've got a roommate, Madame," I announced in front of the concerned doctor. The only way I could imagine Byrne *not* moving her leg was if someone guarded her day and night.

"Are we finally alone?" she asked, when I brought her home from the hospital. "Good. Now we can laugh about this business of you having to take care of me. I would open a bottle of wine but I suppose that's tempting fate. Will you take a rain check?"

I rummaged through the linen closet, looking for sheets to make up the bed that Duncan once occupied. The mirror image of Byrne's, it was nothing more than a twin-size mattress balanced on a plywood box. Touching it disturbed the dust of years of being straddled by an adjustable-height hospital bed on wheels, unmade since his death. I forced myself not to wander into maudlin thoughts. *Duncan died above this bed, not in it*, I told myself. *Turn this into a grand adventure.*

"I'll take a pass on the wine, but you are not getting rid of me that easily," I answered. "It's been years since I've been on a sleepover, and unless you snore, you're stuck with me."

Wipeout waited until I finished tucking in the stiff, musty sheets over Duncan's mattress before she plopped down on the floor between the two twin beds. I was close enough to Wipeout to reach out and massage her soft ears in my hand. But more importantly, I was close enough to Byrne to monitor her breathing.

Lying flat on my back in the dark, listening for any signs of movement, I felt more like a spy than a collected daughter. Byrne didn't snore, but I could hear her lips smack when her throat was dry, and I was worried she'd forget what had happened and get up for a drink of water in the middle of the night. What if Wipeout snored or howled in her sleep and Byrne instinctively kicked out at the intruder? I would have tossed and turned had the rock-hard bed been wide enough to change position without falling off and waking Byrne. I resisted falling asleep knowing that any sudden movement could dislodge the clot in her leg and send it racing up to block the breath from her wheezing lungs.

To mitigate Byrne's need to move, I had to be one step ahead of her. So in the nights that followed, I choreographed a dance, my listening dance. This dance, repeated all through the night, was nothing like the powerful, athletic modern steps of Mark Dendy or Martha Graham. It was more of an *adagio* that comes at the beginning of a classic ballet *pas de deux* and the steps went like this: *lift the edge of my blanket like a twirling skirt, pivot at the waist, take one step into the gap between us and bend toward her head. Hold a hand under her chin, lift a glass of water to her lips, kiss her forehead and then back away. Feel the floor with my feet, reversing the steps, toes first, then heels. Keep quiet, so she can fall back asleep without ever knowing she is following instead of leading.*

When Byrne declared to all that the swelling was in remission, she celebrated by sitting at the kitchen table with a cup of tea and watching me cook supper. I propped her still grotesquely fat leg on a chair underneath the glass surface of the table.

"This stiff bastard is rather a nuisance," she said. "I feel like one of those ghastly Barbie dolls with a naked leg sticking straight out from the waist."

It made sense, Byrne's transferring of The Bastard nickname from the meddling man who had tried to stop her dance theater to the equally unyielding leg that threatened her now. The reflection of the glass table distorted and magnified her blood-clotted limb, making it seem close and throbbing. It was the third person in the room, poised to steal Byrne away if I let my guard down.

"How does chicken curry sound?" I asked. "It's the one dish my mom taught me how to make."

I wondered, as soon as I said it, whether my mother would feel left out if she could see the scene inside Byrne Miller's cozy kitchen. I had never cooked curry for my mother. I hardly even spoke to her. It was always my father who grabbed for the phone, and my mother never protested, even when she knew that it was me on the line from South Carolina.

"Teresa, darling," Byrne's voice interrupted. "I need to discuss something with you, and I'm afraid it can't be put off any longer."

I heard the clink of her stirring teaspoon and froze, staring into a pot of boiling jasmine rice. Maybe Alison, her real daughter, wanted to move in to take care of her mother, and I'd have to step aside. Or, far worse, the doctors could have recommended more qualified help at some kind of assisted living center.

"Will you marry me?" she asked. "It'll be quite a scandal, you being my daughter and all, but these divine meals together are worth everything."

I burned my hand on the rice pot, laughing. "I suppose it's better than living in sin. Wait until Councilman Queener uncovers our latent lesbianism. He'll sue the dance theater for emotional damages."

"Ah, we did get the better of him, didn't we?"

She lifted her cup of tea in the air as if it were champagne, and I heard in her voice the same triumphant gusto as the afternoon when she decided how to handle the Dendy debacle.

ON THAT DAY, she had paced the length of the porch as I waited, finger poised on the record button to resume filming our interview.

"I've got it!" she had exclaimed. "Turn that on again. I know just what to do." She was twitching with the pleasure of her own idea. "Instead of bringing Mark Dendy to my handicapped classes for the residency, as is my custom, I will bring the students to him."

I wanted to share in her enthusiasm, but I couldn't imagine how some sort of change of venue would keep Councilman Queener from cancelling a grant. Or what lessons a cocaine-addicted choreographer sleeping with an empty sherry bottle in the next room could possibly teach Byrne's handicapped students.

"We will give them all balloons to suspend from their wrists and then we'll have a dance parade through downtown Beaufort. Mark Dendy will be the Pied Piper, and all the world will see what wonders dance can work."

It was a brilliant plan. Instead of hiding what was arguably the most important aspect of Byrne's work behind the doors of a classroom, a parade would bring it all to light. Any protest from the pious councilman would seem meanspirited and paranoid. Especially since I would capture the delighted smiles with my video camera and broadcast it to every television set in the county.

In less than a week, Byrne pushed the idea of a dance parade into reality. Her office was transformed into a war room with to-do lists drawn on oversized sheets of construction paper and thumb-tacked to the walls. Dozens of students scattered around the county required specially equipped school buses and chaperones. There were parents to consent and traffic permits to acquire. Board members and volunteers took on individual tasks, and Byrne enlisted the support of the downtown business association called Main Street Beaufort. Mark Dendy was so grateful to Byrne for preventing a company mutiny that he would have led a parade all the way back to New York had she insisted.

Parade day dawned, and it was a gift from the gods of Southern weather. The skies were blue and a light sea breeze kept the humidity bearable. More than a hundred children made their way down Bay Street, some pushed in wheelchairs, others struggling with metal walkers, some pulled behind their caregivers in little red wagons. The balloons on their wrists lifted their chins a little higher.

"Let's be tall," shouted Mark Dendy from the front of the procession. The world-renowned choreographer pranced backward, facing the children like a gleeful band conductor, stretching his expressive hands toward the sky. "Be as tall as a giraffe, taller than the trees!"

I slowly tilted my camera up as a hundred bright red balloons, tethered to wrists, reached toward the sky in unison.

"Now we're small," Dendy commanded and the children scrunched up in their wheelchairs, reining in balloons.

It might have been the influence of cocaine or just his natural exuberance, but Mark Dendy was hypnotic. "Now we're wide, as wide as the Beaufort River," Dendy sang out, leaping in full side split through the air, hands flexed like rays of the sun.

Shoppers and workers streamed out of the storefronts, transfixed by the pure delight of it. Onlookers fell in step behind the wheelchairs and the chaperones. I caught up with Dendy to interview him as he led the parade. My plan was to carefully check the footage of him for dilated pupils when I edited the story for the news that night, but I was worried for nothing.

"If you can start them out understanding creative imagery at an early age, you're building them to become an appreciative audience for the arts in the future," he said.

The minute the words left Dendy's lips, I thought they would be the perfect ending of the story. His passionate, lucid sound bite was exactly the antidote we needed to keep public opinion on Byrne's side. But when it was her turn for an interview, Byrne inspired me to rewrite the script I had just imagined.

"Everyone gets a chance to be marvelous," she said. Her eyes sparkled with conviction and purpose, and her earrings danced on either side of an up-thrust chin. "I want this generation to learn how to imagine and create. In this, we are all of equal promise."

It would have made a spectacular end to a resume tape, uplifting and life affirming. Queener's quest was squelched in an outpouring of public support for the arts in Beaufort. But the footage of the Mark Dendy dance parade stayed on the back wall of the WJWJ newsroom. I never finished editing the resume tape I began the night Byrne called me from the hospital. I couldn't leave her.

43

The Letter

BEAUFORT – 1995

WHATEVER ROOM BYRNE shuffled into, a furry white shadow was right behind her. For the most part, Byrne tolerated this clumsy company, but she drew the line when Wipeout tried to follow her into the bathroom.

"That's far enough, Friend," Byrne would say as she closed the door behind her.

While I made breakfast, Wipeout settled under the glass table, leaning against Byrne's blood-clot stiffened leg.

"Move, Friend," Byrne would mutter when it was time to rise and "No, Friend," when Wipeout nuzzled her chin after she turned out the light to go to sleep.

The tone she used with Wipeout was so low and gravelly that Wipeout often licked Byrne's feet instead of getting out of the way. I told myself that a dog and a dancer who couldn't step over the dog wasn't as dangerous a partnership as it seemed. Wipeout made herself useful – padding to the door when she heard approaching visitors and howling at moons Byrne could no longer see in their entirety.

One night I came home from the TV station to discover Wipeout sitting beside Byrne's bed, transfixed by a shadow puppet show against the wall. There had been sporadic power outages all along the coast, thanks to an approaching hurricane, but Byrne hadn't bothered to turn the lights back on when the electricity was restored. She said she was having too much fun in the dark.

"Oh, my friend and I have managed quite nicely," she told me. "We found this enormous candle and discovered that it illuminates the wall quite dramatically. Shadow puppetry is a little trick I discovered to pass the time after all of my back surgeries."

Each day, her resilience and attitude astounded me. The woman whose husband once blew an entire paycheck on a gown from Saks 5th Avenue was forced to shop for sweatpants at Kmart because elastic waists could stretch around The Bastard's stiffness.

"Clothes are like art," she declared for the benefit of people behind us in the checkout line. "I can still admire exquisite designs without having to own everything I admire."

Apart from the leg becoming The Bastard, it was forgiven. I knew because her walk changed to accommodate it. Each time she transferred weight onto the swollen leg, the opposite foot rose up on its ball in an almost imperceptible *relevé*, for clearance. The Bastard, too fat to pass the other in a straight line, brushed the floor in a semi-circular move she called by its ballet term: *rond de jambe*. Somehow it served to make Byrne's entrances more dramatic. Her movements became as calculatedly slow as a Southern drawl.

If anything, it was her declining eyesight that tested the limits of her determination. Mary and Lisa took turns driving her to Charleston for injections right into the orbs of her eyes. But she made a game out of her impairment, as if it were only temporary.

"Come see what I managed today," she told me after an uneventful newscast. She took my hand, as if I were the one who needed to feel my way between the beds to reach the dresser. "I've reorganized all the drawers."

The top drawer of her dresser was filled with neat stacks of bras and compression stockings. Silky slips and underwear lined the next.

"You're a genius," I said. "Now you won't have to bend down as often and strain The Bastard."

"You know the most wonderful part?" she asked. "I'd forgotten just how many textures there are and how different they feel. It's like closing your eyes and opening a present every day, guessing what's inside by touch."

Lisa helped her rearrange the refrigerator. In the lowest pocket of the side door, she lined up wine bottles, full ones tucked in back. One thumb to an exposed cork and Byrne knew which bottle to grab when a visitor dropped by. She alphabetized dairy products down the right side of the shelves – butter at the top, cheeses the next shelf down, milk in the middle and yogurt at the bottom. She was as proud of her system as if she had convinced Councilman Queener to buy season tickets to her dance theater.

"Could you do me another favor and write out a note for me?" she asked. I knew what the request really meant. Byrne, the keeper of immaculate phone records and writer of elegant thank you letters, could no longer see to put pen to paper.

"Just write in caps, 'Welcome all, but please replace where you found it.' That should do. Make it big enough for the cleaning woman to see. She's no spring chicken, you know."

The refrigerator message was the first of many Byrne asked me to write. There were thank you notes to donors and letters to the editor after particularly well-attended concerts. She insisted her penmanship was simply nowhere near as nice as mine, not that she couldn't see when her sentences marched off a page.

Reading was harder to joke about. Lisa brought her books-on-tape from the library, but Byrne said the actors weren't robust enough in their performances to warrant wasting time with them. I would come home to find her pressed up against the light source of her electric reading machine. She was determined to keep track of the dance theater's bills: $6,000 still owed for a Shapiro and Smith performance, another $9,000 for the celebrated Lucas Hoving protégés Eiko and Koma.

"Look, we're already living in sin," I told her. "It's only fair that I chip in with domestic chores. Let's do the paperwork together."

From then on, when solicitations came in the mail, I read them aloud and wrote out checks in the amounts she decided to send. All she had to do was feel for the corner of the checks and scribble her signature to donate to the ACLU, Common Cause and public television. "It's all about priorities," she said. "They are the extension of your principles. Plus, I want you to keep your job, and that Newt Grinch person is gunning for PBS funding." She donated season tickets too for prizes the station auctioned on live television. If Gingrich's Contract-With-America threats materialized, I'd have to edit a resume tape after all.

One day she handed me a letter from Alison.

"Would you mind reading this aloud to me?" she asked. "There are no secrets between you and me, and I can no longer decipher what she's written. Not that it was ever easy."

I slid wrinkled sheets of yellow, ruled notebook paper from the envelope and quickly scanned the contents. It was an illustration of madness – words joined together randomly and sprinkled with obscenities, pens abandoned midsentence for colored pencils, thoughts interrupted by jingles from TV shows, declarations of sexuality dangled between happy faces and exclamation points.

"Umm," I hesitated. "It's hard to make out the handwriting but basically she asks if you are well. Then she goes on about somebody named Summer. Oh, I guess that's her dog."

Byrne leaned Duncan's cane against the wall. "Alison had the best education, so I admit the grammar tortures me. But you don't have to cover for her." She shifted her weight, lifting through her spine and closed her eyes to recite a line I knew by heart. "Life is hard to bear," she started.

"But do not affect to be so delicate," I finished.

"It is only a letter, my dear. We are all of us beasts of burden, don't you see? I am built to bear the truth."

I knew Alison only as a character with schizophrenia in the story of Byrne's life, crazy in a past tense sort of way. But in my hands were pages of child-like scrawl, written by a woman old enough to be my grandmother. On the final page Alison came to her point:

> "I'll be praying, every night and every day, that the doctor _WILL_ save your eyes. But, PLEASE consider? If I had more "helping hands" than the 97 year-old "Queen Mum" and father Time "turned out the lights" on me – I'd GET THE GUIDE DOG."

I was the one who couldn't see. This was Alison, reaching out to a woman we both loved. Her letter offered all that she had learned of coping with darkness: the companionship of a dog.

> "I can read or watch TV, but specially like to talk to 'Summer.' I tell you _I'd_ feel better, for the mobility and protection you'd get."

I wondered if Alison would be happy or hurt to know about the enormous white dog sitting at Byrne's feet as her letter was read. Living as far away as she did, would knowing a stranger was taking care of her mother give Alison comfort or make her feel replaced?

My own father had not handled the news of my new living arrangement well.

"You've always had a bleeding heart, but this is taking advantage of it," he said, like I should smarten up, check if an inch had become a mile. If he had stopped there, I could have told myself that he was just a worried father, maybe even a jealous one. But he hadn't.

"People always wonder how the Jews get ahead. Well this is how, if you ask me."

The shame of remembering it mingled with the discomfort of reading a letter not meant for my eyes. And then I saw my name spelled out in Alison's handwriting, no segue between service dogs and someone she had never met. Each letter of the word Teresa stood alone, fist-gripped. It were as if Alison's illness arrested her on the cusp of learning cursive; the words didn't stand up straight. Letters leaned in little clusters, straining for connection. The "r" in the middle of my name tilted toward the right, the "e" shrunk down in the middle and the "s" wobbled back to the left again, undecided.

"You already told me about Teresa and I agree it sounds like a dandy idea – and a neat friend."

At some point after she came home from the hospital, Byrne must have called Alison and told her that I moved into the house she once shared with Duncan. If she had been afraid of hurting her daughter's feelings, she must have decided the tradeoff of the truth was more important.

I had been squirming with worry about what Byrne would think of me. Even though she always said the family you're born with is not the one you're stuck with, I had hidden my embarrassment of my father's beliefs from her, rationalizing that I had to be strong before I could be honest. But I had it all wrong. Byrne's honesty was what gave her strength.

44

The Last Dance

LONG LEGS GOT BYRNE her first dance job, but her breasts made her last public performance possible. Her Aunt Cornelia's antique, saffron-colored caftan jutted out in front of her bony shoulders allowing the silky fabric to droop and ripple out of range of her thick, stiff bastard leg. Even so, Byrne had to rely on Duncan's carved cane for balance when the gauze curtain rose. She began to sway and undulate to exotic Middle Eastern music. It was Lillian's bachelorette party, and as the maid of honor, I had convinced Byrne to be the entertainment.

"Have you ever done belly dancing?" I had asked my other mother three months earlier, an idea taking shape as we shared a glass of champagne on the porch. My sister-by-Byrne had just called to tell us that the man she considered her Duncan had finally set the date for their wedding: Thanksgiving.

"In a cabaret number, a lifetime ago," Byrne answered my question. I could picture a 20-something Byrne shimmying with voluptuous breasts and sculpted belly on a Vaudeville pedestal. "I've still got a cast photo somewhere. Fabulous costumes if I recall. It's all about moving different parts of the body in isolation. Very seductive."

I imagined the perfect ritual for Lillian, the bride's last night surrounded by her handmaidens, with a former burlesque dancer teaching us the most alluring moves of all. Byrne lifted her arms above her head and pressed her palms together. Her taut neck stretched from side to side, each cheek coming close to an elbow but never touching. It was like watching a cobra rise from a coiled basket. All she needed was hypnotic music.

"Go inside and bring me the album called *East Meets West*. Wonderful Sudanese jazzman, by way of Brooklyn. Not terribly traditional, but Malik might just do the trick."

I wondered what Byrne's inhospitable neighbor thought in the evenings that followed, when the brittle twang of Ahmed Abdul Malik's 72-string kanoon and sinuous oud wafted between the porches of our two houses.

"We should have some costumes made," I suggested during one of Byrne's screened porch rehearsals.

"A marvelous idea. Loads of see-through silks and tassels," she said. "And rubies for the navels of our nubile maidens."

We bought bolts of chiffon and gauze and took them to a Beaufort seamstress. I made a guest list of the other women in Lillian's wedding party and her closest friends, and Byrne and I guessed on sizes, leaving elastic cords to cinch unmeasured waists, covering seams with long sashes and braided tassels. We scavenged resale shops for bikini tops, halters and lacy bras to decorate with sequins and glue-on jewels. After each loosely constructed costume was finished, I modeled it for Byrne. She ran her hands over the fabric and had me wave ribbons of scarves through the sultry air to judge how they moved.

"Indecently delicious," she declared, satisfied with the last of 20 costumes.

The night before she married her Duncan, Lillian untied a blindfold covering her eyes and became the center of a cushioned cave of opulence. Every surface of the house was caressed by shimmering sheets, which billowed in a breeze created by hidden box fans. Piles of pillows covered the floor in inviting heaps. Sticks of incense scented the air and strands of twinkling Christmas tree lights made ephemeral sculptures of coat racks and bookcases. Wipeout howled with impatience.

I tugged on the cord that pulled up a diaphanous, makeshift curtain, and Byrne stood with both arms extended to her harem, exotic music throbbing all around her.

"Is this even legal?" one of Lillian's nieces squealed as 20 women stripped the clothes from their bodies, dove for the pile of gossamer costumes and glued plastic rubies into each other's belly buttons. The bride stood next to Byrne, matching her rhythmic movements just as she always had through years of modern dance classes. But this time there were no corrections, just hips pivoting in the candlelight.

Near the end of almost every ballet class, the teacher will ask for a combination of steps to travel across the floor. She may physically demonstrate or simply call out the movements in French: *tombé, pas de bourrée, pas de chat, glissade*, all leading up to the *grand jeté*. She will move over to the pianist and work out a tempo while the dancers mark the steps on their own, figuring out which foot goes where and the correct position of the accompanying arms. Then the first student backs as far into the corner of the studio as possible to make room for an explosion of movement. But the climactic jump has no suspense, no drama, without the smooth, gliding, connection steps that build up to it. The lowly, penultimate *glissade* is what gives the *jeté* its power to leap offstage into the wings. My time with Byrne after the death of Duncan and the divorce from Sonny was that *glissade*, and we were both preparing for the *grand jeté* to come.

At first, I wasn't sure there was enough room to leap. Fallout from Newt Gingrich's Contract With America was beginning to smother isolated public television outposts like WJWJ. As the months went on, the station management encouraged me to cover less controversial stories and flatter politicians instead. The news staff had always been exempted from the annual PBS pledge campaigns, for the appearance of objectivity. Now I was asked to stand in front of the anchor desk and beg for funding for the local news. For each $50 pledge, I promised viewers a mug emblazoned with the station's call letters.

When legislators who were considering closing the station held a public hearing to assess community support, I covered the event with my camera as though doing so wasn't obviously self serving. Between programs, we began airing pseudo-commercials: scenes of hurricanes we'd covered and me, valiantly standing out in a rainstorm while text like "dedication" and "community service" scrolled across the bottom of the screen.

Ron saved me copies of *Broadcast Magazine*, folded open to the want ads. "Writing's on the wall, Teresa," he said. "I'd start looking higher up the food chain if I were you."

The whole situation felt so out of my control that I wanted to curl up on Byrne's porch and ignore it. We always had upcoming dance performances to discuss and plans to put into action. The rituals of our life together were reassuring. I felt like I was doing something practical with every to-do list item we crossed off and every recipe we clipped from the newspaper and tried.

There was structure even in tending to Byrne's rose bush. A few scraggly blooms leaned against the white walls outside her office, as if sporadic exhibitionism would grab the attention of the woman inside who used to keep them pruned. But Byrne could no longer see the thorns all around her. Her vision wasn't going to make a miraculous recovery. And with her permanently swollen leg, her days of kneeling down in the warm dirt and spreading mulch between the stems of roses were over.

So how could I tell her, when the blood red roses were overshadowed by pink camellias of a new year, that there was a perfect job opening in Washington, D.C.? Ogilvy Public Relations, one of the largest agencies in the country, wanted someone to run its broadcast department. It would pay three times what I made at the TV station, assuming the station still had funding to pay salaries at all. Given the long odds, I decided not to risk discussing it with Byrne. Ron thought the ad was a formality, published just to feign due diligence when some big city player probably had an inside track. I underestimated both myself and Byrne.

"Listen, darling, until this Newt Neanderthal is voted out of office, your livelihood is in danger," she said over dinner one night, unprompted. "As much as I'd miss you, I think you should try to find a job that isn't dependent on congressional funding."

So it was with a clear conscience that I sent off a resume, along with a rough cut of my Gullah documentary in lieu of a resume tape. Byrne took the message when Ogilvy's creative director called back, asking for more writing samples. The position wasn't an immediate opening. I had plenty of time for second thoughts. There was Wipeout, for one thing.

"My friend here will stay with me of course," Byrne said, nudging the lump at her feet. "Until you find an apartment that takes dogs."

Taking the public relations job would mean giving up my

on-air career. If I were no longer a television "personality," no one would recognize me paddling with Wipeout on the bow of my kayak. I would disappear in a big city.

"Anonymity has its own rewards," Byrne said. "Think of all the men you'll meet. You can be trashy and no one will ever know."

There was no obstacle she could not counter, even the ones I didn't say out loud. Byrne made a point of telling me that her elderly cleaning lady needed more money, so she had hired her to work one extra day a week. She made travel plans to fly to Colorado to visit Alison and Scott, the son-in-law she considered a son. And one day, I came home to find a metal walker folded up and leaned against the wall of the entryway.

"I don't intend to use it," she said. "Except perhaps like a ballet *barre*, for leg lifts."

I knew what she was doing, clearing the way for me to move on without worrying about her or feeling guilty. You can't be everything to a man, she always said. *She doesn't expect me to be everything to her,* I began to hear.

"I'll always be here," she said. "You can come home and live with me forever, after you've seen the world. But only if you bring back marvelous stories and fabulous wines to drink on our screened porch."

She was referring to so much more than comfortable wicker chairs behind an aging mosquito screen. From that porch, she and Duncan had watched the waters of their world fill and empty twice a day, and she was offering me a shared universe. The generosity of her love, the utter un-selfishness of it, flooded me like a spring tide.

I had been tying myself to her so that she would never float away. But Byrne, one by one, unwound the lines. It was unconditional, her encouragement. She did not see it as a sacrifice and therefore extracted no promises in return.

I was free in a way that sang out with sureness. I was free to stretch and test myself and to search for my Duncan.

During the night that followed the day I finally accepted the job in D.C., I heard Byrne getting out of bed. She was feeling for Duncan's cane, and I was about to walk with her to the bathroom door. Our pajama *pas de deux*, she called it. But before I reached her, a beam of light illuminated the hallway. Instead of the cane, she gripped a new, silver flashlight I'd never seen before. Her other hand reached for the wall. The Bastard *ron de jamed* along the wooden floor with a soft swoosh of self sufficiency that silenced me.

When she came back to bed, Wipeout was waiting with alert ears, ready to pounce on the point of light advancing across the floor.

"Wipeout, no! Get out of the way," I said, imagining catastrophe.

Byrne sat down on the edge of her bed and pointed the flashlight high above her head. A sharp circle of light hit the wall, softening into a rim of draining focus.

"Look at this, Friend, better than the candle," she said, in the warbly low tone she reserved for Wipeout.

I saw in her outstretched arms a chance to dance with her. Before the flashlight grew too heavy, I reached around her from the back and took the beam of light into my hands. My *promenade* around the room was slow and wide, as sweeping as the peace that settled in my bones. The light passed over the wall displaying Duncan's photograph, eyes still twinkling and tobacco glowing in the pipe between his lips. It arched over the transom of the bedroom door. Silken robes hanging from a hook fell into folded shadow.

It traced the top of the dresser, past a teddy bear Alison had sent when Byrne was in the hospital and past the sparkling sequins of a scarf draped across the polished surface of the wood. In the blackness of the window where

Duncan used to watch the river pass, our two pale faces were reflected moons. Behind me, I could see Byrne leaning back against a pyramid of pillows, swiveling her hips into the center of the bed to lie down.

I lowered my arms from fifth position overhead to fourth, the flashlight following the corner of the room until my right arm crossed in front of my chest. Now the beam was an extension of my hand, closer to the fourth and final wall. Objects in its path threw deep shadows of their forms: the lamp became a hovering dome, the Navajo vase a braided archway, the glass vitrine a sharp-edged cube. Dangling earrings on their metal jewelry tree took flight with blackbird wings. Byrne reached out as if to catch the birds when the light caught up to her. Her long fingers were branches swaying in a silent wind; Duncan's ring a knot in the tree's grain.

Wipeout rolled over onto her back, staring up at the silhouetted figures through her paws. We were three, then, shifting shapes in the moonless night. Thumbs held high transformed into snapping jaws and flopping ears, wild prey with a beam of light in hot pursuit. A world away but near enough to hear, owls and foraging raccoons were the hoots and scuffles of a score that sneaked inside through cracks in windows and gaps under doors. From underfoot rose a muffled snore and then Byrne and I resumed our duet, leading and following around a sleeping dog.

Byrne was fluid and graceful once again, her hands flowing in and out of the spotlight she could see only in her peripheral vision. A wrist, pivoting under a clenched fist seemed against the wall to be the coy movements of a ballerina turning her cheek to a spurned love. She was only warming up. One by one, fingers unfurled from the shelter of curved palms, each one reaching then receding, contracting then releasing.

This was a modern *adagio*, burst free from tradition and constraint. There was power in the unpredictable, a lesson in the leap. *Anticipate the next move*, her hands demanded of the light I held, *don't hesitate*. And so I moved in counterpoint, swooping under as Byrne flew, spiraling overhead as she reached for the floor. We pulled together, then apart. I felt for the metallic ridges that switched off the heavy flashlight and we continued dancing into the darkness of dreams.

~

Epilogue

THE MILLERS ARE ALL GONE now, and I am reading Duncan's unpublished manuscripts, the ones saved under the sofa in the living room of the house I bought after Byrne died. It is as if I've heard the stories before, or seen them written down somewhere. I touch the delicate, woven rows of antique seed pearls around my neck. The necklace once belonged to Fanny Miller, and Byrne passed it down to me when I told her I had found my Duncan. Suddenly I remember Alison's letters, the ones Byrne asked me to read when her eyes began to fail. There is a sound I recognize in Duncan's writing: the tangled cry of a damaged brain.

I uncurl my fists and let the pages flutter to the floor. If a stiff wind comes along and blows Duncan's pages out of order, and if that wind meets another breeze that holds aloft the letters written by his schizophrenic daughter, and if these pages were to shuffle and settle in a random order – in another place and time – it would read as though the same person wrote them.

Whatever truth or fiction Duncan was trying to tell, the disease attacking his brain sabotaged his intent. Byrne's choice was to acknowledge and confront the man she loved with ugly reality – trusting in the same medical system that had told her electric shock therapy would cure Alison – or create an alternate universe with Duncan as the brilliant writer at its distant core. The logic of it doesn't matter now. I hold in my heart the truth of a love that took light years to reach me.

My husband builds a fire next to the camellia tree overlooking the Beaufort River, and I look out over an indrawn tide for courage. It is time to release Byrne from her only regret, and I start by feeding hundreds of rejection letters into the flames. They curl and buckle before succumbing, kindling for the massive job ahead. I set aside the final versions of Duncan's manuscripts, novels arrested at the point at which he found some satisfaction in them. Those we will bury under the wild azaleas, a time capsule for a future that might judge them in a different light. But the rest, thousands of regurgitated pages rejected even by their creator, I burn in blue-hot flames and in the morning, the dewy soil is covered with a silver carpet of ash.

I cannot will entire novels into print, but I can search among the final manuscripts for the truth I witnessed. Brilliant phrases dangle between lines of Duncan's madness like seed pearls. I dive for them, holding my breath so as not to drown amid the sad, raw prose. I pry them from their jagged shells and kick for the pure air at the water's surface. I string them out, side by side, sparkling in the sun, and marvel at the beauty the world rejected. "Duncan, darling," Byrne would have said. "At last, you are published."

I'm hanging with my fingertips on the lip of a big idea.
I must grab hold of the earth,
or be swept away through an endless sky.
The air is so still that summer scents lie coiled close to the ground.
The palm fronds splinter and tree toads cry.
The night sobs for me.

My mind returns to those moments when I first began to know you.
Seeing through your eyes,
dancing on the edge of dreams.
I was a river coursing through your soft green banks.

We love each other for the sum of what we are.
Implicit with movement, even in repose.

Acknowledgments

WHERE TO BEGIN? With my family, of course, and especially my husband Gary who had the first look at every version of every chapter, red pen in hand, and made sure that a love story about a dancer passed male muster (specifically, no syrupy, soul-mate, coming-of-age, girl power epiphanies).

So many confidants and champions offered their support and encouragement for this rememoir, but chief among them are two women Byrne would have adored: my editor, Susan Kammeraad-Campbell, and my agent (and former modern dancer), Faith Hamlin. Without them this book wouldn't have the legs to dance.

My sisters-by-Byrne (and a few brothers too) helped me remember all that was meaningful about Byrne and Duncan – thank you Ben, Lisa, Larry, Lillian, George, Judean, Joe, Mary, Scott, Becca, Suzanne, Betty, Pam, Jo Ann, Annie, Nancy, Dennis, Madison, Maria, Jeff, Mildred, Bob, Louise, Gordon, Bob, Marge, Catherine, Emily, Jerry, Star, Ted, Ruth, Evelyn, Alice, Ellen, Robert, Paul, Billy and still-missed Harriet. But memories shared in conversation alone can't reconstruct a life. And so I owe a debt of gratitude to Grace Cordial and Dennis Adams who helped me resurrect the records of Byrne's life collected at the Beaufort County Library and to my dear friend Lawrence Downes, who read an early version of the manuscript, chased down leads and suggested connections for my research in New York. Without them this would be a work of fiction.

I am lucky to know many talented writers and artists and even more lucky that they were patient enough to brainstorm and critique this very iterative process. Thanks to Will Balk, Margaret Evans, Lolita Huckaby, Mark and

Susan Shaffer, Lois Battle, Ann Ness, Andrea Schenck, John Zinsser, Scott Graber, Bernie Schein, John Warley, Quitman Marshall, Warren Slesinger, C. Steve Johnson, Karen Peluso, Jacquelyn Markham, Richard Brooks, David Anderson, Rebecca Hirschfeld, Tom Kwas, Lyn Geboy and my literary inspiration – Pat Conroy.

And last, but not least, the beautiful Rosie deserves some credit. Her purring presence during my writer's-block-curing afternoon naps kept everything in perspective.

Book Club
Discussion Guide

1. The world Byrne enters as a burlesque Vaudeville dancer with an open marriage seems incongruent with her traditional Jewish immigrant upbringing. What aspects of her mother's personality play into the woman Byrne becomes?

2. When Byrne tells Teresa about the time Duncan hid a sexual encounter with another woman, she sums up their reconciliation by saying, "Isn't it the truthfulness of friendship that reignites the passion?" Was Byrne acknowledging something deeper than the relief that comes with confession?

3. Early on, Teresa admires Byrne's openness even as she herself keeps secrets from Byrne, especially the truth about her relationship with Sonny and her own father's anti-Semitism. But Teresa's regard for Byrne is rattled when she discovers the truth that Duncan was never published. Ultimately, how does Teresa deal with this?

4. Byrne tells her collected daughters, particularly those in collapsing marriages, to have affairs with married men "to build confidence." She also says monogamy is overrated and that honesty is imperative. How literally do you think Byrne intended for her "womenisms" to be taken?

5. Given what happened when Alison was diagnosed with schizophrenia as a child, is it surprising that Byrne tried to create a world where Duncan did not have to confront or accept the realities of his condition?

6. When Byrne agrees to the open marriage, she tells Duncan "we cannot be everything to each other." This philosophy becomes a key "womenism" she passes down to her collected daughters. In Byrne's own life, did she follow this advice?

7. Considering the stress of their daughter's mental illness, was Byrne and Duncan's honest, but unorthodox, sexual arrangement a way for them each to "walk into another room"?

8. One of Byrne's first "collected" children is Ben, the Navajo dancer in Santa Fe. Does she grow in her ability to mentor by the time she meets Teresa? If so, in what way?

9. Teresa is drawn to the fairy-tale romance of Byrne and Duncan Miller in part because it is so different from her parents' relationship. Is there a connection between young women who enter relationships with abusive men and the type of marital relationships they were exposed to as children?

10. How does Teresa's understanding of Byrne and Duncan's love story change over the course of the book? Were you disappointed or inspired by the complexities she discovers?

11. Does choosing an "other mother" imply a rejection of the parents who raised you or is it a natural part of human connection and development?

12. Share stories of the "other mothers" in your life. Who are these women? How did they impact your life? How did you impact theirs?